Consumer Protection and the Criminal Law
Law, Theory, and Policy in the UK

To what extent should criminal law be used to protect the consumer? In this important new study Peter Cartwright evaluates the role of criminal law sanctions in consumer protection from an economic and social perspective. The author examines the rationales for protecting consumers, and considers the role that legal techniques play in fulfilling these. He then evaluates the interests that consumer law protects, such as physical integrity and economic interests. In addition, he analyses the nature of criminal law doctrines such as strict, corporate, and vicarious liability, and suggests that such doctrines require re-evaluation in the light of the reality of the corporate entity.

This study will be of interest to academics, undergraduate and post-graduate students, and practitioners.

PETER CARTWRIGHT is a senior lecturer in the School of Law at the University of Nottingham. He specialises in consumer protection, criminal law, and banking regulation. His publications include *Consumer Protection in Financial Services* (1999), as well as many articles.

Consumer Protection and the Criminal Law

Law, Theory, and Policy in the UK

Peter Cartwright

CAMBRIDGE UNIVERSITY PRESS

PUBLISHED BY THE PRESS SYNDICATE OF THE UNIVERSITY OF CAMBRIDGE
The Pitt Building, Trumpington Street, Cambridge, United Kingdom

CAMBRIDGE UNIVERSITY PRESS
The Edinburgh Building, Cambridge CB2 2RU, UK
40 West 20th Street, New York NY 10011-4211, USA
10 Stamford Road, Oakleigh, VIC 3166, Australia
Ruiz de Alarcón 13, 28014 Madrid, Spain
Dock House, The Waterfront, Cape Town 8001, South Africa

http://www.cambridge.org

First published 2001

Printed in the United Kingdom at the University Press, Cambridge

Typeface Plantin 10/12 pt.   *System* LaTeX 2_ε [TB]

A catalogue record for this book is available from the British Library

Library of Congress Cataloguing in Publication data
Cartwright, Peter.
  Consumer protection and the criminal law : law, theory, and policy in the
  UK/Peter Cartwright.
    p. cm.
  Includes bibliographical references and index.
  ISBN 0 521 59080 9 (hardback)
  1. Consumer protection – Law and legislation – Great Britain – Criminal
  provisions.   I. Title.

KD2204 .C37 2001
343.4107′1–dc21

                                                        2001025437

ISBN 0 521 59080 9 hardback

To Sue, Emma, and Joe

Contents

Preface

Consumer protection law and criminal law have both received considerable analysis from academic lawyers. The role of legal intervention with the aim of protecting the consumer has come in for scrutiny in a number of seminal works, many of which concentrate upon the role of consumer law in the marketplace. The role of criminal law has also been discussed by a large number of leading commentators, with particular attention being paid to the boundaries of criminal sanctions, and particular concern being addressed to increasing criminalisation. Against this background, it is surprising that so little has been written about the role of criminal sanctions in the protection of the consumer. The criminal law has been the prime technique used by successive post-war governments to implement consumer policy in the UK. Intervention in the civil law to protect the consumer has been less frequent, although a number of important examples of this exist. Strict liability regulatory offences, tempered by statutory defences, remain the paradigm of UK consumer protection law.

This book aims to be the first major monograph to examine the role of criminal sanctions in the protection of the consumer. Although focusing on the UK, much of the analysis in this work is relevant wherever matters of consumer policy are being considered. The book provides a critique of regulatory consumer law, by examining the objectives of consumer policy, the role of criminal law in society, and the extent to which consumer protection is an appropriate topic with which criminal law can deal. The book seeks to achieve its aims in the following ways. First, it investigates the justification for having consumer protection laws, and considers the regulatory techniques available to fulfil consumer policy objectives. Although much of the traditional analysis of consumer protection law has focused on its economic role in correcting market failure, it will be argued that the social objectives of consumer law should be given greater attention. Secondly, the book examines the role, and the use, of criminal law in society, with particular reference to the concept of the regulatory offence. There has been considerable concern from liberal criminal justice scholars at what is perceived as over-criminalisation in general, and it is largely in the regulatory field that the increase in criminalisation has been witnessed. It will be argued that while there is merit in these concerns, criminal law should retain its central function in the protection of the consumer. Rather than a policy of decriminalisation, what is needed is a reassessment of the ways in which regulatory crime operates, with particular attention being focused on the categories of defendant to whom the law applies, and the techniques by which they are held responsible.

The book next examines the law on the basis of the interests that it aims to protect. The two principal interests of concern here are physical safety and economic interests. Where physical safety is at issue, the prime aim of the law is relatively clear. It is concerned to ensure that consumers are not harmed by unreasonably dangerous products. But this simple assertion obscures a plethora of more complex matters. Product safety regulations are a way in which invidious barriers to trade may be erected under the guise of consumer protection. The legislation which contains the majority of the UK's consumer product safety law is based upon a European Directive aimed primarily at facilitating the free movement of goods. It is vital that the role of the criminal law in product safety is assessed against this economic background. Product safety law also provides a useful illustration of the social justification for intervention to protect the consumer. Although it is possible to explain much consumer product safety law on economic grounds of market failure, such as information deficits and externalities, it is also important to consider the extent to which social goals justify intervention. Where consumers' economic interests are being considered more difficulties arise, in particular because the objectives of intervention are less obvious. Should intervention address information deficits that might lead consumers to make inappropriate decisions, or try to ensure that transactions are fair? If the latter, are we concerned with substantive or merely procedural fairness? The law of contract has had to grapple with these issues for some time, but they also have implications for criminal law. For example, quality regulation has generally been viewed as the domain of the law of contract, but the criminal law may also have a role to play here, such as in ensuring that consumers receive goods of acceptable quality. It is perhaps in the area of economic interests that administrative sanctions could have an increasingly important role, and the role of such sanctions in fair trading law is considered in this context.

Consumer law will only achieve its objectives if it is enforced effectively. Considerable empirical research has been undertaken on the strategies adopted by enforcement agencies, most of it concluding that enforcement authorities such as trading standards officers favour compliance to deterrence strategies. Although there have been criticisms of this approach, there appear to be benefits to a strategy which emphasises the primacy of securing compliance, provided prosecution is utilised where informal enforcement fails. The 'tit for tat' strategy favoured by Ayres and Braithwaite bears many similarities to the approach found in the UK and chapter 7 argues that it may be the most appropriate strategy for enforcement authorities to adopt.

The book's discussion of the role of criminal sanctions in consumer protection will reveal the wide variety of roles that criminal law plays in society, from stigmatising immoral conduct to improving trading standards. Criminal sanctions play an important part in protecting consumers by discouraging unacceptable conduct and providing a sanction where that discouragement fails. Many of the objections to the use of criminal law in consumer protection appear premised upon a view of the criminal law as something which should deal only with wicked conduct. However, it will be argued that the regulation of anti-social, harmful, and undesirable conduct is equally the criminal law's business. This is not to suggest that the law is not in need of reform. It will be argued throughout this book that we need to address several important issues, such as the use (and abuse) of corporate and vicarious liability, the relationship between criminal law and other legal forms, and the role of enforcement authorities. It is only in so doing that we will be able to construct a regulatory consumer law which is fit for the twenty-first century.

Acknowledgements

I have incurred many debts in writing this book. First, I would like to thank Geraint Howells, Paul Roberts, and Steve Weatherill, all of whom commented on drafts of chapters in this book. It has certainly been improved by their input. The Learned Societies Fund of the University of Wales, Aberystwyth, and the Academic Purposes Fund of the Society of Public Teachers of Law, enabled me to secure the excellent services of my research assistant Yvonne Williams. Moral support was provided by many, particularly former colleagues Andy Campbell and Gavin Dingwall. As always, I would like to thank my family for their love and support. My wife Sue was a constant source of help and encouragement, and our daughter Emma helped to put it all in perspective. Finally, I would like to thank our son, Joe, whose arrival in the world on 18 October 2000 provided a partial excuse for the late submission of the manuscript.

PETER CARTWRIGHT
Edwalton
31 October 2000

Abbreviations

AC	Appeal cases
Adm LJ	*Administrative Law Journal*
All ER	All England Law Reports
B&S	Best and Smith Reports
BTLC	*Butterworths Trading Law Cases*
Br J Criminology	*British Journal of Criminology*
Cal LR	*California Law Review*
CLJ	*Cambridge Law Journal*
CLP	*Current Legal Problems*
CMLR	*Common Market Law Review*
Consum LJ	*Consumer Law Journal*
Cr App R	Criminal Appeal Reports
Crim LR	*Criminal Law Review*
DLR	Dominion Law Reports
Econ J	*Economic Journal*
EHRR	European Human Rights Reports
F2d	Federal Reporter
FTC	Federal Trade Commission
Harvard LR	*Harvard Law Review*
HL Debs	House of Lords Debates
ICR	Industrial Cases Reports
ITSA MR	*Institute of Trading Standards Administration Monthly Review*
JBL	*Journal of Business Law*
JCLC	*Journal of Criminal Law and Criminology*
JCMS	*Journal of Common Market Studies*
JCP	*Journal of Consumer Policy*
J Legal Stud	*Journal of Legal Studies*
JP	Justice of the Peace
J Pol Econ	*Journal of Political Economy*
KB	King's Bench
Law and Pol Q	*Law and Policy Quarterly*

LGR	Local Government Reports
LMCLQ	*Lloyds Maritime and Commercial Law Quarterly*
LQR	*Law Quarterly Review*
LR	Law Reports
LSG	*Law Society Gazette*
Mich LR	*Michigan Law Review*
MLR	*Modern Law Review*
M&W	Meeson & Welsby Reports
NILQ	*Northern Ireland Legal Quarterly*
NLJ	*New Law Journal*
OJ	*Official Journal*
OJLS	*Oxford Journal of Legal Studies*
QBD	Queen's Bench Division
QJEcon	*Quarterly Journal of Economics*
RTR	Road Traffic Reports
SI	Statutory Instrument
Sol J	*Solicitors' Journal*
Stra	Strange's King's Bench Reports
Sup Ct Rev	*Supreme Court Review*
Tr LR	Trading Law Reports
Tulane LR	*Tulane Law Review*
U Chicago LR	*University of Chicago Law Review*
U Penn LR	University of Pennsylvania Law Reports
Wash ULQ	*Washington University Law Quarterly*
Wash ULR	*Washington University Law Review*
Wisc LR	*Wisconsin Law Review*
WLR	Weekly Law Reports
Web JCLI	*Journal of Current Legal Issues*
Yale LJ	*Yale Law Journal*

1   Consumer protection rationales

Introduction

Laws have been used to protect consumers for centuries. These laws have drawn on a variety of legal forms, including criminal law, tort, and contract, to achieve their objectives. In addition to those laws that specify consumer protection as their primary concern, numerous other provisions have the effect of protecting the consumer, for example by streamlining the prosecution of fraud, protecting property, or facilitating litigation.[1] As a result, the boundaries of consumer protection law are not easily drawn. This book is concerned primarily with those laws that have consumer protection as their main objective, and which use the criminal law to achieve this objective.[2]

This chapter examines the role of law in consumer protection, focusing upon the objectives of consumer protection. In order to achieve this, we need to consider a number of matters. First, we need to identify 'the consumer' whom we are concerned to protect. Secondly, we need to consider the relationship between consumer protection and the market economy. It is sometimes argued that the state, through the law, should play only a restricted role in protecting consumers, because consumer protection is most effectively achieved by the operation of free and open markets. Law should be used to ensure that the markets function as freely as possible. Where markets do not work perfectly, the law should intervene to address this failure, provided this can be done cost effectively. Thirdly, this chapter will consider the extent to which consumer protection should concern itself with social, non-market-based goals. While accepting the importance of market and social goals, it is argued that the distinction between the two is not clearly drawn, and that some approaches could be viewed under either heading. Using the language of efficiency and equity

---

[1] See for example, the Misrepresentation Act 1967, the Theft Act 1968, and the Civil Procedure Rules 1998 (as amended).

[2] It is recognised that many of these statutes will have additional aims, in particular, the protection of honest traders and the encouraging of fair competition.

rather than market and social goals, Ramsay observes that '[a]n efficient policy is ultimately justified by equity since consumers are able to obtain goods and services of a quality, on terms, and at the price that they are willing to pay'.[3] Although helpful for the purposes of structure, the market/social distinction is imperfect in practice. The chapter concludes that the market, underpinned by private law, is an important technique for ensuring that consumers are able to purchase the goods and services that they want, and that intervention which helps the market to function is valuable. However, social goals are being recognised as increasingly important and it is important for any effective consumer protection policy to address both.

Who is a consumer?

Describing something as a consumer protection statute implies that there is someone who can be identified clearly as a 'consumer'. Although the private buyer of goods is perhaps our paradigmatic consumer, she has been joined by a wealth of other economic actors who can lay claim to forming part of that diverse group. As a result, there is the initial difficulty of identifying our subject matter. The first point to note is that there is no universally agreed definition of the term 'consumer', although a number of statutes, both criminal and civil, attempt to define it for their own purposes. One example of such a definition is found in s.20(6) of the Consumer Protection Act 1987, which states:

'consumer'
(a) in relation to any goods, means any person who might wish to be supplied with the goods for his own private use or consumption;
(b) in relation to any services or facilities, means any person who might wish to be provided with the services or facilities otherwise than for the purposes of any business of his; and
(c) in relation to any accommodation, means any person who might wish to occupy the accommodation otherwise than for the purposes of any business of his.

Another example is contained in s.12 of the Unfair Contract Terms Act 1977. This states that a party to a contract deals as a consumer if '(a) he neither makes the contract in the course of a business nor holds himself out as doing so; and (b) the other party does make the contract in

---

[3] Iain Ramsay, *Rationales for Intervention in the Consumer Marketplace* (London, Office of Fair Trading, 1984), p. 12.

the course of a business'. Regulation 2 of the Unfair Terms in Consumer Contracts Regulations 1999 provides a further approach, describing a consumer as 'a natural person who, in making a contract to which these Regulations apply, is acting for purposes which are outside his business'. These definitions suggest that the consumer is a private individual acting in a private capacity. A further paradigm of consumer protection statutes is that the defendant must act in the course of a trade or business.[4] However, some UK statutes which would undoubtedly be regarded as examples of 'consumer protection' legislation fall outside this description. For example, the Trade Descriptions Act 1968 prohibits the supply of false and misleading information in business to business transactions.[5] There is also a suggestion that the Act might prohibit misdescriptions applied by private individuals, albeit in limited circumstances.[6]

It seems that the main characteristics of consumer protection statutes are that the supplier acts in the course of a trade or business, the recipient is a private individual, and the recipient acts in a private capacity. It should be remembered that it is important not to limit the term 'consumer' to contracting parties, as that might exclude the ultimate user of goods and services, such as the plaintiff in *Donoghue* v. *Stevenson* whom Jolowicz describes as 'the law's best known consumer'.[7] Indeed, it is possible to develop a much wider concept of the consumer than has traditionally been envisaged.[8] A private individual who receives services from a non-commercial state authority, such as the user of National Health Service facilities or even the recipient of state benefit, might be aptly described as a consumer. As Kennedy has stated, 'consumerism is just as concerned with the supply of services as with goods. The consumer merely becomes the client, or patient, or whatever rather than the shopper.'[9] We could even go as far as Ralph Nader, the American consumer rights activist, and equate the word 'consumer' with 'citizen'. Scott and Black point out that the consumer interest is involved whenever citizens enter relationships with bodies such as hospitals and

---

[4] For discussion of the meaning of this see Richard J. Bragg, *Trade Descriptions* (Oxford, Clarendon Press, 1991), ch. 2.

[5] See *Shropshire County Council* v. *Simon Dudley Ltd* (1997) 16 Trading Law 69.

[6] See *Olgeirsson* v. *Kitching* [1986] 1 WLR 304, although it is submitted that this case is wrongly decided.

[7] J. A. Jolowicz, 'The Protection of the Consumer and Purchaser of Goods Under English Law' (1969) 32 MLR 1, 1.

[8] For discussion see I. Ramsay, *Consumer Protection: Text and Materials* (London, Weidenfeld and Nicolson, 1989), ch. 1 and C. Scott and J. Black, *Cranston's Consumers and the Law* (3rd edn London, Butterworths, 2000), pp. 8–11.

[9] I. Kennedy, *The Unmasking of Medicine* (The 1980 Reith Lectures) (London, Allen and Unwin, 1981), p. 117. Cited in Ramsay, *Consumer Protection*, pp. 11–12.

libraries.[10] The Molony Committee, which was set up in 1959 to consider and report on changes to consumer law, opined that the consumer is 'everybody all of the time'. However, the committee did not suggest this as a working definition of the term, limiting their ambit to the purchase of or obtaining on hire purchase goods for private use and consumption.[11] This illustrates the numerous contexts in which an individual could be regarded as a consumer. It is interesting to note that when the idea of the Citizen's Charter was taking shape, there was some discussion about whether it should be referred to as the 'Consumer's Charter'. The former title was agreed upon, as the term 'consumer' was seen as 'narrow [and] econocratic'.[12] Equating 'consumer' with 'citizen' has the benefit of enabling us to look beyond the narrow economic function of the consumer, and to consider the individual's wider role in society. This is important in areas such as financial services where a strict economic definition of consumer might exclude private investors.[13] It thus becomes easier to see rights against the state as consumer issues. However, there is the danger that the term 'consumer' could become almost meaningless. Indeed, it could be argued that the legacy of the Citizen's Charter is that citizens have increasing been treated as consumers, rather than consumers as citizens.[14]

This book does not propose to offer a prescriptive definition of the consumer. It is concerned to examine the way in which criminal law is used in the context of consumer protection in the UK, but the UK has no agreed definition of the consumer. Few could deny that the Trade Descriptions Act 1968 and the Consumer Protection Act 1987 are properly described as consumer protection statutes, even though they take different approaches to whom they protect. It is therefore suggested that we should eschew a narrow definitional approach to the concept of the consumer, recognising that statutes may legitimately take different approaches to this issue. Nevertheless, we should recognise that this book is primarily concerned with those statutes which aim to protect the buyers of goods and services from the misbehaviour of traders and which use the criminal law to do so.

---

[10] See Scott and Black, *Cranston's Consumers and the Law*, pp. 8–11.
[11] Board of Trade Final Report of the Committee on Consumer Protection (the Molony Committee) Cmnd 1781/1962, para. 16.
[12] S. Hogg and J. Hill, *Too Close to Call: Power and Politics – John Major in No. 10* (London, Warner, 1995), p. 94.
[13] See P. Cartwright, 'Consumer Protection in Financial Services: Putting the Law in Context' in P. Cartwright (ed.), *Consumer Protection in Financial Services* (Deventer, Kluwer, 1999) and C. J. Miller, B. W. Harvey, and D. L. Parry, *Consumer and Trading Law: Text Cases and Materials* (Oxford, Oxford University Press, 1998), pp. 5–6.
[14] A. Barron and C. Scott, 'The Citizen's Charter Programme' (1992) 55 MLR 526.

Consumer protection and the market system

The perfect market

When examining why we intervene in the market to protect consumers, it is possible to take the so-called 'perfect market' as a starting point. This is helpful even if we doubt that such a system is attainable in reality. Free market economic theory suggests that if the characteristics of a perfect market could be created, there would be no need for regulation. In one of the leading studies, *Rationales for Intervention in the Consumer Market Place*, Ramsay identifies the characteristics of the perfect market as follows:

(i) there are numerous buyers and sellers in the market, such that the activities of any one economic actor will have only a minimal impact on the output or price of the market;
(ii) there is free entry into and exit from the market;
(iii) the commodity sold in the market is homogeneous; that is, essentially the same product is sold by each seller in the particular market;
(iv) all economic actors in the market have perfect information about the nature and value of the commodities traded;
(v) all the costs of producing the commodity are borne by the producer and all the benefits of a commodity accrue to the consumer – that is, there are no externalities.[15]

Those who champion the idea of the perfect market see markets as efficient and effective tools for maximising consumer welfare. The expressions 'free market economics' and 'free market economists' are used in this context for want of a better term. It is recognised that this is not a perfectly homogeneous group. This approach, which is associated primarily with the Chicago School, makes assumptions about the ways in which markets operate.[16] First, it assumes that individuals are rational maximisers of their own satisfaction. In other words, they know what they want, and will make logical, consistent choices in accordance with their wishes. Secondly, it assumes that by their choices, consumers influence producers and so dictate the way that the market operates. By making choices in accordance with their wishes, consumers send signals to traders. If traders do not respond to these wishes they will lose custom and, ultimately, be forced to exit the market. The consumer is therefore sovereign.

[15] Ramsay, *Rationales*, pp. 15–16.
[16] For a useful discussion see Scott and Black, *Cranston's Consumers and the Law*, pp. 26–9.

The market system can be viewed as desirable for two main reasons. First, it is economically desirable because it is efficient. Traders compete with each other to win custom, thereby raising standards and lowering prices. Secondly, it is seen as ideologically desirable that individuals' choices should be respected, rather than a choice made on their behalf by the state. Indeed, many supporters of the free market seem as much influenced by ideological matters as by efficiency arguments.[17] The free market recognises that different consumers are likely to be prepared to endure different levels of product safety and quality for different amounts of money. Where this is the case, a variety of products will be supplied with different levels of quality and safety for different prices. It is for consumers to act rationally in accordance with their own preferences and decide upon the level of safety or quality that they are prepared to purchase.

The perfect market only exists where the requirements set out in Ramsay's list are met, although we may still have competitive markets where not all are present. If we have numerous buyers and sellers competing with each other, no individual trader should be able to influence price appreciably by varying output.[18] By ensuring that there is free entry into and exit from the market, we ensure that anyone who wishes to enter a particular market may do so, and that anyone who does not respond to consumer demand will be forced to exit the market. By having perfect information, we ensure that the choices that consumers make are fully informed, and so likely to give effect to their true wishes. Where externalities do not occur we can be sure that only the parties to a transaction are affected by that transaction, and so the price of the transaction reflects its value to the parties. Free market economics tells us that where these factors are present there is no need for the state to intervene. However, that does not mean that the state has no role in the free market, as we will now see.

The market, the state, and the law

Although free market economics is frequently associated with rolling back the frontiers of the state, this does not mean that the free market requires the state to lose its role in all areas.[19] On the contrary, for the market

---

[17] See C. Fried, *Contract as Promise: A Theory of Contractual Obligation* (Cambridge, Mass., Harvard University Press, 1981) and P. S. Atiyah, 'The Liberal Theory of Contract' in P. S. Atiyah, *Essays on Contract* (Oxford, Clarendon Press, 1990), p. 121.

[18] F. M. Scherer, *Industrial Market Structure and Economic Performance* (2nd edn, Boston, 1980), p. 10.

[19] Andrew Gamble, *The Free Economy and the Strong State: The Politics of Thatcherism* (2nd edn, Basingstoke, Macmillan, 1994), ch. 2.

to function effectively it is vital that the state retains its strength. Frank Knight observed that 'the [market] system as a whole is dependent upon an outside organisation, an authoritarian state . . . to provide a setting in which it can operate at all'.[20] The state should, therefore, not be seen as an alternative to the market, but as an essential part of the market system. Hutchinson similarly comments that '[w]ithout a state willing or able to define and protect property rights, enforce contracts and prevent involuntary transactions, maintain a circulating medium, and curtail monopoly and anti-competitive behaviour, there is no market in any real or meaningful sense'.[21] The state is therefore vital to set up and enforce the structure in which the market operates. This is done through the mechanism of law. Law determines the 'rules of the game' in the first place, and acts as an umpire to interpret and enforce those rules.[22] For example, competition/anti-trust law ensures that markets are open and that competition exists. Property law sets out the rules of property and so determines rights of ownership, and explains how title can pass. Criminal law ensures that such rights are protected. As the market is premised upon the importance of exchange, the rules of contract law have to be set out. There is no inherent conflict between a strong state, strong laws, and the free market.

Although the state has to be strong for the market system to function effectively, the state only imposes its views on citizens in order to ensure that parties are held to their agreements. It is individuals' choices that count, rather than those of the state. As a consequence, laws prohibiting fraud and force are seen as protecting the private rights of citizens rather than enforcing the state's aims on those citizens.[23] The prime method by which choices can be demonstrated and effected is through the private law of contract. The next section considers the use of the private law to protect consumers within the context of the market. It focuses on the role and limitations of the law of contract, but also considers the place of the law of tort. Although contract law could be viewed as a technique of regulation, and so might be thought of as more appropriately placed in our discussion of techniques of regulation, its almost symbiotic relationship with the market has led it to be considered here.[24]

---

[20] F. Knight, 'Some Fallacies in the Interpretation of Social Cost' (1924) 38 QJEcon 582 at 606.
[21] A. Hutchinson, 'Life After Shopping: From Consumers to Citizens' in I. Ramsay (ed.), *Consumer Law in the Global Economy* (Aldershot, Dartmouth and Ashgale, 1997), p. 25 at p. 31.
[22] See M. Friedman, *Capitalism and Freedom* (Chicago, Chicago University Press, 1962).
[23] See J. Raz, 'Promises in Morality and Law' (1982) 95 Harvard LR 916.
[24] For an excellent examination of contract law as a form of regulation see H. Collins, *Regulating Contracts* (Oxford, Oxford University Press, 1999).

The use and limitations of private law

The role of contract

The law of contract is central to the effective working of the market. Contracts provide a mechanism through which individuals can express their preferences, create agreements with others, and ensure that those agreements are fulfilled. Contract law provides a framework through which the market can function. The classical theory of freedom of contract has been central to the development of contract law and its relationship with the market. As Sir George Jessel famously argued: '[i]f there is one thing which more than another public policy requires it is that men of full age and competent understanding shall have the utmost liberty of contracting, and that their contracts entered into freely and voluntarily shall be held sacred and shall be enforced by courts of justice'.[25] Although championed by the 'New Right' in the 1980s, classical theory was originally associated with left-wing movements in the nineteenth century, concerned that the people should be allowed control over their destinies.[26]

Classical theory's emphasis on freedom of contract is a natural consequence of putting faith in the market. Consumer sovereignty demands the means by which the consumer can exercise choice. If we accept that consumers are rational maximisers of their own satisfaction, then it is logical that they should decide the transactions into which they wish to enter, and the terms upon which those transactions will be entered. Intervention by the state beyond that agreed by the parties is therefore anathema to the traditional idea of contractual freedom. Classical theory was characterised by free dealing and non-intervention in substantive matters. It was concerned with fairness, but primarily in relation to procedure rather than substance, acting as an 'umpire' to be appealed to when a foul is alleged.[27] However, it is a moot point whether the law of contract ever championed the kind of freedom to which Sir George Jessel alluded. Despite the significant extent to which classical theory has been emphasised in writing, some commentators question how influential it was in practice. Reiter refers to Jessel's view as 'simply wrong',[28] and Atiyah notes several ways in which contractual freedom was limited,

---

[25] *Printing and Numerical Registering Co.* v. *Sampson* (1875) LR 19 Eq 462 at 465.

[26] See P. S. Atiyah, 'Freedom of Contract and the New Right' in Atiyah, *Essays on Contract*, p. 355 at p. 357.

[27] P. S. Atiyah, *The Rise and Fall of Freedom of Contract* (Oxford, Clarendon Press, 1979), p. 404. For an even stronger defence of individual autonomy see R. Nozick, *Anarchy, State and Utopia* (Oxford, Blackwell, 1974).

[28] B. Reiter, 'The Control of Contract Power' (1981) 1 OJLS 347.

even in the so-called heyday of classical theory.[29] Nevertheless, the philosophy of classical theory was influential, and can be used to explain many of the characteristics of twentieth-century contract law.

Classical theory's aversion to intervention on the grounds of substantive fairness can be justified on a number of different grounds. Collins identifies four main propositions which underlie this, none of which convinces him.[30] It is worth saying a few words about these, as they provide both an authoritative summary of the key characteristics of classical theory and a useful critique of its principal arguments.

First, classical theory's adherents argue that most instances of apparent unfairness turn out to be illusory. For example, most terms which appear to be unfair will be balanced by corresponding benefits, such as a reduction in price. As a result, it is difficult to determine that a voluntary exchange is unfair.[31] Collins accepts that we should not jump to conclusions concerning the unfairness of transactions, and that unfair contracts are more difficult to detect than might first be thought. However, he recognises that unfair contracts do exist, and that the important point is to engage in a detailed examination of the particular circumstances of the transaction, and to take the whole picture into account.[32]

Secondly, it has been argued that approaches which allow contracts to be challenged on the basis of fairness will make it more difficult to construct markets, a prime aim of contract law. Several statutes allow contracts to be challenged on the basis of substantive unfairness, although different terms are used in different contexts. For example, the Unfair Terms in Consumer Contracts Regulations 1999 allow the courts to strike down a term in a consumer contract which 'contrary to the requirement of good faith causes a significant imbalance in the parties' rights and obligations under the contract to the detriment of the consumer'. Also s.137(1) of the Consumer Credit Act 1974 allows a consumer to challenge a credit bargain on the grounds of its being extortionate. Although these provisions look appealing from the point of view of equity, there is an argument that they create uncertainty for the contracting parties, which makes it difficult for those parties to predict how their transactions will be judged. Collins questions this. First, he argues that business people do not regard planning documents as central to transactions and that as a result of this, uncertainty about legal

---

[29] Atiyah, *The Rise and Fall of Freedom of Contract*.
[30] Collins, *Regulating Contracts*, ch. 11.
[31] See M. J. Trebilcock, 'The Doctrine of Inequality of Bargaining Power: Post Benthamite Economics in the House of Lords' (1976) 26 *University of Toronto Law Journal* 359.
[32] *Regulating Contracts*, pp. 258–9.

enforceability will seldom affect entry into transactions.[33] Secondly, he suggests that business people place great emphasis on their expectations, represented by such factors as the long-term business relation and the customs of the trade. As a result, general clauses such as good faith may be helpful in allowing decisions to be made in accordance with expectations. He concludes that most commercial parties 'would expect the legal system to decline to enforce terms in the planning documents that impose extremely harsh bargains'.[34]

The third argument that could be used to criticise intervention is that where the law attempts to regulate fairness, this tends to backfire. Epstein puts forward this view in the context of intervention on the grounds of unconscionability: '[w]hen the doctrine of unconscionability is used in its substantive dimension, be it in a commercial or consumer context, it serves only to undercut the private right of contract in a manner that is apt to do more social harm than good'.[35] One example that has been given is that the setting of interest-rate ceilings may exclude poor consumers from the market altogether.[36] Another is that minimum-wage laws may lead to employers employing fewer people. Collins suggests that this will depend on the market in question, and points out that there is some empirical evidence that measures such as minimum-wage laws have led to a decrease in unemployment.[37] The evidence of the effects of minimum standards of this sort is ambivalent.[38]

Finally, it is sometimes argued that where genuine unfairness does occur, the most effective remedy will be to tackle the market failure that caused it. The issue of market failure is examined in some detail below and so is not considered in detail here. Suffice it to say that steps which correct market failure are desirable in helping the market to function, for example by generating competition and correcting information deficits. However, they cannot create perfect markets and will be limited in the extent that they protect consumers, particularly the most vulnerable. Collins concludes that regulation of unfair contracts can be desirable, and that such measures comprise an important ingredient of the legal system. He favours both 'open textured rules' rooted in private law, and

---

[33] Ibid. p. 269.
[34] Ibid. p. 271.
[35] R. Epstein, 'Unconscionability: A Critical Reappraisal' (1975) 18 *Journal of Law and Economics* 293 at 315.
[36] See D. Cayne and M. J. Trebilcock, 'Market Considerations in the Formulation of Consumer Protection Policy' (1973) 23 *University of Toronto Law Journal* 396.
[37] D. Card and A. B. Krueger, *Myth and Measurement: The New Economics of the Minimum Wage* (Princeton, N. J., Princeton University Press, 1995).
[38] See A. Leff, 'Unconscionability and the Crowd: Consumers and the Common Law Tradition' (1970) 31 *University of Pittsburgh Law Review* 349.

public regulation. Many other commentators doubt whether intervention has the harmful effects that have been suggested.[39] If we accept that intervention may be valid, for example in order to help ensure fairness for the consumer, our next step is to examine some of the ways that intervention in contract law can take place.

Intervention in contract

Under the classical notion of contract the focus of control was upon procedural matters. As a result, doctrines of duress, fraud, and misrepresentation developed.[40] Attempts to tackle the fairness of the substance of contract law were more limited. More recently, however, we have seen increased statutory intervention in the substance of contract law, both by removing undesirable terms and imposing desirable terms.[41] Examples of the former are found in, for example, the Consumer Credit Act 1974, the Unfair Contract Terms Act 1977, and the Unfair Terms in Consumer Contracts Regulations 1999, and of the latter are found in *inter alia* the Sale of Goods Act 1979 and the Supply of Goods and Services Act 1982. The Unfair Contract Terms Act 1977 is concerned primarily with exemption clauses, invalidating some, and subjecting others to a test of reasonableness. The Unfair Terms in Consumer Contracts Regulations 1999 provide, *inter alia*, that a term shall be regarded as unfair if, contrary to the requirement of good faith, it causes a significant imbalance in the parties' rights and obligations arising under the contract, to the detriment of the consumer. Both pieces of legislation allow certain terms to be challenged on the grounds of fairness. The Consumer Credit Act 1974 also allows terms to be challenged on the basis of substantive unfairness. Section 137(1) of the Act allows the court to re-open a credit agreement so as to do justice to the parties, where it finds a credit bargain to be extortionate. There are weaknesses with this provision, and suggestions have been made for its reform. In particular, it suffers from the requirement that the victim has to commence the action. By contrast, under the Unfair Terms in Consumer Contracts Regulations, it is possible for interested groups, such as the Consumers' Association, utilities regulators, and the Director General of Fair Trading, to challenge terms on the grounds of fairness.

---

[39] See M. A. Eisenberg, 'The Bargain Principle and its Limits' (1982) Harvard LR 741 and Gordley, 'Equality in Exchange' (1981) 69 Cal LR 1587.

[40] It has also been possible to create a strict test of incorporation of terms to ensure that particularly unfair terms are not deemed part of the contract. See *Interfoto Picture Library Ltd* v. *Stiletto Visual Programmes Ltd* [1988] 2 WLR 615.

[41] Although common law notions such as undue influence have also become more visible.

When examining implied terms it is helpful to draw a distinction between two situations. First, terms can be implied to give effect to the wishes of the parties. We can classify these terms as those implied in fact. For example, it may be clear that the parties intended a particular term to be part of the contract, but did not explicitly include it. Where this is done, it can be said to be in accordance with the market system and the philosophy of contractual freedom, as the court is merely giving effect to the intention of the parties.[42] The second situation is where terms are implied in law. These implied terms, such as those under the 1979 Act, are mandatory, and so cannot be excluded by the parties. They are therefore implied, not to reflect the wishes of the parties, but to reflect the wishes of the state.[43] Although it might be possible to argue that mandatory implied terms reflect the standards that the parties would have agreed to had they been able to negotiate on the basis of full information, this does not appear to be the basis on which they are implied in reality. The Sale of Goods Act 1979 provides a useful illustration of how terms may be implied in law. For example s.14 of the Act requires that goods be of satisfactory quality and reasonably fit for their purpose. Section 14(2A) states that goods are of satisfactory quality 'if they meet the standard that a reasonable person would regard as satisfactory, taking account of any description of the goods, the price (if relevant) and all other relevant circumstances'. The standard is intentionally vague, allowing the courts to determine what is reasonable in all the circumstances. Section 14(2B) provides a list of factors that may be considered where relevant, such as freedom from minor defects, safety, and durability.

English law does not have a general requirement for terms to be fair. Lord Denning made some steps towards such a provision in the famous case of *Lloyds Bank* v. *Bundy*, but there remains no general test of fairness.[44] There have been suggestions that the law might impose a general duty to trade fairly, or create a general provision which would allow contracts to be challenged on the basis of extreme unfairness, perhaps couched in terms of unconscionability. The traditional free market arguments against such measures have been set out above, but they fail to convince. There are good reasons to be wary of re-writing contracts, but there are sound reasons for challenging provisions that are so unfair that we can classify them as unconscionable. One reason is that it is

---

[42] Although it could be argued that, in reality, the courts imply terms, not on the basis of the parties' intention, but on the basis of how the parties should behave.

[43] For a discussion of paternalism in consumer law see below.

[44] [1974] 3 All ER 757. This can be contrasted with s.2–302 of the Uniform Commercial Code in the USA which gives a power to the courts to refuse to enforce a clause or contract that is unconscionable.

difficult to separate matters of procedure from matters of substance. The willingness of classical theory to challenge contracts on the grounds of procedural unfairness but not substantive unfairness assumes that there is a clear distinction between the two. This is not always so. The point is well put by Kronman when he explains the different advantages one party may enjoy over another and which make the transaction unfair:

the advantage may consist in his superior information, intellect, or judgment, in the monopoly he enjoys with regard to a particular resource, or in his possession of a powerful instrument of violence or a gift for deception. In each of these cases, the fundamental question is whether the promisee should be permitted to exploit his advantage to the detriment of the other party.[45]

Viewed this way, the distinction between procedural and substantive unfairness is muddied. If a consumer finds himself to be the victim of a substantively unfair bargain we look to see why he entered it. We can nearly always point to some procedural factor which has made the resulting contract unfair, but some of these we accept (such as greater knowledge or skill in bargaining) while others we do not accept (such as deception or violence). Part of the task of consumer law is to determine which factors can be taken into account and when. This is a difficult task. Atiyah offers 'a word of caution against the belief that we can wholly separate our ideas of fair procedures from our ideas of fair results'.[46] He goes so far as to conclude that 'when there is some gross imbalance, something serious enough to offend our sense of justice, it will usually be found that some remedy is available'.[47] This brings us to a second argument in favour of having a general power to intervene on grounds of unfairness. Although there are techniques that allow the courts to intervene on grounds of fairness, would it not be more desirable to create a transparent rule which allows them to do this openly, rather than under the guise of some other doctrine? The Unfair Terms in Consumer Contracts Regulations have certainly gone some way towards allowing unfair terms to be removed, but as we have seen, they are subject to important limitations. A general rule against unconscionability, or a general duty to trade fairly would, it is submitted, be desirable, provided it was clearly formulated. This is considered in more detail in chapter 6.

Freedom of contract provides a degree of protection to the consumer, but experience has shown that consumers cannot be expected to fulfil the role attributed to them by market theory. Intervention in the law of contract in the way mentioned above has made significant inroads

[45] A. Kronman, 'Contract Law and Distributive Justice' (1980) Yale LJ 472 at 480.
[46] P. Atiyah, 'Contract and Fair Exchange' in *Essays on Contract*, p. 329 at p. 333.
[47] Ibid. p. 338.

into the notion of contractual freedom and has done much to improve consumer protection. However, it should be remembered that contract law suffers from certain limitations which mean that it is unable always to provide an appropriate degree of protection for the consumer. The main limitations are the doctrine of privity and the existence of transaction costs.

Contract and privity

A major limitation in the ability of the law of contract to protect consumers is the doctrine of privity of contract. The doctrine states that, in general, a contract cannot confer rights or impose obligations on someone who is not party to that contract.[48] For example, a consumer cannot generally sue a manufacturer in contract for producing faulty goods (vertical privity), nor can he sue a retailer in contract for supplying faulty goods which were purchased on his behalf by a friend (horizontal privity). There has been criticism of the doctrine and both academic and judicial support for reform. In *Darlington Borough Council* v. *Wilshier Northern Ltd* Steyn LJ argued that 'there is no doctrinal, logical, or policy reason why the law should deny effectiveness to a contract for the benefit of a third party where that is the expressed intention of the parties'.[49] If the law of contract is seen as having among its functions a deterrent role, it will be important that the person who is best able to determine the characteristics of a product is subject to liability. In some cases, it will be impossible to sue the retailer, for example if he has become insolvent or cannot be traced, and so the consumer may be left without a remedy. The consumer will only have a remedy against the manufacturer in tort if the product is not merely defective, but dangerous.[50] There may be some cases where the court will find a collateral contractual relationship between manufacturer and purchaser, and bypass privity rules, but such situations will be rare.[51] The law relating to privity was recently reformed by the Contracts (Rights of Third Parties) Act 1999. This followed the Law Commission Report *Privity of Contract: Contracts for the Benefit of Third Parties*,[52] and has made it easier for consumers to take action. The main change is that a third party may now enforce a contractual provision, either if the contract contains an express term to that effect, or if it purports to confer a

---

[48] See for example *Tweddle* v. *Atkinson* (1861) 1 B&S 393.
[49] [1995] 1 WLR 68. Mitchell describes privity as 'a rule which is almost universally regarded as unjust'. See C. Mitchell, 'Privity Reform and the Nature of Contractual Obligations' (1999) 19(2) *Legal Studies* 229 at 230.
[50] But see the wording of Part I of the Consumer Protection Act 1987.
[51] See for example, *Carlill* v. *Carbolic Smoke Ball Co. Ltd* [1893] 1 QBD 256.
[52] Law Commission Report no. 242, 1996.

benefit upon him. The third party, in these circumstances, will be given rights as though he were party to the contract. It is not proposed to go into detail about the changes here.[53] The Act does protect consumers in specific circumstances, but leaves the doctrine largely intact.

Tort

In 1951 Glanville Williams identified the principal aims of tort as: appeasement, justice, deterrence, and compensation.[54] There will be both conflicts and overlaps between these aims, and they are by no means exhaustive. Jones argues, for example, that we should add loss distribution and economic efficiency to the list.[55] The effect of tort law is to transfer resources from one party to another in order to return the victim to her position prior to the commission of the tort. The rules of tort law provide a framework for establishing when and how this can be done. If looked at from an economic point of view, tort liability rules provide an incentive for producers to take cost-effective measures to prevent defects. Some of the limitations inherent in the law of contract can be addressed through the law of tort. For example, the consumer who is given a defective product by a friend and suffers injury will have a right of redress against the producer of that product in the law of tort, either under the tort of negligence or Part I of the Consumer Protection Act 1987. However, tort law is subject to its own limitations which may place obstacles in the way of consumers' obtaining access to justice. Whereas contract law is concerned primarily with agreements made by the parties, tort law imposes duties irrespective of the parties' intentions, and irrespective of any contractual relationship.[56] This may seem to be wider than contract, but in some ways it will not be so. First, tort liability often only arises where the plaintiff can prove fault. Under *Donoghue* v. *Stevenson* a manufacturer owes a duty of care in negligence to the ultimate consumer of the manufacturer's product.[57] However, this duty will only give rise to liability where it has been breached: that is, where the plaintiff can prove fault against the manufacturer. Unlike strict liability in

---

[53] For material discussing the proposed changes, see e.g. Mitchell, 'Privity Reform', J. Adams, D. Beyleveld, and R. Brownsword, 'Privity of Contracts – The Benefits and Burdens of Law Reform' (1997) 60 MLR 238, F. Reynolds, 'Privity of Contract' (1997) 113 LQR 53 and S. Smith, 'Contracts for the Benefit of Third Parties: In Defence of the Third Party Rule' (1997) 17 OJLS 643.

[54] G. Williams, 'The Aims of the Law of Tort' (1951) 4 CLP 137.

[55] See M. Jones, *Textbook on Torts* (4th edn, London, Blackstone Press, 1993), p. 14.

[56] Although there will be occasions when tort law depends on the parties entering into a relationship, for example, in relation to negligent statements or liability of employers.

[57] [1932] AC 562.

contract, this is often difficult to establish. Secondly, the law of tort does not, in general, allow recovery for pure economic loss. If a consumer buys a defective washing machine the consumer will be able to recover damages from the supplier in contract. If the washing machine had been given to the consumer as a present, he would not be able to seek redress, either from the supplier or the manufacturer. This is because the consumer is not part of a contractual relationship, and there is no general right in tort to recover damages for the cost of putting a product right, which is classified as pure economic loss. This contrasts with the situation where the washing machine burns a hole in the consumer's kitchen floor. Here the consumer would be able to recover damages for the cost of correcting that as the product has caused property damage outside itself.

Just as there has been state intervention in the law of contract, so there has been in the law of tort. Since the implementation of Part I of the Consumer Protection Act 1987 there has been strict liability for defective products and so seeking compensation for injury caused by defective products is, in theory at least, easier than before the Act. However, the dearth of case law on Part I and the width of the development risks defence raise doubts about the extent to which the provision has improved consumer protection in practical terms. To a large extent, seeking redress under the law of tort remains illusory for many consumers.

Private law and transaction costs

Perhaps the main limitation of private law is that it relies upon the victim for its enforcement. A rational individual will not enforce the law unless the expected benefit exceeds the expected cost, and in the case of many consumer disputes the costs of ensuring redress will be prohibitive. These 'transaction costs', in particular enforcement costs, pose the greatest obstacle to consumers' ability to rely on the market for protection. Transaction costs include search costs, and bargaining costs, as well as enforcement costs. The difficulties of securing optimal information through search are dealt with in detail later in this chapter.[58] Difficulties presented by bargaining costs are obvious. Consumers often do not have the time, skills, or inclination to bargain effectively and make informed decisions accordingly. But it is in relation to enforcement costs that we see particular difficulties. Litigation is time-consuming, uncertain, and expensive, particularly as costs have traditionally been paid by the unsuccessful party. These obstacles are compounded by other factors.

[58] See below, p. 20.

First, many difficulties of substantive law face the consumer. Problems of establishing causation where there has been personal injury, and of showing fault where the action is in negligence, are obvious examples. These obstacles increase the likelihood that an action will be unsuccessful, and so the risks involved in taking action. Secondly, private law remedies will only be effectively utilised where consumers are aware of their rights.[59] There can be little doubt that steps have been taken to improve awareness, with publications such as *Which?* and television programmes such as *Watchdog* informing consumers of action they can take, but there is still a long way to go. The Office of Fair Trading (OFT) has long regarded the publication of booklets and leaflets to explain consumer rights as one of its key functions, and there is evidence that techniques such as distributing leaflets can be beneficial.[60] Furthermore, it is interesting to note that the Financial Services Authority, which has been given the responsibility for regulating financial services in the UK, has, as one of its regulatory objectives, 'public awareness', alongside the more traditional objectives for a financial regulator of market confidence, protection of consumers, and reduction of financial crime. The Authority has said that it will work alongside government departments, business and consumer groups to promote financial literacy, consumer information, and advice. The importance of consumer awareness has also been recognised at an international level. The UN Guidelines for Consumer Protection state that '[g]overnments should develop or encourage the development of general consumer education and information programmes' and that '[c]onsumer education should, where appropriate, become an integral part of the basic curriculum of the educational system. . .'.[61] There can be little doubt that ignorance of the law is one of the principal impediments to consumer protection and that measures to eradicate this ignorance will be an important part of an effective consumer policy.

A further matter for concern with private law is that it may have undesirable distributive effects. Wilhelmsson has argued that by emphasising individual claims consumer law reproduces injustice. As litigation will generally only be undertaken by more affluent and better-educated consumers, only they will be protected effectively.[62] This is examined later in

[59] See the discussion of consumer education in H. Beales, R. Craswell, and S. Salop, 'The Efficient Regulation of Consumer Information' (1981) 24 *Journal of Law and Economics* 49.

[60] H. Genn, *Meeting Legal Needs? An Evaluation of a Scheme for Personal Injury Victims* (Oxford, Centre for Socio-Legal Studies, 1982).

[61] It is interesting to note the UK Government's decision to have citizenship taught in schools as part of the National Curriculum in the light of this.

[62] Wilhelmsson, 'Consumer Law and Social Justice' in Ramsay (ed.), *Consumer Law in the Global Economy*, p. 217.

the context of discussing social justice. Recent developments in the civil justice system have been designed to improve access to justice for less affluent consumers, for example, raising the limit of the county court's small claims procedure, and streamlining case management, but the extent to which they are likely to be successful is unclear.[63] Leff's observation that 'one cannot think of a more expensive and frustrating course than to seek to regulate goods or contract "quality" through repeated law suits against inventive "wrongdoers"' rings true.[64]

Market failure

It is widely accepted that the perfect market considered above does not exist in reality, and it is clear that the private law on which it is based suffers from limitations that make it an inadequate basis for protecting consumers. Howells and Weatherill describe the idea of the perfect market as being 'as alluring as it is unrealistic'[65] and Cranston has likened the free market economist to 'the foolish man who built his house upon the sand'.[66] Certainly, the characteristics of the perfect market could never, it is submitted, be created in their entirety. However, this does not mean that discussing free markets is pointless. One possible consumer protection policy would be to try to create, as far as is possible and cost effective, the conditions of a perfect market. The next section looks at the reasons why market failure might occur and considers the appropriate responses that the law might make to this.

Absence of competition

Markets may fail through the absence of competition. If the market is to function effectively, it is important that no individual firm or group of firms has sufficient power to influence price. However, '[t]he notion that rival suppliers must dance to the consumer's tune is false where the consumer's influence is thwarted because of a lack of competition'.[67] The

---

[63] See Scott and Black, *Cranston's Consumers and the Law*, pp. 110–20.

[64] A. A. Leff, 'Unconscionability and the Crowd – Consumer and the Common Law Tradition' (1970) 31 University of Pittsburgh Law Review 349 at p. 356. However, it may not be as expensive as public regulation. See S. Shavell, 'Liability for Harm Versus Regulation of Safety' (1984) 13 J Legal Stud 357.

[65] G. G. Howells and S. Weatherill, *Consumer Protection Law* (Aldershot, Dartmouth and Ashgale, 1995), p. 1.

[66] R. Cranston, 'Consumer Protection Law and Economic Theory' in A. J. Duggan and L. W. Darvall (eds.), *Consumer Protection Law and Theory* (Sydney, The Law Book Company, 1980), p. 243.

[67] Howells and Weatherill, *Consumer Protection Law*, pp. 2–3.

law can play an important role in avoiding monopolies and, in particular, in controlling abuse of a monopolistic or oligopolistic position. This could be done by removing behavioural restrictions such as cartels, and structural restrictions such as monopolies themselves. In practice, it may be unrealistic to expect perfect competition. In some cases there will be natural monopolies, where it is less costly to society for production to be carried out by one firm than by several.[68] There are different ways of responding to this, and it is not possible to examine them in any detail here.[69] Suffice it to say that some markets will be subject to structural problems that make having numerous competitors unrealistic. Indeed, competition may even be undesirable, for example if it discourages innovation because of the risk of competitors taking up a product developed by their rival. Laws of intellectual property are thus used to suppress competition in the broader public interest. For these reasons, the aim is often said to be 'workable' rather than 'perfect' competition. Although the former term could be criticised as unduly vague and flexible, it is submitted that it reflects a realistic approach to what can, and should, be achieved by way of competition.[70]

Barriers to entry

Free entry and exit are aspects of the market over which governments have a significant amount of control. Subject to international obligations, it would be possible to allow any trader who wishes to do so to enter a particular market, and to allow that trader's business to fail if unsuccessful. In reality, governments elect to impose barriers to entry and exit in certain sectors of the economy. Barriers to entry are generally imposed through prior approval schemes. For example, banks must be authorised by the Financial Services Authority, and anyone accepting a deposit from the public without authorisation commits an offence.[71] Prior approval is seen as justified because of the risks to consumers from unauthorised banks, who may be poorly capitalised, and the risk to the financial system at large from bank failure. Although prior approval has been the subject of criticism, it is widely viewed as an essential element of the banking regulatory framework.[72] Governments show an equal reluctance to allow free exit from the market where banks are concerned. A bank whose

---

[68] A. I. Ogus, *Regulation: Legal Form and Economic Theory* (Oxford, Clarendon Press, 1994), p. 30.

[69] See Ogus, ibid. pp. 30–3.

[70] See Howells and Weatherill, *Consumer Protection Law*, pp. 443–4.

[71] Banking Act 1987.

[72] See for example K. Dowd, *Laissez-Faire Banking* (London, Routledge, 1993).

failure is thought to have implications for the soundness of the financial system will not be allowed by governments to exit the market through insolvency – the so-called 'too big to fail' doctrine. There will be arguments against free entry in other areas too, particularly where the risks posed by a particular sector are seen to be great, such as pharmaceuticals.[73] Although free entry and exit are seen as characteristics of the perfect market, they are characteristics which governments, in general, are not prepared to endure in all sectors. Indeed, it is interesting to note that a recent report for the OFT argued that misleading and false information is particularly likely to be provided where barriers to entry and exit are relatively small.[74] A final point to note is that barriers to entry are not only imposed by governments through prior approval schemes. In some cases, there will inevitably be high entry costs to an industry, for example if a new business has to lay new pipelines for the supply of water or gas. This, too, will make it difficult for new business to enter the market and so will limit the benefits of competition.

Product homogeneity

The requirement of product homogeneity is closely linked to that of perfect information. The market is said to fail where there are qualitative differences within a particular product market, such that consumers are unable to compare like with like. This is most relevant in the context of advertising. Traders can use artificial product differentiation to create illusory differences between similar products, for example through brand advertising.[75] This is considered in relation to information below, and in relation to the protection of economic interests in chapter 6.

Information deficits

One of the characteristics of the perfect market is that economic actors, including consumers, have 'perfect information' about the nature and value of commodities traded. In reality, we know that consumers can face difficulties in obtaining and using information about products they are considering purchasing. They may suffer from information asymmetry in that they know less than another party (generally the supplier) and will frequently suffer from some information imperfections (in the

---

[73] See ch. 5.

[74] *Consumer Detriment Under Conditions of Imperfect Information* (Office of Fair Trading Research Paper II, August 1997), p. 103.

[75] See I. Ramsay, *Advertising, Culture and the Law: Beyond Lies, Ignorance and Manipulation* (London, Sweet and Maxwell, 1996), pp. 6–7 and 30–40.

sense of having less than perfect information). A major element of consumer protection policy has been trying to remedy these information problems.[76] Indeed, it has been argued that this formed 'the key analytical basis for early consumer protection law'.[77] It is for this reason that a significant amount of space is devoted to examining the role of information in consumer protection. However, it should be noted that because of the impossibility of providing perfect information, intervention has generally sought to achieve 'optimal' information. In other words, enough information to enable the consumer to make an informed choice.

It has been argued that there are three main types of information that a consumer is likely to want when considering making a purchase: the price of the product and other products (complements and substitutes), the quality of the product (relative to substitutes), and the terms of trade.[78] If the consumer has this information, and understands it, she is able to make an optimal purchase and thus fulfil her economic role as a maximiser of her own utility. Some commentators have emphasised the significant incentives upon traders to supply information that consumers demand to win custom, and have suggested that they will supply this information even when it is not required by law.[79] Certainly, there will be an incentive on traders to supply information which they believe will lead to an increase in profits. London Economics' recent report entitled *Consumer Detriment Under Conditions of Imperfect Information* argued that we can expect traders to disclose information that is easy to understand, easy to verify, effective in attracting customers, and can be provided cost effectively. We can, therefore, expect traders to disclose the price of products, objectively identifiable quality characteristics (such as materials used or performance achieved), and similar, but only, in general, where they place the trader's products in a favourable light.

While the market may be expected to supply some information, it is unlikely to supply perfect information for a number of reasons. First, there are different classes of goods. Credence goods are those whose characteristics cannot be determined until some point in the future, often long after a contract is entered into, such as a pension. A consumer will not know how the pension is likely to perform over a long period of time, and

---

[76] This has occurred both at national and European level. See S. Weatherill, 'The Role of the Informed Consumer in European Community Law and Policy' (1994) 2 Consum LJ 49. See also W. Whitford, 'The Functions of Disclosure Regulation in Consumer Transactions' (1973) Wisc LR 400.

[77] G. Hadfield, R. Howse, and M. J. Trebilcock, 'Information-Based Principles for Rethinking Consumer Protection Policy' (1998) 21 JCP 131 at p. 134.

[78] See *Consumer Detriment under Conditions of Imperfect Information*, p. 38.

[79] G. Benston, *Regulating Financial Markets* (London, Institute of Economic Affairs, 1998).

will also be unlikely to know what his needs will be in the future. Although it will be possible to know some characteristics of the product at the time of purchase it will not be possible to know many of the key characteristics which would, in an ideal world, influence the consumer's choice. Experience goods are those whose characteristics can only be identified when they are received, used, or consumed.[80] Where experience goods are purchased frequently and are of relatively little importance, it may not matter that their characteristics could not be ascertained in advance. A consumer who buys a chocolate bar he does not like can simply choose to buy another in the future and hope to influence the market in that way. Where a product is only purchased occasionally, however, switching suppliers may have less effect. It may be that news of a consumer's unsatisfactory car will be passed on to others, of course, and that their decisions will be affected by the original experience. This may have an effect on the market although it will be of little comfort to the original purchaser. Concerns will be particularly great where safety is at issue, even in the absence of externalities. Finally, search goods are those goods, the characteristics of which can be ascertained prior to purchase, for example a poster. Whether a consumer will obtain perfect information about search goods will, to a large extent, depend on his decision about the likely benefits from making a search as against the costs involved. This is considered below.

Even where products cannot be described as credence goods, many will have some characteristics of credence goods. For example, a consumer may be able to identify many of the physical characteristics of a motor car before purchase, but he will never know all the factors that could influence his decision to buy. He may have some data that car A is more reliable than car B, but he will never know if and when the particular car he buys will break down. This information is, of course, something that cannot be supplied, either by the market or as a result of regulation.

Even where it is possible for the market to disclose information that would be useful to consumers, a trader may be unwilling to disclose it. Information may be expensive to collate, or too complex to influence many consumers. Alternatively, it may be vague and difficult for consumers to verify. As a consequence, the trader may make a rational decision not to supply it. From this, we may conclude that certain types of information are more likely to be supplied than others. Price, for example, is more likely to be communicated then quality. This point is developed by G. Akerlof in relation to second hand cars in his seminal article 'The Market for "Lemons": Qualitative Uncertainty and the Market Mechanism'.[81]

---

[80] See Ogus, *Regulation*, pp. 132–3.
[81] (1970) 84 QJEcon 488.

He argues that if consumers are unable to distinguish between high-quality and low-quality cars they will assume that all cars are of average quality. This will have the effect of reducing the market price for high-quality cars and so reducing the profits of dealers selling high-quality cars. There will, therefore, be no incentive to sell high-quality cars. It should further be remembered that traders do not only supply information through direct means. The existence of guarantees and warranties may provide a more reliable indication to a consumer of the quality of a product than claims about its performance. There will be a particular incentive to provide such facilities where there are likely to be repeat purchases.[82]

Another reason why full information may not be disclosed is because it puts the trader's product in an unfavourable light. For example, a trader is unlikely to disclose that his product is outperformed in a material way by a substitute product. We might respond that this does not matter, provided the information is supplied by the competitor. However, traders often appear reluctant to engage in comparative advertising, partly through fear of reprisals, but also because comparative information may lead to an overall reduction in demand for the type of product. For example, an advertisement that X's aeroplanes are safer than Y's or that A's cigarettes cause fewer deaths than B's may lead to a reduction in the consumption of X's and A's products as well as Y's and B's.[83] A second response to the argument that traders will not supply objective information is to say that if there is a demand for that information, third parties will emerge who will provide it. There will be occasions where this occurs, but it should be remembered that information has the characteristics of a public good. This means that individuals may benefit from it without having to pay the price of that benefit. There may therefore be a tendency for others to 'free ride', and a resulting under-provision of the commodity.[84]

A further reason why consumers might not receive perfect information is that traders may choose to supply information in an opaque manner. For example, we noted above that price is a type of information that the market will be likely to supply, but there is no guarantee that information supplied will convey the whole price. It is possible for certain aspects of the cost of a product to be hidden, particularly when products are bundled together with add-ons, such as in the case of maintenance contracts.[85] Similarly, it seems unlikely that an unregulated market would provide clarity in supplying information about the cost of credit because of the

---

[82] See George L. Priest, 'A Theory of the Consumer Product Warranty' (1981) 90 (6) Yale L J 1297 and *Consumer Detriment Under Conditions of Imperfect Information*, p. 40.
[83] See *Consumer Detriment Under Conditions of Imperfect Information*, p. 38.
[84] See Ogus, *Regulation*, pp. 33–5.
[85] *Consumer Detriment Under Conditions of Imperfect Information*, p. 85.

ease with which the price of credit can be disguised. Where a misleading price indication is given it may be possible to take action on the basis of fraud legislation, but there will be many cases where the information cannot be classed as false or misleading, but is, at best, incomplete.

There will be cases where the structure of the market is such that traders are not under an incentive to give an objective indication of the characteristics of products. A seller acting under commission will be under an incentive to sell the products that provide the best commission, rather than those that best meet the customer's requirements, particularly if there is unlikely to be regular trading between trader and consumer.

The actions of consumers will also dictate the extent to which the market supplies perfect information. The rational consumer will look at the expected gain from searching for information and will weigh this against the costs of searching. There may be many cases where the consumer will consider it so difficult to seek out information which in an ideal world he would like to have, that he takes a chance and does not search. A rational supplier will, of course, take this into account when deciding what to disclose.

The view that the market will supply information because consumers will demand it assumes that consumers know the best questions to ask in order for them to maximise their utility. Where a product is complex, for example, a computer, it may be possible for a trader to convince a consumer that she has given him all the information he could want, when she has omitted to supply information for which, if the consumer had understood more about computers, he would have asked. This will provide an opportunity for abuse, particularly where the trader is acting on commission. Furthermore, even if all possible information about a product is supplied, the consumer will not necessarily be able to make a truly informed decision about whether to purchase the product. This is because consumers suffer from bounded rationality: in other words, their ability to deal with information is limited. Because of this, consumers do not, in general, want to be told everything about a product.[86] They want to be told about those characteristics which will help them to make an informed decision. As traders are aware of consumers' cognitive limitations, they are able to take advantage of this.[87] They might do this by presenting information in a biased way, by making information complicated, and by concentrating on particular attributes, known as 'focal points of competition'.[88] There is overlap here with what was said about

---

[86] J. Jacoby, 'Perspectives on Information Overload' (1984) 10 *Journal of Consumer Research* 432.

[87] M. Cohen, 'Insights into Consumer Confusion' (1999) 6 J C Policy 210.

[88] *Consumer Detriment Under Conditions of Imperfect Information*, pp. 51–4.

the incentives upon traders to disclose some information but not other. One of the factors they will consider is what information the consumer is likely to rely upon. We have said that consumers cannot take in all information about products, and so will only, in reality, want limited information. It might seem desirable, therefore, that traders should supply only that information that consumers are likely to rely upon. However, a rational trader may decide to present some information in a clear way, and other information in an opaque way, in the hope that consumers will be drawn to the former. *Consumer Detriment* gives the example of extended warranties on electronic appliances. Knowing that the focal point of competition is likely to be the price of the primary purchase (the electronic appliance) a trader may push the sale of a complement, such as an extended warranty, at a relatively high price. Although there will apparently be an incentive for competitors to reveal the high price of the complement, it is not clear to what extent this happens in practice.

From the above discussion, we can conclude that traders are under an incentive to supply that information which they deem most effective in maximising profits. This will not always be the same information that maximises consumers' ability to make the best choice. As a result, regulation may be desirable to rectify this market failure. One final point to note here is that in trying to rectify some aspects of market failure, other types of failure may be generated. For example, markets which have low barriers to entry and a large number of buyers and sellers meet some aspects of the perfect market, but these markets may present significant difficulties in relation to consumer information.[89] In practice, a trade-off between the different characteristics may be necessary.

Absence of externalities

If the market mechanism is to resolve consumers' grievances, then it is important that only those who are party to a transaction will be affected by that transaction. Only they take the benefits from the transaction, and only they suffer from any detriment imposed by it. As we have seen, the law of contract does not generally impose benefits and burdens upon those who are not party to the contract. However, third parties will be affected by decisions made by others within the market framework. As a result, the requirement that there are no externalities, sometimes called 'spillovers', cannot always be achieved. A simple example relates to a contract for the sale of a defective car. If a consumer pays £100 less for

---

[89] For example second-hand cars and home improvements. See Hadfield, Howse, and Trebilcock, 'Information-Based Principles', p. 153.

a car with defective tyres than he would for a car with safe tyres and drives it home, that may be appropriate *vis à vis* the seller. However, the sale of that car imposes additional costs in terms of the danger that it poses to third parties.[90] Externalities exist where some harm or benefit results from an activity which is not taken into account by the market price. Unless this is 'internalised' (borne by the parties), the price of the product does not reflect its true cost. Because the costs of externalities are not borne by those who cause them, there is little incentive from an economic point of view for the parties to deal with them.

Some internalising can take place through the private law. For example, the law of tort can distribute resources from the tortfeasor to the victim. Negligence may enable those who are injured by a defective car to recover damages for the loss they have suffered. Nuisance can provide a means for those affected by pollution to seek a remedy from the polluter. However, that is unlikely to be a satisfactory solution for a number of reasons. First, transaction costs present an obstacle to reliance on tortious remedies. Pollution may adversely affect a wide range of people, all with an interest in seeing the pollution stopped, but none with sufficient incentive to bear the cost of litigation. If one victim takes action successfully to prevent the pollution, all the other victims will benefit without the need to bear the cost of the litigation. They will therefore be under an incentive to free ride on the actions of others. Secondly, if we value the protection of individual autonomy, the law of tort is unlikely to provide an appealing solution.[91]

Commentators have used the principles of the market system to explain how, in theory, it is possible to overcome externalities through 'utility maximising contracts' made with all the third parties affected.[92] Calls have therefore been heard for a re-arrangement of private property rights rather than regulation imposed by the state.[93] However, it is recognised that, in practice, this will be unrealistic. Ogus identifies several problems with achieving this. As well as the problems of transaction costs and free-riders identified above, there is the difficulty of taking into account the number of people who may be affected over a long period of time. This is particularly evident in areas such as environmental law, where a harmful

---

[90] For this reason there is an offence of supplying an unroadworthy road vehicle under s.75 of the Road Traffic Act 1978.

[91] See for example M. Sagoff, 'On Markets for Risk' (1982) 41 *Maryland Law Review* 755.

[92] Ogus, *Regulation*, p. 19.

[93] See S. Breyer, 'Typical Justifications for Regulation', chapter 1 in S. Breyer, *Regulation and its Reform* (Cambridge, Mass., Harvard University Press, 1982) and G. Calabresi and A. Melamed, 'Property Rules, Liability Rules and Inalienability: One View of the Cathedral' (1972) 85 Harvard LR 1089.

activity may affect future generations.[94] For these reasons, it may be better to impose regulation, for example through standards, in order to ensure that those affected by the decisions of others are protected.

The discussion of market-based approaches to consumer protection reveals the benefits and limitations of the market and private law. There can be little doubt that competitive markets bring many benefits to consumers. In practice, however, the market is unlikely to work perfectly for the reasons discussed above. One further point to note is that even where a market is competitive, there may be reasons why consumers are unable to be protected through market mechanisms. Hadfield, Howse, and Trebilcock note a number of reasons for this.[95] First, repeat transactions may be rare, and so traders are under little incentive to ensure consumer satisfaction. Secondly, entry and exit costs are low, so fly-by-night traders may be common. Thirdly, traders may be outside the jurisdiction, making private law redress difficult. Fourthly, sellers may have insufficient assets against which a judgement can be enforced. Fifthly, the costs of a bad transaction may be delayed, for example, because the goods in question are credence goods. Finally, the size of the transaction may be small, giving the consumer little incentive to go to court. These factors illustrate that even where markets are competitive (albeit imperfect) consumer protection may be a mirage. A further point to note is that markets focus upon the efficient allocation of resources rather than the fair allocation of resources. If consumer protection is about fairness as well as efficiency, the market may be found wanting. It is to the issue of social justice and social policy that we now turn.

Consumer protection and social policy

In addition to market-based reasons for regulation, there are also justifications which may be described as ethical, non-economic, public interest, or social.[96] Ogus identifies these goals as distributive justice, paternalism, and community values, although, as we will see, some examples of intervention can be explained on more than one of these grounds.[97] Furthermore, it should be emphasised that the distinction between market and social goals is imperfect. For example, intervention which appears

---

[94] See Ogus, *Regulation*, pp. 19–20.

[95] Hadfield, Howse, and Trebilcock, 'Information-Based Principles', pp. 155–6.

[96] Ramsay refers to 'ethical goals' (*Consumer Protection*, p. 47), Prosser to 'public interest' rationales (T. Prosser, 'Regulation, Markets and Legitimacy' in J. Jowell and D. Oliver (eds.), *The Changing Constitution* (4th edn, Oxford, Oxford University Press, 2000)), p. 229, and Ogus to 'non-economic justifications for intervention' (*Regulation*, p. 46). I use the broad term 'social justifications'.

[97] Ogus, *Regulation*, pp. 46–54.

to be 'social' may improve the market, and mechanisms aimed at addressing market failure may have desirable social benefits. The following sections examine the main social justifications for intervening to protect the consumer.

Distributive justice

A distinction can be drawn between corrective and distributive justice. Corrective justice involves protecting individual entitlements by providing a remedy for the correction of a wrong, such as a breach of contract or a tort.[98] It focuses primarily upon individual claims made under private law. By contrast, distributive justice is concerned with the redistribution of power and resources on the basis of what is just, or equitable, rather than on the grounds of what is economically efficient.[99] The aim of distributive justice is to redistribute from one group to another, such as from the affluent to the poor, the strong to the weak, or simply from traders to consumers. Distributive justice can be associated with a number of ideological movements, including socialism,[100] and liberalism.[101] One of the reasons for using the term free market economics rather than economic liberalism in this chapter is that the term liberalism can be used to describe those who favour distributive justice. In the words of Paul Krugman: 'I am a liberal – that is, I believe in a society that taxes the well-off and uses the proceeds to help the poor and unlucky.'[102] Many commentators who identify themselves as liberals would not support such distributive measures. Friedman argued that 'one cannot be both an egalitarian . . . and a liberal', although even he accepted that the state had a role in supplying a basic provision for the poor.[103]

Some commentators have examined distributive justice from the perspective of a transfer from trader to consumer on the assumption that the latter is the weaker party. Inequality of bargaining power between traders and consumers, in particular, has been used to justify distributive measures.[104] However, this can be criticised as masking more subtle

---

[98] Ramsay, *Rationales*, p. 57.
[99] Ogus, *Regulation*, pp. 46–51.
[100] V. George and P. Wilding, *Ideology and Social Welfare* (New York, Harvester Wheatsheaf, 1994), cited in Ogus, *Regulation*.
[101] See J. Meade, *The Intelligent Radical's Guide to Economic Policy* (London, Allen and Unwin, 1975).
[102] P. Krugman, *Peddling Prosperity: Economic Sense and Nonsense in the Age of Diminished Expectations* (New York, Norton, 1993), cited in D. Henderson, *The Changing Fortunes of Economic Liberalism: Yesterday, Today and Tomorrow* (London, Institute of Economic Affairs, 1998), p. 20.
[103] Friedman, *Capitalism and Freedom*, p. 163.
[104] In the words of Ramsay, '[i]t is . . . difficult to find official or unofficial writings of the 1960s and 70s on consumer protection which do not refer at some point to this rationale'. Ramsay, *Consumer Protection*, p. 57.

distinctions. By treating consumers as a homogeneous entity who all deserve the same kind of protection, the law may fail to recognise the huge
differences between consumers. By improving the position of consumers
as a whole, we may not see a distribution to the most needy groups
within the consumer collective. As we have seen, Wilhelmsson argues
that consumer law may conceal and even reproduce injustice by placing emphasis on information regulation and individual claims, both of
which will tend to benefit affluent middle-class consumers.[105] Perhaps,
therefore, we need to examine the distributive effects of policies among
different groups of consumers and producers, and decide to whom, and
from whom, we should distribute.[106] There is evidence that bodies such
as the OFT are doing this.[107]

Distributive justice and vulnerability. One group of consumers to
whom we might wish to distribute are the vulnerable.[108] In a recent
report for the OFT, Ramil Burden argues that consumers may be vulnerable for two reasons. First, they may find it more difficult to obtain
or deal with the information needed to make purchasing decisions, and
secondly they may suffer greater loss than other consumers by making inappropriate purchasing decisions.[109] Burden identifies seven vulnerable
groups, namely the elderly, the young, the unemployed, those with a limiting, long-standing illness, those in low-income households, members
of ethnic minorities, and those with no formal educational qualifications.
Burden recognises that there will be substantial overlap between groups,
and concludes that less than one-third of the population of Great Britain
features in none of the vulnerable groups. However, membership of a
group does not necessarily make a person vulnerable; it is merely an
indication of vulnerability.

So how should consumer law take particular account of the needs of
vulnerable consumers? First, if we take the approach of Burden and say
that one aspect of vulnerability is the difficulty of obtaining and assimilat-
ing the information necessary to make an appropriate purchase, then this
can be partially rectified by information remedies, in particular disclosure. However, if we are trying to ensure a degree of distributive justice

[105] See Wilhelmsson, 'Consumer Law and Social Justice'.
[106] Ramsay, *Rationales*, p. 13.
[107] John Bridgeman when Director General of Fair Trading described the OFT's approach
to prioritising its resources as 'Cost Benefit Analysis with a social distribution element'.
J. Bridgeman, 'A Speech to the Year Ahead Symposium', 28 January 1998.
[108] Other possible groupings would be poor consumers (see D. Caplowitz, *The Poor Pay
More* (New York, Free Press, 1963)) or disadvantaged consumers (see A. R. Andreasen,
The Disadvantaged Consumer (New York, 1975), cited in Wilhelmsson, 'Consumer Law
and Social Justice').
[109] R. Burden, *Vulnerable Consumer Groups: Quantification and Analysis* (OFT Research
Paper 15, April 1998), p. 5.

we need to take particular account of the needs of the most vulnerable when establishing the regulatory scheme. For example, one reason why members of ethnic minorities might be particularly vulnerable is because of their difficulty in understanding English.[110] An appropriate regulatory response might be to insist that some information be supplied in minority languages. Such provision would be distributive, in the sense that the cost of regulation would be born initially by traders, and then passed on equally to all customers, but would benefit a specific, and potentially vulnerable, group. Similarly, if one difficulty is that information tends to be disclosed in a way which vulnerable consumers find difficult to follow, then there is an argument for dictating how disclosure takes place. This happens in areas such as the price of consumer credit, but more could be done to achieve this. Measures such as this are also market-correcting, in that they enable the vulnerable consumer to make the informed choice in accordance with his preferences that is essential for the market to function effectively. This illustrates the difficulties with separating market and non-market approaches to regulation.

The second aspect of vulnerability identified by Burden is based upon the greater welfare loss suffered by a vulnerable consumer through purchasing inappropriate goods and services, or failing to purchase appropriate goods and services.[111] This loss may result from information deficits, and so may be solved, to some extent, by information remedies such as disclosure. However, there may be other causes of such welfare loss. One factor to bear in mind is that a consumer may purchase a product which is appropriate at the time of purchase, but becomes inappropriate over time. An example is an investment product which requires regular payments to be made over a long period of time. Low-income consumers are likely to be particularly vulnerable to job insecurity and resulting income volatility. Such problems are extremely difficult for consumer law to resolve, unless there has been mis-selling. Another possible solution would be the introduction of what might be referred to as 'Let the Poor Pay Less' rules. One example of such a measure is the social *force majeure* clause.[112] This applies where the consumer is affected by some unforeseen special occurrence such as illness or unemployment for which he was not at fault

---

[110] This will, of course, depend on a number of factors, such as the community in question and the age and gender of the individual concerned. For example, recent research has found that just 10 per cent of Bangladeshi women in the UK who were aged from fifty to seventy-four years were able to speak English, while the figure for young men from the same community was 92 per cent.

[111] See also F. Cowell and K. Gardiner, *Welfare Weights* (OFT Research Paper 20, January 2000).

[112] Wilhelmsson, '"Social Force Majeure" – A New Concept in Nordic Consumer Law' (1990) 13 JCP 1.

and which causes him difficulty in paying his debts. In such an event, the consumer will be given certain benefits. For example, he might have a defence against liability to pay damages in case of delay, or even be able to terminate a long-term contract.[113] Other forms of consumer bankruptcy laws have similar effect. A re-distribution from creditors and from one group of consumers to another through the market framework takes place on the basis of distributive justice. It is important that where such measures are used they apply where there has not been fault on the part of the consumer. Were it otherwise, there would be a risk of moral hazard, with the consumer being under little incentive to take the consequences of his actions.

A further reason why consumers might be vulnerable is because they have a limited choice of products. The consumer may be able to obtain all the relevant information about a product, but this will be of little use if she is unable to purchase that product. Of course, we cannot expect all consumers to have the means to purchase all products. Nevertheless, where the product in question is something we would class as a necessity, we might see it as appropriate for the law to make it easier for vulnerable consumers to have access to that product.[114] In some ways, consumer law may exacerbate this problem through mechanisms such as product safety standards and credit ceilings, which may reduce the numbers of products available. For example, safety standards may take the cost of goods beyond the less affluent, and credit ceilings might make it uneconomic to lend to poorer consumers, leading creditors to exit the market, or create a black market.[115] However, such measures have received a more sympathetic hearing from some commentators.[116] It is possible for the government to insist that traders supply to vulnerable consumers, even where this is uneconomic, but this is generally limited to utilities.[117] Where vulnerability results from lack of choice, the best regulatory response may be the creation of new products or means of supply.[118] Of course, a consumer's lack of choice may not be due solely to the price of a product, but because of problems of access. This is likely to be a significant problem for those with a long-standing illness or disability. Similarly, some products are only available for those with bank accounts, computers, or

---

[113] Ibid.
[114] For example by placing duties on utilities providers. See Scott and Black, *Cranston's Consumers and the Law*, pp. 220–7.
[115] Cayne and Trebilcock, 'Market Considerations'.
[116] G. Howells, 'Seeking Social Justice for Poor Consumers in Credit Markets' in Ramsay (ed.), *Consumer Law in the Global Economy*.
[117] See e.g. Telecommunications Act 1984 s.3(1)(a).
[118] For example, using Post Offices for banking.

telephones.[119] While substitute products will generally be available for these consumers, they are likely only to be available on less favourable terms. There comes a point where the only effective method for ensuring access to vulnerable consumers is through the welfare state rather than through consumer law. Furthermore, where access is denied on grounds such as race or gender, anti-discrimination measures, which are increasingly viewed as part of consumer law, may provide a solution.[120]

There are other ways in which consumers may be vulnerable. First, they may be more susceptible to trickery than their less credulous fellow consumers. Secondly, they may be particularly susceptible to pressure, for example from aggressive selling techniques. These issues are central to the discussion which emerges in chapter 6 about how the law protects certain types of interests, and are examined in more detail there. Suffice it to say that consumer law, interpreted broadly, can play a significant part in ensuring distributive justice.

Paternalism

The doctrine of paternalism justifies intervention by the state contrary to the wishes of the person whom that intervention is designed to benefit. It has been described as 'the interference with a person's liberty of action justified by reasons referring exclusively to the welfare, good, happiness, needs, interests or values of the person being coerced'.[121] Where paternalism is the sole justification for intervention, the law is invoked regardless of the desires of the individual. We use paternalistic laws in contract, for example, to prevent people from causing themselves harm through their own 'ill considered or disadvantageous promises'.[122] This appears to place paternalism squarely at odds with the market mechanism, with the individual's wishes being replaced by the state's. Product safety laws could be classed as paternalistic, because they deny consumers the choice of which risks they are prepared to accept, as could interest rate ceilings, as they dictate the terms on which credit agreements will be valid. Other examples of laws that could be described as paternalistic are

---

[119] *Vulnerable Consumers and Financial Services: The Report of the Director General's Inquiry* (January 1999), para. 3.16.

[120] See for example I. Ramsay and T. Williams, 'Racial and Gender Equality in Markets for Financial Services' in Cartwright (ed.), *Consumer Protection in Financial Services*, p. 267, and I. Ramsay, 'Consumer Credit Law, Distributive Justice and the Welfare State' (1995) 15 OJLS 177.

[121] G. Dworkin, 'Paternalism' in R. Wasserstrom (ed.), *Morality and the Law* (Belmont, Calif., Wadsworth Publishing, 1971), p. 108. Cited in Ogus, *Regulation*, p. 51.

[122] A. Kronman, 'Paternalism and the Law of Contracts' (1983) 92 Yale LJ 763 at 798.

the requirement that goods must be of satisfactory quality and reasonably fit for their purpose,[123] and the provision that liability for death or personal injury cannot be excluded by any contract term.[124] Consumers are unable to 'contract out' of these provisions, and so the protection is there whether they want it or not. Of course, consumers are not obliged to enforce their rights if they do not want to, but they are obliged to pay for the law's protection. A provision which states that all goods must be of reasonable quality is, in effect, a compulsory insurance policy against goods turning out to be substandard.[125] However, unlike some other areas of compulsory insurance, such as third-party cover for drivers, it cannot be explained on grounds of externalities. It is designed for the benefit of the consumer, and the consumer must accept it.

Justifications for intervention based on paternalism are frequently criticised on both ideological and practical grounds. In relation to ideology, freedom of contract provides an illustration. Freedom of contract means freedom to make choices, including those that the state would not have made. Sometimes, these choices will appear to be, and end up being, contrary to the best interests of one of the parties. But the essence of freedom means that in return for being able to make our own choices, we are obliged to accept responsibility for those choices. Consumer sovereignty, in the words of Schelling, 'includes the inalienable right of the consumer to make his own mistakes'.[126] We may wish to take the chance of a washing-machine being faulty in return for getting it more cheaply than if it were sold with a warranty. Sale of Goods legislation denies us this freedom by dictating what is in our own interests. This reveals a practical objection to paternalistic legislation: that it raises costs. Because of the role of mandatory implied terms as a form of compulsory insurance policy, the price of goods may be higher than if that policy were not present. If implied terms were not mandatory, consumers would still be able to purchase such a guarantee, but would not be obliged to. A further argument against paternalistic measures such as mandatory implied terms and minimum safety standards is that they may remove low-quality, cheap products from the market place, thus denying their benefits to less affluent consumers. This was considered above in relation to distributive justice. A final objection to paternalistic legislation is

---

[123] Sale of Goods Act 1979 ss. 14(2) and 14(3).
[124] Unfair Contract Terms Act 1977 s.2(1).
[125] See P. S. Atiyah, 'Freedom of Contract and the New Right', ch. 12 in Atiyah, *Essays on Contract.*
[126] T. Schelling, *Choice and Consequence* (Cambridge, Mass., Harvard University Press, 1984), pp. 144–6.

that consumers who are guaranteed goods of satisfactory quality may be under little incentive to take care in choosing their products. This is the problem of moral hazard.

One response to the criticisms that a classical theorist might make of paternalism is that classical theory is based upon the premise that consumers' choices reflect their true wishes. Hart observed that: '[c]hoices may be made or consent given without adequate reflection or appreciation of the consequences; or in pursuit of merely transitory desires; or in various predicaments when the judgment is likely to be clouded; or under inner psychological compulsion; or under pressure by others of a kind too subtle to be susceptible of proof in a law court'.[127] This suggests that when decisions are made, they are not always made with a perfectly clear head, with full knowledge of all the facts, and in the absence of pressure. Commentators have recognised the variety of factors that construct our preferences, from advertising and marketing to class, family, and experiences in the workplace.[128] Trebilcock argues that our challenge should be to identify the choices that would be made 'in the absence of social, economic, liberal, legal, or other influences that have shaped these preferences'.[129] Thus, the role of the law should be to try to identify those choices which we would have made were we not subject to those influences. This is not totally convincing. As Hutchinson observes, there would be no preferences without such influences.[130] However, we must nevertheless consider how preferences are formed and decisions are made in order to decide whether the decision should stand. Classical theory recognises that certain factors, such as threats or fraud, will make a transaction involuntary. Challenging a contract agreed under such circumstances is perfectly consistent with free market theory. The question is how far beyond that the law should go: which threats, pressure, and ignorance give relief and which do not?

If we accept that decisions are made without being in possession of all the facts and recognising the consequences, we can interpret this as a type of information failure. In some cases this can be rectified by disclosure, in other cases it might only be addressed by mandatory standards. Consumer credit law bestows the right to cancel a regulated consumer credit agreement where the agreement has been signed off trade premises

---

[127] H. L. A. Hart, *Law, Liberty and Morality* (Stanford, Stanford University Press, 1963), pp. 32–3.

[128] See J. K. Galbraith, *The Affluent Society* (4th edn, London, André Deutsch, 1984).

[129] M. J. Trebilcock, *The Limits of Freedom of Contract* (Cambridge, Mass., Harvard University Press, 1993), p. 243.

[130] Hutchinson suggests that: 'The real challenge ... is not to wish away the informing context and then hazard a guess at what hypothetical choices would be made, but to work towards creating a context in which people can and must fully develop and experiment with their preferences'. Hutchinson, 'Life After Shopping', p. 32.

following oral representations. This 'cooling-off period' is designed to protect consumers from high-pressure sales techniques, and to give them time to reflect upon the agreement they have signed.[131] It prevents the consumer from binding himself while his judgment is impaired. This is often classified as paternalistic as it applies regardless of the agreement formed between the consumer and the trader. However, it could also be explained on the basis of information failure. The cooling-off period allows the consumer a time for reflection, to peruse all the relevant information, seek advice if necessary, and see if the agreement truly reflects his wishes.

This approach to provisions which appear to be paternalistic is particularly relevant when looking at vulnerability. It has been argued, for example, that poor consumers are more likely to make objectively inappropriate decisions than their more affluent counterparts.[132] They therefore frequently cannot fulfil their paradigmatic role of rational, utility-maximising consumers. The Crowther Committee, for example, made reference to the difficulties for consumers in obtaining redress through 'lack of energy and initiative' and the problems for those who 'lack the ability to budget or to manage their income'. Cayne and Trebilcock argue that evidence suggests that 'the poor are hopelessly entangled in a complex web of psychological and cultural imperatives which further debilitate an already vulnerable condition'.[133] There is research to suggest that the poor are more likely than most to exhibit psychoneurotic symptoms, engage in impulsive action, and be unable to engage in long-term planning. However, this is controversial. Where vulnerability results from illness or ignorance rather than poverty it may be easier to justify measures that appear to be paternalistic. For example, Breyer points to the cancer patient who might purchase a drug even though all the available information suggests that it is worthless or even harmful.[134] Similarly, there is ample economic evidence to suggest that consumers underestimate certain types of risks and overestimate others. However, this is by no means limited to the poorly educated.[135] As a result, we may be better setting minimum standards which reflect the sorts of terms for which the

---

[131] Consumer Credit Act 1974 ss.67–73. Note also the Consumer Protection (Cancellation of Contracts Concluded Away from Business Premises) Regulations 1987 SI 1987/2117.

[132] As opposed to making decisions which turn out to be inappropriate because of changes in circumstances and create increased welfare losses because of the poverty of the consumer.

[133] Cayne and Trebilcock, 'Market Considerations', p. 406.

[134] S. Breyer, 'Typical Justifications for Regulation' in *Regulation and Its Reform* (Cambridge, Mass., Harvard University Press, 1984).

[135] For discussion of some of the literature see G. G. Howells, *Consumer Product Safety* (Aldershot, Dartmouth and Ashgale, 1998), pp. 18–23.

consumer would have bargained, had she been able to make a voluntary, fully informed decision.

A second way in which many provisions which are commonly described as paternalistic can be justified is on the grounds of externalities. Product safety laws, sometimes criticised on grounds of paternalism, can frequently be justified on this basis. Even if a consumer has perfect information about the risks posed by a product, third parties are unlikely to and so may be put at risk. The existence of externalities can also be used as a justification for measures which protect solely economic interests. For example, credit ceilings on mortgages may make it less likely for consumers to default and find themselves homeless, thus saving the state the cost of re-housing them. Laws requiring seat belts to be worn in cars and helmets on motorcycles could also be justified because of the cost to the National Health Service of dealing with injuries.

The discussion above reveals that many provisions which can be described as paternalistic can also be justified on economic grounds such as information failure and externalities. Of course, that does not mean that paternalism is a valid ground for intervention, but merely re-classifies measures which have been categorised as paternalistic. Another way of reconciling paternalism with individual choice and free market theory is to argue that consumers consent to the state overruling their immediate wishes in order to protect them from themselves.[136] Howells suggests, for example, that consumers are generally happy for experts to make decisions on their behalf about the risks that products pose, and the levels of danger to which they should be subjected. He calls for 'a certain humility about one's own abilities to look after one's own interests in an increasingly complicated environment'.[137] He argues that the meaning of autonomy should change, so that instead of making decisions on risks which they are ill equipped to do, consumers instead should influence the decisions of those to whom decision-making power is entrusted. This seems a pragmatic solution. Although it is written in the context of product safety law, the logic can be used to justify intervention in other areas.

Instead of attempting to reconcile measures which might appear to be paternalistic with the free market, it is also possible to justify paternalism on its own terms. We could see it as entirely proper for the law to intervene in the best interests of others, particularly the vulnerable, regardless of their expressed interests. In the words of Kennedy: 'there is real value as well as an element of real nobility in the judicial decision to throw

---

[136] The doctrine of 'rational paternalism'. See B. Barry, *Political Argument* (New York, Humanities Press, 1965), pp. 226–7.
[137] Howells, *Consumer Product Safety*, p. 17.

out, every time the opportunity arises, consumer contracts designed to perpetuate the exploitation of the poorest class of buyers on credit'.[138] Other calls for a more paternalistic approach have come from Goldring, who argues that paternalism should not be seen in a derogatory way, particularly where there is imbalance of market power. He continues: '[t]he power imbalance of the consumer compared to that of the production enterprise requires a strong intervening force – the state. To the extent that such intervention is necessary, consumers must surrender a degree of their power to make decisions and choices – a power which in this context is often meaningless – to the state.'[139] The Crowther Committee, whose report led to the Consumer Credit Act, and who frequently emphasised the importance of a market-based approach to consumer protection, also showed some sympathy for paternalism. The committee suggested that: 'there is a level of cost above which it becomes socially harmful to make loans available at all, even if the cost is not disproportionate to the risk and expense incurred by the lender'. It continued: '[t]here may be a case where, in view of the poor financial standing of the borrower, interest at 100% would not yield excessive profit to the lender; but if the borrower falls into a risk category as low as this, then we feel he ought not to be eligible for loans from the private sector'.[140] The question as to when, and in what way, the state should take decisions away from consumers in their own interests is one of the most difficult for consumer law to address.

In conclusion it is perhaps best to say that most of the consumer law provisions which can be justified on grounds of paternalism can also be justified on other, more market-based rationales, such as information failure and externalities. In addition, it should be noted that they can frequently be justified on other social grounds, such as distributive justice. For most consumer protection laws, paternalism will be but one justification.

Community values and future consumers

As well as ensuring that consumer policy takes account of distributional matters and protects consumers from themselves, there may be a role for the law in protecting the wider interests of the community and, indeed,

---

[138] D. Kennedy, 'Form and Substance in Private Law Adjudication' (1976) 89 Harvard LR 1685, 1777.

[139] J. Goldring, 'Consumer Law and Legal Theory: Reflections of a Common Lawyer' (1990) 13 JCP 113 at p. 129.

[140] Report of the Committee on Consumer Credit (1974) Cmnd 4596 at para. 6.6.6.

of communities and individuals in the future.[141] There may be public interest grounds for protecting certain values that are not reflected by decisions in the market. Ramsay identifies trust and confidence as prerequisites for flourishing markets.[142] Unlike information, trust cannot be purchased. However, it has been said that '[t]rust and similar values ... have real practical economic value; they increase the efficiency of the system, enable you to produce more goods or more of whatever values you hold in high esteem. But they are not commodities for which trade on the open market is technically possible or even meaningful.'[143]

We can argue, therefore, that consumer law should help to develop trust and confidence in order to help the market function, and to ensure that consumers are protected. Measures to protect the consumers of financial services have frequently been justified on the basis of the need to promote trust and confidence. Ramsay notes that the Consumer Credit Act 1974 and the Financial Services Act 1986 were both intended to stimulate consumer confidence in financial markets. It is also interesting to note that one of the Financial Services Authority's statutory regulatory objectives is the promotion of public awareness and another is ensuring market confidence.[144] Both can be seen as economically important. Community values also demonstrate respect for consumers as citizens. Hutchinson sees a need for consumer law to move towards a concept of citizenship in which we shift 'the civic fulcrum from that of shoppers, with their individual parcels of rights and acquisitions, to citizens, with their social responsibilities and well-being'.[145] This analysis has implications, of course, for whom we describe as consumers, and what we consider consumer law to be.[146] Regulation aimed at promoting community values helps us to create the sort of society we want to have. This rationale might also be used to justify measures to protect matters such as taste, decency, and respect for race and gender. These are values that society holds dear but which can easily be offended, for example by advertising.[147]

---

[141] See R. Stewart, 'Regulation in a Liberal State: The Role of Non-Commodity Values' (1983) 92 Yale LJ 1555, Ramsay, *Consumer Protection*, p. 53 and Ogus, *Regulation*, p. 54.

[142] Ramsay, *Consumer Protection*, p. 53.

[143] K. Arrow, *The Limits of Organisation* (New York, Norton, 1974), p. 23. Quoted in Ramsay, *Consumer Protection*.

[144] The others being consumer protection and the reduction of financial crime.

[145] Hutchinson, 'Life After Shopping', p. 38.

[146] For a recent examination of citizenship from a social policy perspective see R. Lister, 'New Conceptions in Citizenship' in N. Ellison and C. Pierson (eds.), *Developments in British Social Policy* (London, Macmillan, 1998), p. 46.

[147] See generally Ramsay, *Advertising, Culture and the Law.*

Another aspect of community values of interest to the consumer lawyer is that of protecting future generations. The market may play a role in protecting current consumers, but it is a legitimate goal of consumer policy to ensure the protection of future generations. This might be viewed as a form of externality which the market cannot easily internalise, or a form of distributive justice, with the beneficiary being those yet to be born. There are moves to amend the UN Guidelines on Consumer Protection to make reference to sustainable consumption as a key aim of consumer law, illustrating the need for the law to consider tomorrow's consumers as well as today's.

Conclusion

In order to evaluate the role of criminal law in consumer protection, it is necessary to examine the rationales for protecting the consumer. Much attention has been placed in the literature on the role of law in addressing market failure, with consumer protection grounded in the use of private law mechanisms. Although the correction of market failure is an important goal of consumer policy, it should not be viewed as a panacea. It should also be remembered that consumer law is capable of fulfilling social policies, and that there are social justifications for using the law to regulate business in the interests of the consumer. Furthermore, an undue emphasis on private law remedies obscures the considerable obstacles presented by transaction costs. The next step is to consider the techniques that can be used to achieve consumer protection objectives in practice. This is done in chapter 2.

2 Techniques of regulation

Introduction

The previous chapter examined why we protect the consumer. A second question to consider is how to provide that protection. To some extent, this choice will be influenced by the specific objective being addressed. Lack of competition might be tackled by opening up markets and strengthening competition law, and inadequate information by, for example, the imposition of mandatory disclosure requirements. However, identifying an area where consumers are not adequately protected by the market does not mean that the law should necessarily become involved. In some cases it will be extremely difficult, or extremely expensive, to provide a solution. Even where market failure exists, it is generally agreed that government should only intervene where it is cost effective to do so.[1]

One way of characterising the techniques available is by the extent to which they intervene in the market. At one extreme is prior approval, which requires a product or trader to be authorised before entering the market. In the case of consumer products, this approach is likely to be reserved for sectors that are particularly hazardous, such as pharmaceuticals. In the case of traders, it is likely to be reserved for professionals whose activities pose a considerable degree of harm when undertaken poorly.[2] At the other extreme, we might allow an industry to regulate itself, for example by a code of practice. Self-regulation is most likely to be used where industries are trusted to put their own houses in order, and where statutory intervention might be unduly burdensome. Between these two extremes are standards and information remedies. The term standards is used in a number of different contexts, as will become

---

[1] G. K. Hadfield, R. Howse, and M. J. Trebilcock, 'Information-Based Principles for Rethinking Consumer Protection Policy' (1998) 21 JCP 131 at 156. It is submitted that a distributive element should be built in to any assessment of cost-effectiveness.

[2] For the difficulties in identifying precise justifications for prior approval of traders see A. I. Ogus, *Regulation: Legal Form and Economic Theory* (Oxford, Clarendon Press, 1994), ch. 10, especially pp. 216–20.

apparent. UK consumer law has relied upon the use of broad statutory standards, and much of the substantive law considered in this book is contained in such standards. However, it should be emphasised that the dividing line between the different types of regulation mentioned is imperfect. For example, prior approval regimes require standards to be met, and broad statutory standards are often designed to correct information deficits by prohibiting the supply of false and misleading information. As we will see, the control of information has been perhaps the most influential technique in relation to consumer law, and a significant part of this chapter will be spent examining the role of information in consumer protection.

Prior approval

Sometimes referred to as screening, licensing, or authorisation, prior approval is the regulatory technique involving the highest degree of intervention. The essence of prior approval is that a regulatory agency or similar body is given the power to screen out and exclude suppliers or products which fail to meet minimum standards.[3] Instead of relying on prosecutions or law suits to hold errant traders to account, prior approval enables the regulator to block the subject at point of entry to the market and withdraw permission to continue in the market already obtained. Examples of prior approval include licensing of high-skill occupations such as solicitors and doctors, and licensing of potentially dangerous products such as medicines.[4] Related to the positive licensing that characterises prior approval regimes is negative licensing. This is where a trader need not be licensed before engaging in a business, but can be banned from that business for failing to meet minimum standards.[5]

Prior approval can be justified on a number of different grounds. First, it can be seen in terms of correcting market failure, for example, by tackling information deficits and dealing with externalities. In relation to information, it may be extremely difficult for consumers to obtain accurate information about the risks of being treated by an unqualified doctor or purchasing a medicine containing a particular substance. It might, therefore, be seen as important that doctors and medicines are approved in advance by experts who can identify these matters and make

---

[3] S. Breyer, *Regulation and its Reform* (Cambridge, Mass., Harvard University Press, 1982), pp. 575–6. This can be contrasted with certification, which is perhaps better interpreted as an information remedy.
[4] See C. Scott and J. Black, *Cranston's Consumers and the Law* (3rd edn, London, Butterworths, 2000), ch. 12.
[5] See s.3 of the Estate Agents Act 1979.

these judgements. However, there are other ways of tackling information deficits which are less onerous and interventionist, such as certification.[6] In relation to externalities, we might argue that potentially hazardous products such as medicines can cause harm to third parties, and so impose costs which are not internalised by the market. As Ogus points out, a failure by a doctor in treating a contagious disease might lead to an epidemic. Private law mechanisms such as contract and tort, and information remedies such as disclosure and certification, will not address these risks.[7] As well as market-based rationales, we can identify social justifications for prior approval. For example, we might wish to ensure that vulnerable consumers are protected where an error of judgement may carry with it severe consequences.[8] This might partially explain why we insist that banks and other credit providers have to be approved in advance, although the approval of banks can also be explained on grounds of avoiding systemic risk, which should be categorised as an externality.

The strengths of prior approval as a tool of consumer protection are clear. It gives those responsible for its implementation considerable power to decide who and what can and cannot enter the marketplace. As a result, it should be able to help to ensure that only those who are fit and proper to operate in a particular market are able to do so, and that only acceptable products can be supplied. This can bring substantial social benefits, for example, by weeding out dangerous products and incompetent professionals, who would not be held to account by isolated prosecutions or civil actions. However, it should be remembered that prior approval carries with it disadvantages. First, prior approval will, inevitably, deny consumers choice and replace this with a choice made by the regulator. If we could be confident that the regulator's choice reflected that which would have been made by fully informed consumers there might be little cause for concern, but this will not always be the case. As a result, prior approval can therefore be criticised on the libertarian grounds of limiting choice. Secondly, prior approval will be expensive to conduct and to comply with. One effect may be increased prices, leading to certain goods being taken out of the reach of the less affluent. Another effect is that where research and development costs are high, for example, in the case of pharmaceuticals, important investment will be discouraged, and fewer innovative products will find their way on to the market. Even where investment continues, prior approval will tend to lead to a time lag before new products can be placed on the market. These delays may lead

[6] See T. Moore, 'The Purpose of Licensing' (1961) 4 *Journal of Law and Economics* 93.
[7] Ogus, *Regulation*, p. 217.
[8] See ibid. pp. 216–19 and Iain Ramsay, *Consumer Protection: Text, Cases and Materials* (London, Weidenfeld and Nicolson, 1990), p. 72.

to the deaths of consumers who could have been saved if the product had been available earlier. As will be seen shortly, some of these objections can also be made to other forms of regulation, in particular standards, but the effects are even greater where prior approval is concerned. A third fear with prior approval is that it will be used for anti-competitive purposes. Prior approval of drugs protects existing manufacturers from competition, and will tend to benefit larger companies who are better placed to bear regulatory costs. The anti-competitive effects of prior approval for professions is also well documented.[9] A further risk with prior approval is that it may provide regulators with an incentive to make less than rational decisions.[10] In the case of prior approval of medicines, there are two types of mistake that can be made. First, an unsafe drug can be certified as safe, and secondly, a safe drug may be certified as unsafe. As the second type of mistake is less likely to be identified than the first, there may be an incentive upon regulators to be over-cautious.[11] An additional risk of prior approval is that of moral hazard. If a consumer believes that all products or traders in a particular sector have been closely vetted and approved, he may rationally decide to take little care in exercising choice. This is of particular concern in areas such as financial services where the consumer's confidence may be compounded by the existence of compensation schemes.[12]

Despite the reservations expressed above, there are many strengths of prior approval. It is difficult to estimate the costs of licensing, and particularly hard to know what benefits would have existed were a more liberal scheme of regulation in place. It is submitted, however, that prior approval regimes should be limited to areas where the risks of making incorrect decisions can have particularly grave consequences, where it is particularly difficult to obtain reliable information, and where externalities are present. However, if such a scheme is to be successful it is vital that it is properly resourced and carefully constructed. Inadequate resourcing may allow errant traders or products to slip through the net, and this is of particular concern where consumers are liable to exercise

[9] A good deal has been written about the ways in which prior approval advances the interests of professional groups. See W. Gellhorn, 'The Abuse of Occupational Licensing' (1976) 44 U Chicago LR 6 and A. Maurizi, 'Occupational Licensing and the Public Interest' (1974) 82 J Pol Econ 399.

[10] R. Parish, 'Consumer Protection and the Ideology of Consumer Protectionists' in A. J. Duggan and L. W. Darvall (eds.), *Consumer Protection Law and Theory* (Sydney, The Law Book Company, 1980), p. 229 at p. 231.

[11] See K. Shrader-Frechette, 'Uncertainty and the Producer Strategy: The Case for Minimising Type II Errors in Rational Risk Evaluation', ch. 9 in *Risk and Rationality* (Berkeley, University of California Press, 1991).

[12] See Hadfield, Howse, and Trebilcock, 'Information-Based Principles' (1998) 21 JCP 131 at 154.

little control because of their misplaced confidence in the scheme. Careful construction will mean that an appropriate mixture of sanctions is available to the enforcement authority. It has been forcibly argued that where the only sanctions are severe, such as licence suspension or revocation, deterrence will be low as traders will realise that they will only be subjected to those sanctions in extreme circumstances.[13] Prior approval regimes differ greatly in the range of sanctions for which they provide.[14]

Standards

Standards have been an important mechanism for protecting the consumer for centuries.[15] Unfortunately, the term 'standards' is capable of so many different meanings that identifying our subject matter is problematic.[16] Interpreted broadly, standards are minimum duties imposed upon traders, and may be enforced through the criminal or civil law.[17] Although they are generally treated as separate from other techniques, such as prior approval and information remedies, this may mask the degree of overlap that exists between these regulatory forms. For example, a product or professional may only meet the requirements of prior approval if certain standards are fulfilled,[18] and one of the aims of standards may be to improve the supply of accurate information to consumers.[19] Many regulatory schemes involve a mixture of these techniques.

One way of dividing standards is between specification standards and performance standards, although other categorisations are possible.[20] A specification standard either requires a trader to use particular materials or methods of production, or prohibits the use of particular materials or methods of production. For example, a statute might provide that only X material can be used in a particular product, or prohibit Y material from being used in that product. By contrast, a performance standard determines the conditions to be met when a product or service is supplied,

[13] I. Ayres and J. Braithwaite, *Responsive Regulation* (Oxford University Press, 1992).
[14] Contrast the Consumer Credit Act 1974 with the Financial Services and Markets Act 2000.
[15] See A. I. Ogus, 'Regulatory Law: Some Lessons from the Past' (1992) 12 Legal Studies 1.
[16] See Scott and Black, *Cranston's Consumers and the Law*, ch. 4.
[17] See Breyer, *Regulation and its Reform*, p. 96.
[18] For example, a bank will not gain authorisation under the Banking Act 1987 unless it meets capital and liquidity requirements.
[19] For example, under the Trade Descriptions Act 1968.
[20] For example, Stone uses the language of 'constraints', with 'factor constraints' covering what we might call specification standards, and 'performance constraints' equating to performance standards. See Christopher D. Stone, 'The Place of Enterprise Liability in the Control of Corporate Conduct' (1980) 90(1) Yale LJ 1 at p. 36.

but gives the trader freedom to choose the method of meeting those conditions. For example, a statute might say that all ladders must be able to withstand a certain amount of force, but allow the manufacturer to choose how to fulfil that. Ogus identifies a third category of standard, which he calls target standards. A target standard 'prescribes no specific standard for the supplier's processes or output, but imposes criminal liability for certain harmful consequences arising from the output'.[21] He gives the example of the requirement that toys must be designed so that 'they do not present health hazards or risks of physical injury by ingestion, inhalation or contact with the skin'.[22] The duty is therefore to prevent the result from occurring, regardless of how it is achieved. They therefore bear some similarity to performance standards, although they are more closely linked to the harm resulting.

The most obvious use of standards is in the field of product safety, but they can also dictate quality standards that goods and services must meet. Standards may be backed up by the criminal law, for example, under the General Product Safety Regulations, or the civil law, for example, under the Sale of Goods Act 1979. It is conceded that there are definitional difficulties here. For example, Ogus limits his definition of standards to provisions, the breach of which constitutes an offence.[23] Ramsay, on the other hand, envisages standards as being enforceable through a variety of legal techniques, including criminal law, civil law, and removal of a licence.[24] For the purposes of this discussion, an expansive definition is being adopted.

One concern with the use of standards is that, similarly to prior approval, it may impose unacceptable costs. Where standards are the responsibility of a regulatory agency, that agency has to formulate them, monitor the behaviour of regulated firms to ensure that they are compliant, and enforce the standards, if necessary through the courts. Regulated firms have the costs of negotiating with the regulator and complying with the standards, for example, by retraining or recruiting staff, and changing methods of production. These costs have to be weighed against the (generally social) benefits of standards. This balancing of costs and benefits is tricky, particularly as it may be extremely difficult to identify the precise benefits that standards bring. Standards need not, however, be organised in this way. In the UK, for example, it is common for bodies such as the British Standards Institution (BSI) and private trade organisations to devise their own standards. As these standards are neither set,

[21] Ogus, *Regulation*, p. 151.
[22] Toys (Safety) Regulations SI 1989/1275.
[23] Ogus, *Regulation*, p. 150.
[24] Ramsay, *Consumer Protection*, p. 71.

monitored, nor enforced by a regulatory agency, they are perhaps best seen as a form of self-regulation. Although there are concerns that such self-regulatory standards may inhibit competition and innovation, they may be useful in setting minimum quality standards, and helping courts to determine whether general standards, such as satisfactory quality or reasonable safety, are met.[25] There is often consumer as well as trader input into the committees which adopt draft standards, thus providing some degree of control and influence.

It is useful to consider the advantages and disadvantages of the main types of standards considered above. Specification standards have the virtues of certainty and simplicity. They enable suppliers to know precisely what to do in order to meet their legal obligations. This also has particular advantages from the point of view of law enforcement. It is relatively easy for the regulator to determine whether or not a specification standard has been breached, resulting in a reduction in monitoring costs. Where resources are limited, this is particularly valuable. In the words of Hadfield, Howse, and Trebilcock: 'the choice between product-specific regulation and general safety standards . . . has to respond to the fact that it may be much less costly to verify that a product contains a particular design or device than to determine whether products of widely varying designs meet a given standard of safety performance'.[26] Furthermore, it has been noted that where the regulator's monitoring technology is relatively poor, it may be easy for suppliers to challenge claims that standards have been breached. It is easier to counter these defences when specification standards are used.[27] The main disadvantage of specification standards is that they are liable to discourage market and social innovation.[28] By dictating precisely how a standard is to be met, little or no flexibility is allowed for devising more effective methods. There is also the risk that they can quickly become out of date, and that replacing them may be a lengthy process. The United States has gone so far as to prohibit the use of specification standards in safety regulations.[29]

---

[25] H. Collins, *Regulating Contracts* (Oxford, Oxford University Press, 1999), pp. 295–6.

[26] Hadfield, Howse, and Trebilcock, 'Information-Based Principles', p. 161.

[27] Stone, 'The Place of Enterprise Liability', 41.

[28] Stewart defines market innovation as encompassing 'development and adoption of new products and processes that will increase market measures of output per unit of labor or other input and thus increase productivity as measured by traditional national income accounting'. Social innovation, on the other hand, 'includes the development and adoption of new products and processes that are less polluting and safer or that otherwise deliver improved social performance, thereby facilitating the underlying goals of environmental, health and safety regulation'. Richard B. Stewart, 'Regulation, Innovation and Administrative Law: A Conceptual Framework' (1981) 69 Cal LR 1256 at p. 1261.

[29] G. G. Howells, *Consumer Product Safety* (Aldershot, Dartmouth and Ashgale, 1998), p. 41 and ch. 4, especially pp. 208–9.

Performance standards have the advantage over specification standards of flexibility, in that they allow the supplier to decide how to meet the required standard, and therefore provide an incentive to develop better materials and processes. This flexibility means that it will be more difficult to use performance standards for anti-competitive purposes. The European Union's (EU's) 'New Approach' to technical harmonisation and standards emphasises the importance of performance standards, although specification standards remain important in some areas, such as food.[30] However, from the point of view of the regulator, it may be difficult to determine whether or not the standard has been complied with. Monitoring costs will therefore be higher. Target standards allow even more flexibility than performance standards, as they are linked to harm caused rather than output produced. However, where it is necessary to show that the supplier caused a particular harm there may be problems, for example in establishing causation.[31] Also, from the point of view of compliance, it may be difficult for the trader to estimate compliance costs, because of the difficulty in knowing precisely what will cause the harm.[32]

As well as comparing different types of standard, we might compare standards with other types of regulation, such as prior approval, information remedies, and self-regulation. As mentioned above, although there is a close relationship between standards and prior approval, standards in themselves are a less interventionist form of regulation. As a result, they are less likely to lead to firms being excluded from the marketplace. However, there is evidence that standards, particularly specification standards, can be used for anti-competitive purposes. It has also been argued that there may be a tendency for standards to 'over deter' and impose costs in excess of the social benefits that originally justified the regulation.[33] This will obviously depend on a wide variety of factors, such as the type of standard and the industry in question. A further concern with standards is that they may not be set at an appropriate level. Because consumers are likely to be prepared to endure different levels of safety or quality, it is seen as desirable that regulators do not impose standards at too high a level. Apart from denying consumer choice, this might have the effect

---

[30] See Ogus, *Regulation*, ch. 8.

[31] Stone identifies problems with what he calls 'harm based liability rules' (HBLRs), which bear similarities to target standards. He notes the unpredictability of costs, the difficulties in establishing an appropriate penalty and the absence of clear signals sent by such rules as weaknesses. See Stone, 'The Place of Enterprise Liability', p. 1.

[32] Ogus also notes that the overlap between target standards and liability in tort may lead to wasteful duplication of legal proceedings. However, he recognises the arguments for target standards where transaction costs make the enforcement of private rights difficult. Ogus, *Regulation*, p. 166.

[33] Stone, 'The Place of Enterprise Liability', pp. 38–9.

of removing some products from the price range of some consumers. In some cases, this might avoid the benefit that the standard was supposed to bring. For example, setting standards which have the effect of raising the price of ladders beyond the means of less-affluent consumers might result in consumers standing on chairs or tables instead.[34] For these reasons, some commentators point to advantages presented by information remedies.

Despite these reservations, standards clearly bring benefits. General contractual standards such as those that require goods to be of satisfactory quality should help to ensure that unsatisfactory goods are excluded from the market, although they suffer from the weaknesses of the private law considered above. General criminal law standards such as the requirement that producers only place safe products on the market should help to ensure that unsafe products are excluded from the market, but still allow the producer flexibility and encourage innovation. As these standards are enforced by public officials, they obviate the weaknesses traditionally posed by private law. It has been suggested that safety regulation of this type may be the most 'unambiguously valuable' form of consumer protection regulation, because by supporting general expectations of safety, it reduces the information and search costs that consumers face in all markets.[35] Standards of this sort can be the most effective way of overcoming information deficits. Specification standards do give cause for concern to the extent that they inhibit innovation and competition, but they may nevertheless be valuable where there is no better way of fulfilling the desired objective, and where the costs of enforcing other types of standard would be prohibitive.

Information remedies

There are several ways in which the law can help to provide information that the market has not supplied, but which would be desirable for consumers. The most obvious ways are through disclosure regulation, and by prohibiting the supply of false and misleading information.[36] These are now examined.

---

[34] See M. Weidenbaum, 'The Case Against the UN Guidelines for Consumer Protection', 1987 JCP 425.

[35] Hadfield, Howse, and Trebilcock, 'Information-Based Principles', p. 158.

[36] Other possibilities are standardised scoring systems and consumer education. See H. Beales, R. Craswell, and S. Salop, 'The Efficient Regulation of Consumer Information' (1981) 24 *Journal of Law and Economics* 49.

Disclosure regulation

One solution to information deficits is to require traders to supply consumers with information, thus enabling rational choices about products to be made. Disclosure regulation is a way of ensuring that valuable information is supplied, thus helping the market to function. It is therefore likely to be favoured by those who see the correction of market failure as the prime rationale of regulation. It also helps to overcome the fear of over-regulation through more traditional forms of control.[37] Where disclosure regulation operates effectively, the consumer carries out her analysis of the product in question, its advantages and disadvantages, and makes an informed choice. The consumer is helped to protect herself according to her own preferences, and once her choice is made, her decision is respected.[38] This approach is compatible with the idea of the consumer as a rational utility maximiser, and so with the market system. This approach avoids giving a regulator the task of producing a common standard which applies to all consumers regardless of their preferences.[39] This can be seen as economically efficient and ideologically desirable for the reasons discussed in chapter 1.

Disclosure regulation exists in a number of areas, from food labelling to consumer credit.[40] For example, the Consumer Credit (Advertisements) Regulations 1989 provide detailed disclosure requirements for different types of advertisement, and the Food Labelling Regulations 1996 require food to be marked or labelled with particular information. Disclosure is also important in other areas. In relation to product safety, for example, there may be mandatory warnings about the risks posed by particular products, such as hazardous chemicals or tobacco.[41] In relation to quantity there are rules about how weight or other quantity should be disclosed,[42] and in relation to price there are detailed provisions for the disclosure of unit pricing of goods.[43]

---

[37] See e.g. Breyer, *Regulation and its Reform*, p. 184.

[38] Although there is some doubt about the extent to which consumers, in reality, use information to make rational decisions. See R. L. Jordan and W. D. Warren, 'Disclosure of Finance Charges: A Rationale' (1966) 64 Mich LR 1285, 1320–2. The Molony Committee suggested that consumers frequently made decisions 'on instinctive but not always rational thought processes'. Molony Committee, para. 891.

[39] See Beales, Craswell, and Salop, 'The Efficient Regulation of Consumer Information' 491 at 514.

[40] See Scott and Black, *Cranston's Consumers and the Law*, chapter 9 and Ogus, *Regulation*, ch. 7.

[41] See the Tobacco Products Labelling (Safety) Amendment Regulations 1993 SI 1993/1947.

[42] See for example s.48 of the Weights and Measures Act 1985.

[43] See the Price Marking Order 1999.

There is debate about whether traders would disclose information to consumers even in the absence of a legal requirement to do so. It has been argued that firms have an incentive to disclose information to consumers in order to win custom, and that regulators may design rules which prevent product providers from communicating effectively with consumers.[44] However, chapter 2 has already examined the reasons why an unregulated market might not supply the information that would most benefit consumers, and mandatory disclosure would appear an obvious solution to some of these difficulties. Disclosure regulation helps consumers to make informed comparisons between substitute products by ensuring that valuable information is supplied in a manner which is not misleading, and which helps comparisons to be made.[45] Even price, which it is generally argued traders are under an incentive to reveal, can be presented in a misleading manner if a regime is not in place to control that.[46] More difficulty is raised by the issue of quality disclosure, because of the problems of effective communication of useful, objective criteria.[47] There are quality disclosure regimes, for example for fruit, vegetables, eggs, and wine, and compositional labelling schemes, for example, for textiles.[48] Extending such grading systems to other products is problematic, although performance characteristics can frequently be disclosed, and symbols such as BSI kitemarks may convey quality information simply and effectively. The Government's proposal to replace approved voluntary codes of practice with core principles, and the ability to show compliance with these by using a logo, will be a form of quality disclosure.[49] In the area of safety, too, disclosure can be important. For example, the requirement to label poisons in a simple manner is an effective and simple way of protecting consumers from inherent risks.[50]

Although some criticisms of mandatory disclosure have come from commentators associated with the political right, writers from the centre-left have been sceptical of the value of this form of regulation. Cranston argued that: 'the major problem with disclosure regulation is not in

[44] G. Benston, *Regulating Financial Markets* (London, Institute of Economic Affairs, 1998).

[45] D. Llewellyn, *The Economic Rationale for Financial Regulation* (Financial Services Authority, London, 1999), p. 33.

[46] A good example relates to the requirement to reveal the cost of credit by giving the annual percentage rate (APR) prominence in advertisements.

[47] G. Akerlof, ' "The Market for Lemons": Qualitative Uncertainty and the Market Mechanism' (1970) 84 QJEcon 488.

[48] Scott and Black, *Cranston's Consumers and the Law*, pp. 346–7.

[49] *Modern Markets: Confident Consumers* (CM 4410, 1999), pp. 26–9 and below.

[50] See W. K. Viscusi, W. A. Magat, and J. Huber, 'Informational Regulation of Consumer Health Risks: An Empirical Evaluation of Hazard Warnings' (1986) 17 *RAND Journal of Economics* 351.

securing business compliance, but rather that consumers are unaware of the information disclosed, do not appreciate its significance or simply do not employ the information provided in the market place'.[51] The Crowther Committee, whose report led to the Consumer Credit Act 1974, thought that the disclosure of the cost of credit in a set format would have a number of benefits. First, it would enable comparisons to be made, both with other credit providers and with the return the consumer would receive on savings; secondly it would make creditors conscious of how their charges related to other providers; and thirdly it would ensure that consumers do not over-extend their financial resources 'by ill-informed and rash use of credit facilities'.[52] However, it is unclear in practice to what extent credit disclosure has achieved its objectives. Some research from the USA suggests that there was a difference in the impact of credit disclosure between different socio-economic groups, and that ignorance was still common among less-affluent consumers.[53] As consumers suffer from bounded rationality, information remedies will always be of limited use, especially where information has to be complex or technical to be accurate. A particular difficulty is that consumers' needs in relation to information differ greatly. Information asymmetry is likely to be at its greatest where vulnerable consumers are concerned. The Director General of Fair Trading recently described 'vulnerable consumers' as 'those who through age, infirmity or another disadvantage, have difficulty in obtaining and understanding the information they need',[54] thereby suggesting that there is a close relationship between vulnerability and information deficits. The difficulties faced by vulnerable consumers, for example, those on low incomes, may not be addressed adequately by information remedies. Trebilcock and Cayne cite research on the psychological characteristics of the poor which indicates that they may be less able to protect themselves than others when information is supplied.[55] Also, as was noted in chapter 1, information remedies will be of little use where consumers are denied access to products through poverty, disability, or discrimination.

---

[51] Scott and Black, *Cranston's Consumers and the Law*, p. 372. It has been suggested that poor consumers are particularly unlikely to benefit from measures such as unit pricing. See K. B. Monroe and P. L. La Placa, 'What are the Benefits of Unit Pricing?' (1972) 36 *Journal of Marketing* 16.
[52] *Report of the Committee on Consumer Credit* (Crowther Committee) Cmnd 4596/1971 paras. 3.8.3 and 3.8.13.
[53] L. Mandell, 'Consumer Perception of Incurred Interest Rates' (1971) 26 *Journal of Finance* 1143. Cited in Scott and Black, *Cranston's Consumers and the Law*, p. 366. See also G. Schucker, 'The Impact of the Saccharin Warning Label' (1983) 2 *Journal of Public Policy and Marketing* 46.
[54] J. Bridgeman, 'A Speech to the Year Ahead Symposium', 28 January 1998.
[55] D. Cayne and M. J. Trebilcock, 'Market Considerations in the Formulation of Consumer Protection Policy' (1973) 23 *University of Toronto Law Journal* 396 at p. 40

Disclosure regimes can only go so far in providing consumer protection but, if thoughtfully designed, they can be tailored towards the needs of vulnerable as well as 'typical' consumers, for example by ensuring that information is provided in a simple and consistent manner.[56] Disclosure will also be of value where a message about safety or quality can be communicated simply, for example, by a single word or logo.[57] It is accepted that disclosure regulation will have its limitations, and few would argue that it is a panacea for consumers' problems, but it has an important role to play. Sunstein suggests that disclosure and education strategies are important to consumers as citizens, as without information this role becomes impossible.[58] As Leff memorably observed: 'for a Government to try to design high quality information is much cheaper than its trying to design high quality goods, and much better than its trying to design high quality people'.[59]

Regulating false and misleading information

It should be remembered that it is not merely the absence of information that causes difficulties for consumers, but also the supply of false and misleading information. It has been argued that 'because such prohibitions do work to restrict the information communicated to consumers, the prohibitions should be treated with some care'.[60] However, it would be wrong to see these prohibitions as being at odds with the market system. The requirements necessary for the successful operation of the market include not complete information but optimal information. This means that the information should not be false or misleading, and also that it should not be so complex as to lead to confusion. There are social as well as economic justifications for stamping out false and misleading information, particularly where that information is given dishonestly. In the words of Trebilcock and Cayne: 'the community will not and should not tolerate dishonesty, whatever the economic consequences of preventing it'. They further point out that the market cannot work efficiently if people are misinformed about the choices open to them.[61]

---

[56] But see I. McNeil, J. Nevin, D. Trubek, and R. Miller, 'Market Discrimination Against the Poor and the Impact of Consumer Disclosure Laws: The Used Car Industry' (1979) 13 *Law and Society Review* 695.

[57] Viscusi, Magat, and Huber, 'Informational Regulation'.

[58] C. Sunstein, *Free Markets and Social Justice* (New York, Oxford University Press, 1997), p. 319.

[59] A. A. Leff, 'The Pontiac Prospectus' (1974) 25 *Consumer Journal* 35.

[60] Beales, Craswell, and Salop, 'The Efficient Regulation of Consumer Information'.

[61] Cayne and Trebilcock, 'Market Considerations', p. 422.

Where false information is concerned, there is no social utility in its supply, and so it should be prohibited.[62] Where information is misleading rather than false there are more difficulties. The chief problem is that information may mislead some consumers but not others. Advertisements, for example, may often be interpreted by the viewer in different ways. Controlling information which is capable of different meanings is extremely difficult and is examined at some length in chapter 6. Where information is supplied in large quantities similar problems arise because, as we have already seen, different consumers are able to store and process different amounts of information. In these latter two cases the law's main difficulty is to find an appropriate standard against which information can be judged. This is far from easy.

It is interesting to consider briefly the indicators that the OFT in the UK uses to identify markets and practices that require close examination. The indicators are: where products or services are complex, where goods or services are purchased infrequently, where the purchases are by individual consumers who have little or no knowledge of the product or service, and where purchases are by groups in the population who have particular difficulty in obtaining and interpreting information.[63] This reveals two matters of interest to us. First, it shows the central importance of information in protecting the consumer. Secondly, it demonstrates that the OFT recognises that certain groups will face particular difficulties, not just in obtaining information with which they can make informed choices, but also in processing that information. It may be that encouraging the supply of information will not be enough, and that issues of distribution need to be assessed. These issues were considered above.

Self-regulation

Self-regulation might sound like a contradiction in terms, and it could be viewed as an absence of, rather than a form of, regulation. Regulation, in its traditional sense, 'contains the idea of control by a superior; it has a directive function',[64] and it is difficult to reconcile this with the concept of regulation by oneself. Indeed, '[a]t its simplest it may refer to the capacity and tendency of all individuals and organizations to regulate their own

---

[62] Where the false information is supplied accidentally, we may not want to prosecute the supplier as it may be unduly harsh, particularly if the trader has taken all reasonable steps to ensure that false information is not supplied. Most regulatory statutes allow this as a defence.

[63] J. Bridgeman, 'Giving the Consumer a Fair Deal' (http://www.oft.gov.uk).

[64] Ogus, *Regulation*, p. 2.

conduct'.[65] The term is sometimes used in this way in the financial services field, for example, to refer to a firm's system of control over its employees.[66] One of the difficulties is that the term 'self-regulation' almost defies classification owing to the several different meanings which can be attached to it.[67] Daintith states that self-regulation 'has come to be used particularly of situations in which an activity is controlled in the public interest not by the State itself but by an organization whose members engage in the relevant activity'.[68] In the context of consumer law, perhaps the main example of such self-regulation is s.124(3) of the Fair Trading Act 1973. This imposes on the Director General of Fair Trading the duty 'to encourage relevant associations to prepare, and to disseminate to their members, codes of practice for guidance in safeguarding and promoting the interests of consumers in the United Kingdom'. Although something of a 'legislative afterthought',[69] great emphasis has been put upon it as a technique of protecting consumers in the UK. In the terminology developed by Black, this is 'sanctioned self regulation', where self-regulatory codes are voluntary, but the OFT sets minimum standards for their design and operation.[70] Because of the importance of this technique in the context of consumer protection, it is upon this that we shall concentrate. Again, however, it should be remembered that self-regulation is not perfectly separate from the other regulatory techniques considered.[71]

It is worth considering some of the strengths and weaknesses of OFT codes as they illustrate some of the strengths and weaknesses of self-regulation as a regulatory technique. The first strength of self-regulatory codes is that they reduce many of the costs associated with legislation, in particular those associated with rule-making and Parliamentary time.[72] As the OFT moved to a system of approving rather than negotiating codes, its input is largely limited to setting minimum standards and ensuring that they are met. Although there have been efforts to pass consumer protection legislation which is addressed at specific industries, such as the Property Misdescriptions Act 1991, it is impractical to pass separate statutes to deal with all sectors. Furthermore, the flexibility of

---

[65] R. Baldwin, C. Scott and C. Hood, 'Introduction' in R. Baldwin, C. Scott, and C. Hood (eds.), *A Reader on Regulation* (Oxford, Oxford University Press, 1998) p. 1 at p. 27.

[66] J. Black, 'Constitutionalising Self-Regulation' (1996) 59 MLR 24.

[67] Ibid. pp. 26–8.

[68] T. Daintith, 'The Techniques of Government' in J. Jowell and D. Oliver (eds.), *The Changing Constitution* (Oxford, Oxford University Press, 2000).

[69] Ramsay, *Consumer Protection*, p. 281.

[70] Black, 'Constitutionalising Self-Regulation', pp. 26–8.

[71] Note, for example, the use of BSI standards mentioned above.

[72] See Ramsay, *Consumer Protection*, p. 282.

codes means that they can be changed in the light of new judicial or statutory developments, or in the light of changes in business practice.[73] However, concern has been expressed that the content of codes is only likely to bring benefits if there is a threat of legislation in the background. Writing in 1984 a former Director General of Fair Trading argued that 'Discussion of the value of codes of practice and self-regulation as opposed to regulation needs to take place against a background of political reality... trade associations no longer perceive legislation as a realistic threat if no code of practice is concluded.'[74] An additional benefit of codes of practice is that they can contain provisions that would be difficult to introduce into legislation, such as delays in servicing and periods for which spare parts will be available.[75] Unfortunately, one reason that these provisions would be difficult to put in legislation is that they are difficult to test. They may be similarly difficult to test when challenged as part of a code.

It has been argued that codes are more likely to be effective than legislation because they are written and enforced by those with specialist knowledge of the industry in question. However, too much can be made of this. It is rare for legislation to be drafted without liaison with interested parties, and so there will generally be expert input into the legislative process. Furthermore, there must be a concern that knowledge of the industry is as likely to work against consumers as for them. The European Consumer Law Group argued that 'when traders elaborate and monitor the rules themselves, they are concerned primarily with the interests of trade and not with the interests of consumers'.[76] It has been argued that in some cases, codes can be a useful pilot for legislation, a good example being the Association of British Travel Agents (ABTA) Code which influenced the content of the Package Travel Regulations 1992. However, there may be a fear that the experience of a code could be used as an argument against legislation.[77] For example, a successful code could be used as an argument that there is no need for legislation, whereas an unsuccessful code could lead to the argument that legislation would not have done any better. However, although there is a need for caution, there will be cases where a code can form the basis for at least some part of a

---

[73] For example, the changes to the Code of Banking Practice following a series of cases on spouses providing guarantees.

[74] Gordon Borrie, *The Development of Consumer Law and Policy: Bold Spirits and Timorous Souls* (London, Sweet and Maxwell, 1984), p. 196.

[75] Gordon Borrie, 'Law and Codes for Consumers' (1980) JBL 315 at p. 322.

[76] European Consumer Law Group, 'Non-Legislative Means of Consumer Protection' (1983) 6 JCP 209 at 211.

[77] Ibid.

regulatory regime. Codes can reduce the cost to consumers of obtaining redress by providing for dispute-resolution mechanisms, improving the supply of information and raising consumers' awareness of their rights. It is in the broad area of access to justice that codes play an important part. In 1991 the OFT published its 'Guidelines for the Support of Individual Codes' which set out what the OFT believed to be best practice and provided that the OFT would offer support to codes which met this best practice. The Guidelines covered matters such as the organisation of the code, its preparation, content, provision for complaints handling, monitoring and publicity, and enforcement. In 1993 the Office introduced a further requirement, which was independence in redress and disciplinary procedures. In the late 1970s and early 1980s Pickering and Cousins investigated the economic effects of voluntary codes of practice in the UK, and concluded that on balance the social benefits of codes outweigh the costs.[78] A recent Director General of Fair Trading has argued that in situations where some form of regulation is necessary, 'self-regulation can represent an effective and economic alternative to statutory regulation. By using the expertise of those actively engaged in the industry, and through employing a lighter and more responsive touch than may be possible with statutory regulation, it can prove highly effective.'[79]

Despite the strengths of codes, there are obvious limitations to them as a form of regulation. First, the codes discussed here are voluntary and so do not apply to those who are not members of the relevant trade association. It is possible to have statutory codes but the Government has stated in its White Paper *Modern Markets: Confident Consumers* that it is unwilling to impose codes of practice on industry.[80] It is only in the case of very few sectors, for example, travel, that being outside a trade association is likely to be particularly damaging to business. Codes consequently appear to have relatively little impact on the trading activities of those outside the association. Very often, it is the traders operating outside recognised trade associations who pose the greatest threat to consumers.[81] A second difficulty is that there is a major conflict between the role of trade associations as representative of member businesses and as regulators of the business when a consumer is in dispute with a member business. Many trade associations admit to a conflict here, in particular

---

[78] See in particular J. F. Pickering and D. C. Cousins, *The Economic Implications of Codes of Practice* (Manchester, UMIST, 1980).

[79] *Consumer Affairs: The Way Forward* (London, OFT, October 1998).

[80] See *Modern Markets: Confident Consumers*, para. 4.11.

[81] See G. Borrie, 'Trading Malpractices and Legislative Policy' (1991) 107 LQR 559 at p. 571.

when faced with an errant member.[82] The ultimate sanction is to be ejected from the association, but this brings its own difficulties. First, the member can carry on trading outside the association. Secondly, the association will not only lose influence over the member, but will also lose that member's revenue. Some associations admitted to the OFT that they were in business to gain membership and said that they would not expel their members.[83] Thirdly, there is the risk of both the member and the industry attracting harmful publicity following an expulsion. These factors go some way to explain the low levels of expulsion from trade associations, and the relative rarity of other sanctions being imposed. The imposition of a fine of £105,000 imposed under the ABTA Code on a tour company following changes that were made to consumers' holiday arrangements appears to be exceptional.[84] In addition, there may be a question-mark on competition and constitutional grounds whether trade associations should have the power to discipline traders, particularly when this may affect the trader's ability to earn a living.[85] A further major problem with codes is their lack of visibility. High-profile codes are the exception. A number of respondents to the OFT's consultation document on voluntary codes of practice commented that codes not only suffered from a lack of visibility, but were also too lengthy, variable, and complicated to make an impact on most consumers. Evidence suggests that while consumer dissatisfaction remains extremely high, the numbers of people using redress schemes attached to codes is low. In 1998 the OFT found that 63 per cent of consumers said that they were aware of trade association voluntary codes, and consumers generally believed that codes offer reassurance, help to resolve problems, and are an indicator of a quality firm. However, knowledge of specific codes was rare. When unprompted, only 34 per cent of consumers mentioned at least one product or service for which there is a code. The only sectors which were identified by more than 10 per cent of consumers when unprompted were electrical/electronic goods and holidays/travel.[86] The OFT recognised in its Report *Raising Standards of Consumer Care: Progressing Beyond Codes of Practice* that the redress schemes provided for in codes are viewed as neither consumer friendly nor genuinely neutral, either by consumers

---

[82] *Raising Standards of Consumer Care: Progressing Beyond Codes of Practice* (London, OFT, 1998), para. 2.16.
[83] Ibid.
[84] *The Times*, 9 August 1990.
[85] *Progressing Beyond Codes of Practice*, para. 2.17. See also *Thorne* v. *Motor Trade Association* [1937] AC 797.
[86] *Raising Standards of Consumer Care: Report on a Conference held at New Hall College Cambridge* (London, OFT, February 1999), Appendix C, p. 29.

themselves or their advisors.[87] Both trade associations and consumer advisors often steer consumers away from these procedures: the former because they are seen as neither impartial nor easy to use, and the latter because of the cost to the association. Consumer bodies said they often suspected that schemes were run to 'get traders off the hook' rather than to provide independent redress. The OFT cited the need to publicise schemes and the need for truly independent alternative forms of redress and disciplinary procedures as key elements in any new approach. Of course, if the lack of visibility of codes has little impact on the buying decisions of consumers in the first place, this acts as a disincentive to firms' signing up. An additional problem with codes is that they may lead to cartels. Although the Department of Trade and Industry (DTI) has concluded that there are no significant restrictions on competition in any of the OFT supported codes, there are still competition risks attached to them. If the standards that codes lay down are seen as normal rather than as minimum standards of conduct, there may be a tendency for firms not to raise their standards. This is particularly concerning where associations adopt what might be called 'lowest common denominator standards', which a number of respondents to the OFT's consultation paper felt were common.[88]

The DTI White Paper *Modern Markets: Confident Consumers* states that the Government proposes to give the Director General the power to approve codes of practice, allowing members of approved codes (those who adhere to them) to use a logo denoting approval. The DTI has consulted further on the details of the proposed scheme in its *Policy Paper on Codes of Practice*.[89] The Director General will continue to encourage codes to be prepared, but the prime responsibility for producing the codes will be with the businesses concerned, acting through their sponsors (those submitting the code for approval).

The outline core principles contained in the White Paper identify the sorts of matters that consumers should see. These include, for example, truthful adverts; clear, helpful, and adequate pre-contractual information; clear, fair contracts, an effective complaints handling system run by the business and, if problems cannot be resolved in-house, an effective and low cost redress mechanism. The outline core principles then examine what should happen behind the scenes. First, they state that 'the sponsor should have a supervisory body for the code made up of people from the sector and consumers, with some independent members'.

---

[87] *Progressing Beyond Codes of Practice*, para. 2.18.
[88] Ibid. para. 2.14.
[89] DTI (2000).

Secondly, they provide that 'the sponsor should tailor the core principles to develop its own code, taking into account the needs and characteristics of the sector such as the size of businesses within it, and keep it up to date'. Thirdly, 'businesses in the sector should agree to deliver on the principles in the tailored code and report regularly to the sponsor on the operation of the code'. Fourthly, the sponsor should provide 'an effective and low cost redress mechanism in the event of an unresolved dispute between a member and a consumer'. Fifthly, 'the sponsor should put into place an effective system to underpin compliance and to address breaches by members'. Sixthly, 'the redress and compliance systems should, wherever necessary or possible, include an independent element'. Seventhly, 'the sponsor should publish a report on compliance with the code and on complaints about its operation'.

The Director General will be given several powers to act in relation to 'core principles', which set out what consumers should see. First, the Director General will have the power to promote the core principles and to encourage good practice by keeping those principles up to date. Secondly, he will have the power to approve or reject codes and publicise these decisions. The Director General will test codes which are submitted for approval against the core principles before deciding whether to approve or reject them. Thirdly, he will be able to publicise to consumers the benefits of the overall scheme and the benefits of dealing with businesses that comply with approved codes. Fourthly, he will have the power to provide and market a seal of approval for approved codes so that consumers can see whether a trader is committed to code principles. Finally, he will be able to remove the seal from codes that fail to deliver.

The Government has decided not to go down the route of imposing codes where the voluntary approach has not worked. In the words of the White Paper '[c]odes need the support of businesses if they are to be truly effective and an imposed code would not have that support'.[90] Where the voluntary approach does not work, the Government favours using a new procedure for dealing with unfair trading practices. This is considered in chapter 6.

Our examination of codes of practice, and their likely successors, demonstrates that self-regulation can bring benefits for consumers. However, where self-regulation is being considered as an alternative to enforced regulation, it should be examined very closely. The experience of self-regulatory codes is unlikely to instil a great deal of confidence in someone searching for an effective method for regulating business in the interests of the consumer. But it should be remembered that

[90] *Modern Markets: Confident Consumers*, para. 4.11.

self-regulation does not exist in a vacuum. The key to its effective util-
isation is in the design of a system of oversight which obviates the less
desirable risks of self-regulation but recognises the advantages that can
result. In the words of Scott and Black: '[t]he choice for policy makers is
not self-regulation *or* public regulation, but rather a question of how to
harness the self-regulatory capacities of business to deliver public policy
objectives through the combination of public and self-regulation'.[91]

Improving access to justice

It was mentioned in the previous chapter that private law can be viewed
as a technique of regulation. We have seen that the private law presents
both opportunities for, and obstacles to, the pursuit of consumer justice. To some extent, these obstacles can be tackled by improving access to justice. One example is the small claims procedure of the county
court, described by Sir Thomas Bingham MR as 'a procedure for re-
solving low value claims . . . with a minimum of formality and expense'.[92]
Although the procedure was designed primarily as a means of improving consumer redress, the statistics suggest that it is more commonly
used by traders than by consumers.[93] Nevertheless, consumers use the
scheme as plaintiffs in around one-third of cases, and the procedure
has significant advantages over more traditional litigation. The changes
introduced by Lord Woolf's report on access to justice, including increased management of cases by the court, dealing with cases in ways
which are proportionate and trying to ensure that parties are on an equal
footing, should improve matters further, although their precise effect is
difficult to gauge at this stage.[94] In particular, we are likely to see increased use of alternative dispute resolution. Collective initiatives such as
group or class actions may also minimise some of the risks of unsuccessful litigation.[95] Indeed, collective initiatives and small claims procedures
are consistent with the market system as they improve the consumer's
ability to achieve redress under the private law by overcoming the traditional obstacles presented by transaction costs. Provision is made in the
Civil Procedure Rules 1998 for representative actions and group litigation
orders. Again, the likely success of these measures is difficult to judge,

---

[91] Scott and Black, *Cranston's Consumers and the Law*, p. 66.
[92] *Joyce* v. *Liverpool City Council* [1995] 3 All ER 110 at p. 119.
[93] R. Baldwin, *Small Claims in the County Courts in England and Wales* (Oxford, Clarendon Press, 1997), p. 25.
[94] *Access to Justice. Final Report by the Rt. Hon. Lord Woolf* (HMSO 1996).
[95] See G. G. Howells and S. Weatherill, *Consumer Protection Law* (Aldershot, Dartmouth and Ashgale, 1995), pp. 534–50.

and detailed discussion of such provisions is beyond the scope of this book.[96]

Self-regulation is also important when it comes to dispute settlement. When deciding whether to support a code of practice, the OFT will consider the mechanisms available for complaints handling, and will require there to be a low-cost independent scheme of redress available as an alternative to the courts. Most codes contain conciliation and arbitration procedures which help to resolve disputes with trade association members. These schemes tend to be flexible, cheap to use, informal, and reasonably expedient, at least when compared with litigation. However, the OFT has recognised that they are sometimes viewed by consumers and consumer advisors as biased towards the industry, and there is evidence that consumer advisors often suggest that consumers take action under the small claims procedure as an alternative.[97] Private ombudsman schemes also allow aggrieved consumers to challenge the behaviour of business by complaining to a (reasonably) independent adjudicator. Ombudsmen can frequently go beyond the legal position in order to impose a just settlement in an individual dispute. For example, the Banking Ombudsman's terms of reference allow him to settle disputes 'by reference to what, in his opinion, is fair in all the circumstances', rather than on the basis of the strict legal position. As a result, compliance with the law will not necessarily give the bank immunity. Ombudsmen manage to settle the majority of cases through conciliation, and so their adjudicatory role is generally secondary. Although there is the question about how independent such schemes are, they may provide a valuable additional source of redress for consumers.[98]

Conclusions

The aim of this chapter has been to identify the regulatory techniques that can be used to control business in the interests of consumers. These vary from prior approval to self-regulation, all involving different degrees of intervention. The weaknesses of the private law were examined in the previous chapter, and the regulatory techniques discussed here overcome some of these deficiencies. All the techniques have advantages and disadvantages and all can be used as part of an effective consumer protection regime. The difficulty is deciding when each technique should be used. Although sometimes used for reasons of protectionism, prior approval

[96] See Scott and Black, *Cranston's Consumers and the Law*, pp. 120–33.
[97] *Progressing Beyond Codes of Practice*, para. 2.18.
[98] See R. James, *Private Ombudsmen and Public Law* (Aldershot, Dartmouth and Ashgale, 1997).

provides an important mechanism for controlling the most hazardous industries and products. A carefully constructed standards-based regime can also provide effective protection by ensuring that a balance is drawn between protecting consumers from new products and allowing them the benefits of such products. The emphasis that consumer law and regulatory scholars have placed on information remedies is understandable, given the influence of law and economics thinking in this area. Insofar as information regulation removes false and misleading information it is difficult to challenge it. However, it is in the area of disclosure regulation that much debate has ensued. Critics from the right have frequently labelled it as unnecessary, while those from the left point to its inadequacies. Perhaps the appropriate conclusion to draw is that carefully designed disclosure regimes, which address the needs of vulnerable as well as 'average' consumers, can have a positive effect. Empirical research findings have not been conclusive, and more needs to be done to identify the best ways of educating and informing consumers. Self-regulation, both the least coercive and the least determinate form of regulation, has been a central part of the regulatory process in the UK. Because of the wide variety of regimes falling under the self-regulatory umbrella conclusions are difficult to draw. However, our examination of codes of practice made under the Fair Trading Act 1973 reveals the benefits and risks of relying on this particular form of regulation.

3   The role of criminal sanctions in consumer protection

Introduction

In the previous chapters, it was argued that the civil law plays an important role in the protection of the consumer, but suffers from limitations which make intervention from the state desirable. English law has tended to use the criminal sanction as the prime method of protecting the consumer, with the creation of new offences a frequent response to consumer problems. This chapter examines the place of the criminal law in society, with particular reference to regulatory offences and consumer protection. It begins by examining when conduct is properly classified as criminal, and when conduct should be classed as criminal. It then considers the main theories of punishment, and thereby seeks to explain what criminal law seeks to achieve by punishing the defendant. Finally, the chapter considers the extent to which there is a separate category of law, known as regulatory crime, and the extent to which consumer law is part of such a category.

When is conduct criminal?

There are two important questions which are sometimes confused by commentators: first when *is* something criminal, and secondly when *should* something be criminal? As Smith and Hogan have commented, 'writers who set out to define a crime by reference to the nature of the act . . . inevitably end by telling us, not what a crime is, but what the writer thinks it ought to be; and that is not a definition of a crime'.[1] We can adopt an institutional approach to the first question by saying that it is criminal when it is deemed to be so by the law-maker. We can identify it as criminal by seeing that it is enforced by the state by prosecution in the magistrates' or Crown Court, and with the standard of proof of

---

[1] J.C. Smith, *Smith and Hogan Criminal Law* (9th edn, London, Butterworths, 1999), p. 20.

beyond reasonable doubt. So one characteristic of criminal law is that it is subject to certain procedural rules. It is argued that one can only identify criminal activity in this formal way. In the words of Lord Atkin: '[t]he criminal quality of an act cannot be discerned by intuition; nor can it be discovered by reference to any standard but one; is the act prohibited with penal consequences?'[2] This view was shared by Glanville Williams, who declared that 'a crime is an act capable of being followed by criminal proceedings having a criminal outcome',[3] and Andrew Ashworth, who argued that '[t]he only reliable test is the formal one: is the conduct prohibited, on pain of conviction and sentence?'[4]

A number of commentators have tried to identify when something is criminal by examining the nature of the act, the degree of culpability involved, the degree to which it is immoral, and so on.[5] The difficulty with this is that it is always possible to find offences which fall outside any such definition. Whenever Parliament creates a new offence, or decriminalises conduct, the act becomes or ceases to be criminal, but the essential characteristics of the underlying conduct stay the same: 'the act does not change in nature in any respect other than that of legal classification'.[6] However, even this procedural approach is subject to uncertainty. The European Court of Human Rights has stated that proceedings should be regarded as criminal if they are brought by a public authority, and either (a) they have culpability requirements, or (b) they have potentially severe consequences such as imprisonment. This will apply even if a State Party's law categorises the proceedings as civil.[7] There may be provisions of English law which UK lawyers might describe as civil, but which would meet this test.[8]

Although crimes might be seen as little more than acts, omissions, or states of affairs which Parliament or the courts have decided should be criminal, there will tend to be certain factors which lead Parliament or the courts to that conclusion. In particular, it has been argued that crimes tend to be acts which have a harmful effect on the public, and do more than merely interfere with private rights.[9] This 'public' nature of crime is reflected in the extent to which the state has control over a

---

[2] *Proprietary Articles Trade Association* v. *Attorney General for Canada* [1931] AC 310 at 324.

[3] 'The Definition of Crime' [1955] CLP 107.

[4] A. Ashworth, *Principles of Criminal Law* (3rd edn, Oxford University Press, 1999), p. 2.

[5] For a useful discussion see C. M. V. Clarkson and H.M. Keating, *Criminal Law: Text and Materials* (4th edn, London, Sweet and Maxwell, 1998), chapter 1.

[6] Smith, *Smith and Hogan Criminal Law*, p. 15.

[7] *Benham* v. *UK* (1996) 22 EHRR 293.

[8] Particularly if 'severe consequences' is taken to include removal of a licence.

[9] See Smith, *Smith and Hogan Criminal Law*, ch. 2.

prosecution, and is most evident when crimes are compared with civil laws.[10] If someone is to bring an action under the civil law, she needs standing (generally, to have been injured), can drop the action at any point, and may relieve the defendant of his liability if she wishes. Under the criminal law, by contrast, any citizen may generally bring a private prosecution, but cannot necessarily drop the case of her own volition, nor release the defendant from liability once he is convicted. The state's control over proceedings might therefore be seen as a key characteristic of criminal law.

When should conduct be criminalised?

As might be expected, there is no agreed test for when conduct should be made criminal.[11] Although this might appear to be an unpromising start, it is nevertheless important to examine possible approaches to this question. Criminalisation has been a typical government response to social ills. However, some eminent commentators have argued that this is both ideologically inappropriate and practically ineffective.[12] So much first-rate commentary has been produced on the role of the criminal law that it is impossible to do full justice to it here. This chapter will approach the literature by examining the recent work of Ashworth as a guide to contemporary debates. This work brings together two centuries of liberal scholarship in an informed and coherent way, and so is an appropriate model to examine. Ashworth has attempted to identify what he calls 'a principled core of criminal law', which he sees as consisting of four inter-linked principles.[13] It should be emphasised that Ashworth regards these as core principles rather than absolute rules, and therefore some derogation from them is viewed as permissible, provided those derogations are justified on a principled basis. By examining these principles, and their relationship with the work of other jurists, we can consider the extent to which consumer protection is an appropriate subject for regulation by the criminal law.

---

[10] Note, for example, the comment by Marshall and Duff that 'to believe that a certain kind of conduct should be criminal is to believe, at least, that it is conduct that should be declared wrong by the community; that it is a matter on which the community should take a shared and public view, and claim normative authority over its members'. S. E. Marshall and R. A. Duff, 'Criminalization and Sharing Wrongs' (1998) 11 *Canadian Journal of Law and Jurisprudence* 7 at p. 13. Cited in Ashworth, *Principles of Criminal Law.*

[11] See, for example, P. J. Fitzgerald, 'A Concept of Crime' [1960] Crim LR 257.

[12] See, for example, S. Kadish, *Blame and Punishment* (New York, Macmillan, 1987), Ashworth, *Principles of Criminal Law.*

[13] A. Ashworth, 'Is the Criminal Law a Lost Cause?' (2000) 116 LQR 225, 253–6.

Ashworth's core principles

Ashworth's first principle is that the criminal law should be used, and only used, to censure persons for substantial wrongdoing. It has been noted that the reaction of government to many wrongs, including those by businesses which may cause harm to consumers, has been to create new criminal offences. A number of commentators, Ashworth included, have been critical of what they perceive as this unprincipled over-criminalisation. Ashworth notes that of the thirty-nine new statutory offences created in 1997, only thirteen required proof of *mens rea*.[14] It is therefore not just the criminal law which is seen as an appropriate response to a multitude of social ills, but strict liability criminal law. The prevalence of strict liability is striking for a number of reasons. First, the House of Lords has recently reaffirmed the presumption in favour of *mens rea* in criminal offences in the case of *B* v. *Director of Public Prosecutions*.[15] Although it could be argued that this should reduce concern, as the judiciary can be relied upon to imply *mens rea* where it is not expressly included in a statute, this is not the case. The majority of offences that make no mention of *mens rea* will remain interpreted as strict liability offences despite the restatement of the presumption, as their lordships have made it clear that a number of factors can rebut the presumption, including where the offence is regulatory.[16] Secondly, the Government has set out some principles of criminalisation. Lord Williams of Mostyn stated that offences should only be created 'when absolutely necessary', and that when considering whether to create new offences, the Government will take into account whether: 'the behaviour in question is sufficiently serious to warrant intervention by the criminal law; the mischief could be dealt with under existing legislation or by using other remedies; the proposed offence is enforceable in practice; the proposed offence is tightly drawn and legally sound; and the proposed offence is commensurate with the seriousness of the offence'.[17] Although this appears to demonstrate support for minimalism in criminalisation, it is doubtful that this is carried through into practice. The number of new offences, and the wide variety of conduct with which they deal, suggests that the Government is less principled in its use of the criminal law in practice than in theory.

There are initial difficulties with applying Ashworth's test. First, we might ask when conduct is to be regarded as involving substantial

---

[14] Ibid. at 227.
[15] [2000] 1 All ER 833.
[16] *Sweet* v. *Parsley* [1970] AC 132.
[17] HL Debs vol. 602 WA 57 (18 June 1999) cited in Ashworth, 'Is the Criminal Law a Lost Cause?' p. 229.

wrongdoing. Other commentators such as Packer have asserted that conduct should only be criminalised when wrongful, but this term could have a number of different meanings.[18] Clarkson and Keating argue that wrongful could mean immoral, causing harm to others, or causing harm to others or to the perpetrator.[19] It is worth saying a few words about this in the context of consumer protection. First, if wrongful is to mean immoral, it is unlikely that many consumer protection offences would meet Packer's test.[20] Most consumer protection offences could not easily be viewed as immoral. Indeed, even outside the regulatory sphere there are many offences which it would be difficult to describe as immoral. As a result, immorality is not generally viewed as a necessary precondition to the imposition of criminal sanctions. Whether immorality is a sufficient condition for criminalising conduct has been the subject of considerable debate. The argument that it is sufficient is generally associated with Lord Devlin. In his 1959 lecture 'The Enforcement of Morals' and subsequent work, Lord Devlin famously argued that the criminal law should be used to defend public morality, regardless of any obvious harm to others.[21] This thesis was strongly opposed by Hart, although Hart agreed that law should play a role in enforcing morality to some extent, and accepted that paternalistic laws could be acceptable.[22] Secondly, if 'wrongful' means causing harm to others, then consumer protection statutes will generally meet the first stage of Packer's test. Although there is no need for injury to a consumer to have actually taken place, consumer law protects against potential harm, and so there is likely to be agreement that this is wrongful.[23] Central to John Stuart Mill's view of criminal law is the concept of 'harm to others'. He argued that criminal law should only be used to prevent harm to others, and not solely to prevent people from harming themselves.[24] Of course, there are some practical difficulties in applying this. Should harm, for example, include preventing offence? Some areas of consumer law will be concerned with offensive conduct, for

---

[18] Herbert L. Packer, *The Limits of the Criminal Sanction* (Stanford, Stanford University Press, 1969).

[19] Clarkson and Keating, *Criminal Law: Text and Materials*, p. 4.

[20] Unless we take the approach of Gross and say that the rights enjoyed by consumers and others are moral as well as legal rights, 'since entitlement to the security and freedom that they represent is a matter of fundamental social consensus and not a matter simply of legal enactment'. H. Gross, *A Theory of Criminal Justice* (New York, Oxford University Press, 1979), p. 15 cited in Clarkson and Keating, *Criminal Law*, p. 6.

[21] Although we could say that preventing harm to others is part of public morality.

[22] H. L. A. Hart, 'Immorality and Treason' (1959) 62 *Listener* 162.

[23] If actual harm had to be proved, there could be no offence of attempted murder. It is assumed that all commentators would accept potential harm as coming within the test of 'wrongful'.

[24] J. S. Mill, *On Liberty* (1859).

example, the regulation of advertising.[25] If 'wrongful' includes harm to the perpetrator alone, then the law is in the realms of paternalism. There is considerable debate about the extent to which the criminal law should have a paternalistic role.[26] Despite some high-profile cases, particularly in the area of sexual expression and the causing of bodily harm, where judges seem to have taken a moralistic and, arguably, paternalistic stance, the idea of paternalism has been the subject of criticism in the UK.[27] Paternalism involves the idea of prohibiting behaviour, purely from the point of view of protecting an individual and irrespective of his wishes. In some cases, we prohibit the action of the 'victim', for example by prohibiting the use of certain drugs and insisting on the wearing of seat belts in cars. In other cases we prohibit the perpetrator from acting in a particular way towards his 'victim', despite his having the victim's consent, for example, by regarding consent to assault as invalid where actual bodily harm is intended and/or caused.[28] In both situations the law is imposed contrary to the wishes of the victim. Paternalism in the context of consumer law is relevant where we deny the consumer choice by criminalising the actions of a trader. For example, the state might deny the consumer the choice to buy a dangerous product at a knock-down price in the belief that the consumer should not expose himself to that risk. Paternalism is examined in more detail in chapter 1 of this book. Suffice it to say that the criminal law may be used to protect consumers, even when the consumer consents to the harm, or at least the risk of harm, in question.

If we can overcome the initial obstacle of identifying what is meant by wrongful, we face the additional hurdle of describing when wrongdoing is to be regarded as 'substantial'. It might be argued that 'substantial' is synonymous with 'serious'. There will be some offences which are unquestionably serious, some which are difficult to regard as serious, and some about which there is likely to be dispute as to their seriousness. The two main components of seriousness are perhaps severity of harm and culpability.[29] Ashworth argues that harmfulness must be judged in terms of its effect on valued interests 'which may be individual

---

[25] For example, the Code of Advertising Practice requires advertisements to be decent as well as legal, honest, and truthful. Breach of the Code is not, however, an offence.

[26] It is rejected by J. Feinberg in *Harm to Self* (New York, Oxford University Press, 1986).

[27] One of the few works to support the approach of the House is W. Wilson, 'Is Hurting People Wrong?' [1992] *Journal of Social Welfare and Family Law* 388.

[28] *Brown* [1994] 1 AC 212.

[29] Feinberg identifies five main tests for whether harm should be criminalised: gravity of harm; probability of harm; magnitude of risk; value of the conduct; and reasonableness of the risk of harm. J. Feinberg, *The Moral Limits of the Criminal Law: Harm to Others* (New York, Oxford University Press, 1984), pp. 215–16.

interests or some form of collective interests'.[30] Offences may certainly be serious without causing material harm to an individual where there is sufficient culpability (for example, attempted murder or conspiracy). More difficult, and perhaps more relevant in the context of consumer law, is whether offences can be serious if there is considerable harm, but little or no culpability. Ashworth argues not, stating that intention or recklessness would be a requirement of the paradigm of crime that he espouses.[31] Empirical evidence suggests, however, that the public does regard the degree of harm inflicted as an important element of offence-seriousness.[32] Many regulatory offences deal with matters which involve potentially significant harm, such as product safety and environmental protection. Some of these are offences of strict liability, although they tend to be subject to due diligence defences. Other consumer protection offences might involve relatively little harm and little culpability, for example, innocently giving a misleading price indication which meant that a customer was over-charged by a few pence. Because of the existence of due diligence offences, traders should not be convicted unless they fail to show that they have taken all reasonable precautions and exercised all due diligence. As a result, it could be argued that there will always be a degree of culpability to a conviction where a due diligence defence is available.

The next principle is that criminal laws should be enforced with respect for equal treatment and proportionality. Ashworth argues that the principle of equal treatment, i.e. 'that those who commit wrongs of equivalent seriousness in relatively similar circumstances should be subject to censure of a similar magnitude', is an important principle of criminal law.[33] He accepts that this is not an absolute rule, and that there may be some circumstances, such as labour and family disputes, where 'the principle of equal treatment might be regarded . . . as outweighed by the need to protect other values and to assign a more peripheral role to the criminal law'.[34] However, he suggests that the burden should fall on the legislature, court, or prosecutor to show why offences should not be treated in the usual way.

This is particularly important to us in relation to regulatory offences, a category of offence which is examined in detail below. A characteristic of regulatory offences is that they generally are enforced by agencies or

[30] Ashworth, 'Is the Criminal Law a Lost Cause?', p. 240.
[31] Ibid. p. 241.
[32] Leslie Sebba, 'Is Mens Rea a Component of Perceived Offense Seriousness?' (1980) 71 JCLC 124.
[33] Ashworth, 'Is the Criminal Law a Lost Cause?', p. 245.
[34] Ibid.

authorities which adopt compliance strategies in preference to formal prosecution.[35] Although discretion is exercised at most levels of law enforcement it is clear that regulatory agencies tend to use warnings far more frequently, and prosecute far less frequently, than the police.[36] Can this flexible approach to enforcement be defended? Ashworth identifies two possible justifications: that it is more effective in the long term, and that it is more economical. He appears convinced by neither. The first argument is questioned on the basis that 'it remains to be demonstrated that extra law-abidance is produced, and, if so, that it can only be achieved by means of a compliance approach to enforcement'.[37] The second is dismissed for its potentially unfair effects: '[i]f one person who wrongs another is convicted of a crime whilst another who commits an allegedly more serious wrong is not, this is a manifestation of warped priorities and clear injustice'.[38] In relation to the first point, although it has been suggested that deterrence, or sanctioning strategies, would have the effect of reducing contraventions of regulatory legislation, the evidence on this is inconclusive. As we shall see in chapter 7, enforcement authorities argue strongly that compliance strategies facilitate their enforcement of regulatory legislation. In relation to the second point, if the justification for compliance strategies were merely that they save money, this would be a matter for concern.[39] Certainly, enforcement authorities argue that they are underfunded, and this is a matter which should be addressed. But it is by no means certain that a higher level of funding would necessarily lead to a greater number of prosecutions. Research by Hawkins on enforcement of environmental law found that some authorities felt that they could prosecute more frequently if they wanted to with a minimal effect on resources.[40] This is, however, a matter that needs further investigation. A further point on consistency is that there are measures in place that aim to ensure that enforcement is carried out equally within a particular sphere of activity, for example, co-ordination of enforcement activity on food and trading standards by the Local Authority Co-ordinating Body on Food and Trading Standards (LACOTS).[41] This addresses, for example, the risk of inconsistency within trading standards.

[35] See ch. 7.
[36] Ashworth, 'Is the Criminal Law a Lost Cause?', p. 247.
[37] Ibid. p. 248.
[38] Ibid. p. 249.
[39] Some studies assume that the rarity of prosecutions is down to inadequate resources. See R. Cranston, *Regulating Business: Law and Consumer Agencies* (London, Macmillan, 1979) and J. E. Conklin, *Illegal But Not Criminal* (Englewood Cliffs, Prentice Hall, 1977).
[40] K. Hawkins, *Environment and Enforcement* (Oxford, Oxford University Press, 1984), ch. 10.
[41] See ch. 7.

What it does not do is address the differences between different enforcement agencies, for example between trading standards officers and the police/Crown Prosecution Service (CPS). This is one of Ashworth's main concerns, although he recognises that the police use discretion, and caution a higher percentage of offenders than was previously the case; for example, around 38 per cent of offenders are now cautioned rather than prosecuted.[42]

The next principle is that persons accused of substantial wrongdoing ought to be afforded the protection appropriate to those charged with criminal offences. By this, Ashworth means the minimum protections contained in Articles 6.2 and 6.3 of the European Convention on Human Rights. Article 6.2 states that '[e]veryone charged with a criminal offence shall be presumed innocent until proved guilty according to law'. Article 6.3 states that '[e]veryone charged with a criminal offence has the following minimum rights ...' Those rights include the right to be informed of the nature and cause of the accusation against him and the right to have adequate time and facilities to prepare a defence. It is not proposed to examine this principle here. It is difficult to argue against the need for procedural safeguards, although there might be debate about how far they should extend.

Next is the principle that maximum sentences and effective sentence levels should be proportionate to the seriousness of the wrongdoing. Under this heading, Ashworth calls for a revision of maximum penalties, and a re-assessment of sentence levels and of differentials between them.[43] Again, of course, we face difficulties in establishing seriousness. However, few could dispute that the most serious offences (those which involve the most actual or potential harm and those which involve the highest degree of culpability) should generally carry the highest penalties, and that the least serious offences should carry the lowest penalties. Consumer law sometimes fails to achieve this. For example, breach of the General Product Safety Regulations gives rise to a maximum of three months imprisonment, whereas breach of lottery regulations can lead to a prison sentence of two years. As will be seen in chapter 5, a major criticism of product safety law is that the sentences for breach of its provisions are inadequate. Difficult sentencing issues are also raised where the defendant is a corporation. The issues surrounding corporate liability are considered in the next chapter.

Censure, minimalism, and crime as a last resort. Fundamental to Ashworth's conception of criminal law is that it exists primarily as a

---

[42] See Ashworth, 'Is the Criminal Law a Lost Cause?', p. 247.
[43] Ibid. p. 255.

means of censure. Indeed, he states: '[m]y conception of criminal law gives primary place to its censuring function'.[44] He contrasts this with the approach of Braithwaite who, in Ashworth's view, perceives criminal law as one of a number of mechanisms for preventing harm – a major goal of social policy. One question which emerges here is whether conduct should only be criminalised as a last resort. This approach is rooted in concern at over-criminalisation. It reflects the view that the criminal law should not be used where there is an alternative available. Where consumer protection offences are at issue, it is clear that there may be alternatives to the use of the criminal law. These include civil remedies in contract and tort, administrative sanctions such as the removal of a licence, and civil penalties. Chapter 1 examined the limitations of the private law, and the difficulties in relying on private law remedies to provide adequate consumer protection. The limitations of the private law may be somewhat overcome by removing the burdens that are traditionally placed on the victim by way of transaction costs. Group actions could be used, and powers given to an administrative body to take action on the consumer's behalf. Instead of fining defendants, they could be given civil penalties, which would, arguably, remove the stigma of a conviction.[45] It should be remembered that there is considerable overlap between civil and criminal law and this is one reason why it is so difficult to distinguish the two. This overlap is most apparent in relation to criminal law and tort, where many criminal offences will also be torts, and most observers have concentrated on this.[46] However, as is explained in chapter 6, there is also overlap between criminal law and contract in the consumer protection field. Ashworth lends his support to alternative approaches, perhaps called civil violations or administrative offences, seeing them as providing a method of ensuring quick and effective justice. These would generally be punished by way of fine, and would not attract a custodial sentence. Although they would be subject to simple procedures, there would remain minimum rights for defendants, such as access to a criminal court.[47] Although there is a role for such approaches, it is submitted that this does not mean that the criminal law should be removed from the area of consumer protection. This view is developed below.

A pre-requisite of effectiveness? Should criminal law only be used where it is effective? Packer argues that criminal law should only be used to deal with conduct that is wrongful, but also that it must be *necessary*

[44] Ibid. p. 250.
[45] See D. Tench, *Towards a Middle System of Law* (London, Consumers' Association, 1981).
[46] See for example Williams, 'The Definition of Crime' [1955] CLP 107.
[47] Ashworth, 'Is the Criminal Law a Lost Cause?', p. 255.

to use the criminal law to condemn or prevent that conduct.[48] This ties
in with the minimalist idea that crime should be a last resort, but also
reflects the idea that conduct should not be criminalised where that will
be ineffective in controlling the conduct. Ashworth sees criminal law as
having a role in censure and this may justify classifying conduct as criminal even where the criminal law is likely to be a blunt instrument in
preventing that conduct. He argues that if conduct is serious or harmful
enough to justify criminalisation, 'there is at least an important symbolic
reason for declaring it to be criminal'.[49] However, he also concedes that
criminalising conduct may have a damaging effect, for example, by producing black markets for drugs or leading to police corruption.[50] In such
cases there may be a strong pragmatic argument against criminalisation.

The sufficiency of effectiveness. A related question to that of whether
effectiveness is a prerequisite of criminalisation is whether it is sufficient
to criminalise conduct. Here, Ashworth's approach is in the negative.
There are two factors to his argument: first, that culpability is central
to the idea of wrongdoing, and many of the areas where criminal law
might be introduced on the grounds of effectiveness may lack culpability. Secondly, that many of these areas involve only minor wrongs, and
that the criminal law should not be used for minor wrongs. On the first
point, it is true that the areas where criminal law has been justified on
the basis of effectiveness involve regulatory offences. As many of these
offences do not require proof of *mens rea*, it could be argued that they
can be committed without culpability. Having said this, the vast majority of regulatory offences contain due diligence defences which allow the
defendant to escape liability by proving that he (or it, in the case of a
company – most defendants here are likely to be corporations) has taken
all reasonable precautions and exercised all due diligence to avoid the
commission of the offence. These defences are frequently referred to as
'no negligence' defences, suggesting that the defendant will be acquitted when he shows he was not negligent. As a result, it could be argued
that only negligent defendants, and therefore culpable defendants, will
be convicted. There are, however, difficulties with this analysis. First, establishing a due diligence defence is not exactly the same as showing an
absence of negligence. It is a narrower test, although some comments indicate that it may be interpreted quite broadly in practice. Secondly, there
may be disagreement about whether evidence of negligence is evidence of

---

[48] Packer, *The Limits of the Criminal Sanction*, pp. 262–4.
[49] Ashworth, *Principles of Criminal Law*, p. 36.
[50] Kadish, *Blame and Punishment*.

culpability for the purposes of the criminal law. On the second point, although there is an argument for not criminalising minor harm, it is important to note that there will be occasions when harm appears to be minor, but where the broader picture tells a different story. In the consumer protection field, an obvious example is over-pricing. Over-pricing might appear to amount to minor harm in an individual case, but may appear more serious if it affects a large number of transactions. In practice, it appears that enforcement authorities exercise their discretion carefully to ensure that minor infringements are not punished. While that allows the potential for punishing minor harms, it does much to obviate the harshness of strict liability in practice.

A related question is whether criminal law is effective in providing protection. There is little doubt that it has been perceived to be so by successive governments, but the issue is far from resolved. In particular, if we tie this point in with the idea that conduct should only be criminalised as a last resort, we might conclude that alternative sanctions, such as administrative or civil penalties, could do the job just as effectively. Certainly, if the deterrent effect of criminal law is the formal punishment that is imposed (generally a fine), then civil penalties should be able to deter just as effectively. What civil penalties lack is a condemnatory edge, but if the wrongs we have in mind are not deserving of condemnation, then this might be welcomed. However, it is submitted that while the criminal law may be one of society's primary forms of condemnation, not all offences carry that condemnatory message. Regulatory offences, in particular, appear to lack the stigma usually associated with the criminal law. As long as we recognise that criminal law is about more than censure for moral wrongdoing we should not be alarmed at the use of criminal sanctions in the regulatory sphere.

To conclude this part of the chapter, it is important to note that, trite as it may sound, there is considerable disagreement about the role of criminal law, and about when conduct should be classified as criminal. Ashworth's core principles provide a helpful and well-constructed paradigm for analysis. Were they accepted as prerequisites for criminalisation, it seems likely that many consumer protection offences would have to go. But as we have seen, it is possible to question Ashworth's assumptions about the proper role of criminal law. As will be seen later, these assumptions are particularly relevant where regulatory offences are concerned. Before we examine the concept of the regulatory offence, however, it is important to say something about the aims of punishment. If punishment is a defining characteristic of the criminal law, an investigation into why we punish is important to our discussion.

The objectives of punishment

Related to the question of when something should be classed as criminal is that of what we are seeking to achieve by imposing penal sanctions upon the defendant. The first point to make is that consumer protection offences are generally trying to achieve two main things: the protection of the consumer and the protection of the honest trader. Although most discussion has taken place in relation to the former, it is clear that the protection of honest traders can be viewed as an important function and aim of consumer protection legislation.[51] However, we can dig more deeply, and ask what, precisely, punishment is designed to achieve. Put another way, how is the use of penal sanctions supposed to ensure the aims set out above? To answer this, we need to look briefly at the main theories of the objectives of punishment. These can be identified as: deterrence, incapacitation, rehabilitation, retribution, and restoration. These theories will be briefly examined in order to consider how effective criminal law can be in tackling the wrongs of business against consumers. As will become apparent, one of the difficulties with the criminal law is that many of its techniques and principles have developed with individual defendants in mind. Although some defendants in consumer protection cases are individuals, many will be corporations. This raises particular difficulties which are examined in the next chapter.

Deterrence. One of the main justifications for imposing punishment on an offender is to deter similar conduct in the future. Deterrence works mainly at two levels. First, by punishing an individual he may be deterred from committing an offence in the future. This is called individual deterrence. Secondly, the punishment of that individual may deter others from committing similar offences in the future. This is referred to as general deterrence. Despite the influence of deterrence theories in criminal justice policy, there is dispute about the extent to which punishment deters in practice. High reconviction rates might suggest that individual deterrence is a chimera, and society may be persuaded not to commit offences by a wide range of factors other than punishment, including moral inhibitions and fear of censure of their associates.[52] If these fears and inhibitions result from the conduct being criminal, then we can say that the criminal law has an important deterrent function. Indeed, there is a body of literature which sees criminal sanctions as part of a

---

[51] See, for example, the Trade Descriptions Act 1968.
[52] See J. Andenaes, 'The General Preventive Effects of Punishment' (1996) 114 *University of Pennsylvania Law Review* 949.

message from the state to society about the unacceptability of conduct.[53] This might form part of a third deterrent-based category, sometimes called educative deterrence. Educative deterrence emphasises the role of criminal sanctions in creating a climate in which laws are complied with because they are laws. Punishment strengthens the habit of compliance. This has a relationship with the function of the criminal law in shaming, and so has some connections with rehabilitative and restorative approaches discussed below.[54]

The limitations of deterrence where the defendant is a corporation are of particular concern in the context of consumer protection offences.[55] Wells argues that: '[m]ost corporate crime theory has been deterrent-based, in the sense that the purpose of instituting sanctions has been to discourage violations and encourage good practice'.[56] But how effective is the criminal law in deterring corporate wrongdoing? This may depend on the types of sanctions available. Writing in 1972 the Law Commission stated that it believed that the criminal law could have a strong deterrent effect on corporations because of the publicity that results from their prosecution.[57] Although this has been doubted,[58] there is evidence that publicity can be effective. As has been observed, the use of brand image in advertising and the efforts of corporations to regain a clean image after a disaster shows the importance to them of their status and image.[59] If conviction is a deterrent, it is perhaps because of the impression that is given by being branded a criminal that effects this, rather than the level of formal punishment imposed. In the words of Ball and Friedman: 'the word "crime" has symbolic meaning for the public and the criminal law is stained so deeply with notions of morality and immorality, public censure and punishment, that labelling an act as criminal often has consequences that go far beyond mere administrative effectiveness'. They conclude that 'businessmen abhor the idea of being branded a criminal', and that fear of prosecution is an effective deterrent to business people.[60]

---

[53] T. Mathiesen, *Prison on Trial* (London, Sage, 1990), Gross, *A Theory of Criminal Justice*.
[54] See J. Braithwaite, *Crime, Shame and Reintegration* (Cambridge, Cambridge University Press, 1989).
[55] For an excellent account of the criminal liability of corporations see C. Wells, *Corporations and Criminal Responsibility* (Oxford, Clarendon Press, 1993).
[56] Ibid. p. 31.
[57] Law Commission (1972), para. 88.
[58] See Iain Ramsay, *Consumer Protection: Text, Cases and Materials* (London, Weidenfeld and Nicolson, 1989), p. 190.
[59] Wells, *Corporations and Criminal Responsibility*, p. 37.
[60] Harry Ball and Laurence Friedman, 'Use of Criminal Sanctions in the Enforcement of Economic Legislation: a Sociological View' (1965) 17 *Stanford Law Review* 197 at 216–17.

Some writers emphasise the utility of other deterrent-based sanctions. Fisse and Braithwaite have called for punitive injunctions which would require resources to be devoted to the development of new preventative measures.[61] Such sanctions would ensure that some account is taken of the harm done, and that steps are taken to minimise the risk of such harm in the future. Other sanctions which could have a deterrent effect include corporate probation,[62] community service,[63] incarceration,[64] or, ultimately, corporate dissolution.[65]

Incapacitation. The most obvious form of incapacitation is imprisonment. Imprisonment may be an element of a deterrence or rehabilitation-based regime, but could be seen as a reaction to the apparent failure of such regimes.[66] Even if imprisonment fails to deter or rehabilitate, at least it protects the public for the period that the defendant is incarcerated. However, offenders may pose more of a threat when released, and research casts some doubt on the success of incarceration in reducing crime.[67] Where consumer protection offences are concerned, imprisonment is not always an option. The Trade Descriptions Act 1968, for example, allows an offender to be imprisoned, whereas the Property Misdescriptions Act 1991 does not. Where the defendant is a corporation, of course, there is no possibility of it being imprisoned, but all consumer protection offences contain senior officer provisions which allow for the conviction of those individuals who consent to or connive in the commission of an offence by their corporation, or to whose neglect the commission of the offence is attributable.[68] Many of these provisions allow for imprisonment. Imprisonment is relatively rare following conviction for a consumer protection offence. Of the 1,156 convictions under s.1 of the Trade Descriptions Act cited in the Annual Report of the Director General of Fair Trading for 1998 just fifty defendants received prison

---

[61] See B. Fisse and J. Braithwaite, 'Allocation of Responsibility for Corporate Crime: Individualism, Collectivism and Accountability' (1988) 11 *Sydney Law Review* 468 and the discussion in Ashworth, *Principles of Criminal Law*, pp. 116–24.

[62] See B. Fisse, 'Reconstructing Corporate Criminal Law: Deterrence, Retribution, Fault and Sanctions' (1983) 56 Cal LR 1141 at 1222.

[63] See J. Gobert, 'Controlling Corporate Criminality: Penal Sanctions and Beyond' [1998] 2 Web JCLI.

[64] See D. Meister, 'Criminal Liability for Corporations that Kill' (1989–90) 64 Tulane LR 919 at p. 946, where he argues that a corporation could be forbidden to engage in particular activities.

[65] Clarkson and Keating, *Criminal Law*, p. 248.

[66] R. A. Duff and D. Garland, *A Reader on Punishment* (Oxford, Oxford University Press, 1996), p. 25.

[67] See A. von Hirsch and A. Ashworth, *Principled Sentencing* (2nd edn, Oxford, Hart, 1998).

[68] See, for example, s.20 of the Trade Descriptions Act 1968.

sentences. Of the 286 convictions under Part II of the Consumer Protection Act 1987 which deals with offences under safety regulations, just
one defendant was imprisoned. A further point to note is that although
corporations cannot be 'imprisoned', it may be possible to take a similar
form of action against them, as mentioned above.

Although it is customary to concentrate upon imprisonment when
examining incapacitation, the concept can be viewed more widely. The
main way in which a trader can be incapacitated is by having her licence
revoked. Several consumer protection statutes provide for the licensing
of traders, including the Consumer Credit Act 1974. Although licensing
is viewed as an administrative function, revocation of a licence may well
follow conviction for a criminal offence. In this way, incapacitation is a
very important tool in the armoury of consumer law enforcement.

Rehabilitation. A rehabilitative theory of punishment would attempt to persuade offenders to comply with criminal law in the future,
not through fear of punishment, but by creating in the offender 'the
capacity for social participation and responsibility'.[69] Although rehabilitation might be viewed as one of the more laudable aims of the criminal
law, it been castigated by critics as reactionary, failing to respect the
rights of the defendant.[70] Duff and Garland observe that '[o]ne of the
most striking changes of the last twenty years has been the extent to which
consequentialist ideas [such as rehabilitation] have been abandoned, and
retributivist ideas revived'.[71] It is unclear to what extent rehabilitation is
an issue in consumer protection offences. There is debate, for example,
about the extent to which white-collar offenders may be susceptible to rehabilitation. One difficulty here is that rehabilitation may be interpreted
in different ways. It has been argued that 'if rehabilitation is taken to
be a kind of transformation of character in which offenders are turned
into law-abiding citizens by the application of some generalizable penal
technique, then the reconviction rates alone indicate that rehabilitation
remains an impossible goal'.[72] Certainly, it appears that part of the process of rehabilitation is a recognition that one has done wrong, and it is
doubtful whether such recognition is present on the part of many who
commit consumer protection offences. Cranston, for example, concludes
that 'the businessman's conception of himself does not change following
a conviction for a consumer offence, and neither is there any loss of status

---

[69] E. Rotman, *Beyond Punishment*, p. 1, cited in Duff and Garland, *A Reader on Punishment*.
[70] See J. G. Murphy, 'Marxism and Retribution' (1973) 2 *Philosophy and Public Affairs*
217.
[71] Duff and Garland, 'Introduction' in *A Reader on Punishment*, p. 9.
[72] Ibid. p. 24.

among his commercial associates'.[73] To the extent that a feeling of shame is necessary, it is unlikely that those who commit consumer protection offences will be rehabilitated. There may be good reasons for traders possessing this attitude. As the majority of such offences are not committed intentionally, the perpetrator is unlikely to feel that he has acted in a morally reprehensible manner. The most shame he is likely to feel is that he could have done more to have prevented the offence occurring. Furthermore, the main sanction for breach of consumer protection offences is the fine, and rehabilitation is unlikely to follow from being fined. If the offender is to change wilfully, it seems likely that prison or some community or education-based punishment would be necessary. Such sentences cannot be handed out to corporations, and will only rarely be handed out to those behind a corporation.[74]

However, it is important not to over-state the limitations of rehabilitative theory. Rehabilitation may be about more than the kind of transformation suggested above. For example, Morris is critical of traditional rehabilitative regimes, but has also argued that punishment has an educative element which may help offenders to recognise their wrongs, and change their behaviour. This is presented as paternalistic rather than rehabilitative, as it concentrates on the interests of the offender, rather than the interests of society.[75] However, the distinction between the two is far from stark, and it is possible to view this as a form of rehabilitation. There is also some connection between rehabilitation and educative deterrence, which is considered above. Indeed, if rehabilitation is to encompass re-education, then it may have a role in consumer protection. Many offences are committed carelessly rather than intentionally, and an important role of the legal system is to bring those offences to the attention of the offender. Many traders will be keen to avoid committing offences and the criminal process may help them to achieve this. This can, and frequently will, be done without a prosecution, as part of a compliance strategy rather than through punishment. It would be wrong to describe this form of re-education as rehabilitation in the usual sense. However, it is important to remember the role that criminal law enforcement, both formal and informal, can play in ensuring compliance through education aimed at eliminating the careless commission of offences. This is considered in more detail in chapter 7.

---

[73] Cranston, *Regulating Business*, p. 172.

[74] Although a more imaginative approach to corporate sentencing would allow similar penalties to be imposed on corporations. See above.

[75] H. Morris, 'A Paternalistic Theory of Punishment' (1981) 18 *American Philosophical Quarterly* 263.

Retribution. Retribution, the origins of which can be traced to the Bible, is the aim of punishment which provides us with the most difficulties.[76] The expression has echoes of revenge about it, and Stephen argued as far back as the nineteenth century that it is 'morally right to hate criminals'.[77] This view is not in favour with many commentators. However, retributive theories of punishment find support in the guise of 'just deserts'. Under this theory, criminals are punished because they deserve to be, not because their punishment will reduce offending, either by themselves or others, in the future. It is interesting to note that although retributive theories might appear likely to be associated with the political right, this is frequently not the case. Just deserts theory is founded on respect for the individual, and aims to ensure that the punishment offenders receive is fair, determinate, and proportionate.[78] Indeed, the success of retributive theories has been due to a combination of practical and philosophical factors. On the practical level, research has suggested that rehabilitative and deterrence-based punishment has little effect on crime. For example, the Serota Report stated that if reconviction rates are used to measure the effect of sentencing policy 'there is virtually nothing to choose between different lengths of custodial sentence, different types of institutional regime, and even between custodial and non-custodial treatment'.[79] On a philosophical level we have already seen that rehabilitative regimes in particular have been criticised for giving inadequate respect for the victim – in Kantian terms, treating him as a means rather than an end.[80]

Retribution will sometimes be of significance where consumer protection offences are concerned. Where a trader produces goods which are known to be dangerous, there will be considerable stigma attached to that conduct, and we might expect the criminal justice system to punish on behalf of society, reflecting society's distaste at what has happened. Perhaps the best example of this is in the case of the Ford Pinto, where a calculation by the defendant's actuaries that redesign would be more expensive than paying compensation for deaths caused by the fault to the car led to public outrage.[81] However, retributive approaches allow the severity of the sentence to be related to the seriousness of the offence, and it is doubtful that the consumer protection laws in the UK would provide a sufficient sanction for a corporation or its senior officers in a

---

[76] See Leviticus 24: 17–22.
[77] See J. F. Stephen, *A History of the Criminal Law of England*, vol. II (1883), pp. 81–2.
[78] Duff and Garland, 'Introduction', p. 12.
[79] Serota Report (1977 ACPS para. 8).
[80] I. Kant, *Groundwork of the Metaphysic of Morals* (1785).
[81] See F. Cullen, W. Maakestad, and G. Cavender, *Corporate Crime Under Attack* (Cincinnati, Anderson, 1987).

case such as that involving the Pinto to receive their just deserts.[82] In other cases, where offences are committed accidentally or carelessly, it is less likely that retribution will found a justification for punishment, although the culpability in failing to have procedures in place to prevent contraventions from occurring may, in some cases, be high.

Restoration. Restorative theories of punishment are complex. In the words of Ashworth '[a] restorative theory might be chiefly concerned to achieve compensation or a reconciliation that restores the status quo ante'.[83] The main difficulty with a restorative approach concerns its relationship with the theories considered above. For example, 'just deserts' includes the concept of ensuring that offenders do not benefit from an unfair advantage by interfering with another's rights. Punishment under that approach can be seen as restoring equilibrium. Braithwaite comments that '[r]estorative justice aims to restore harmony based on a feeling that justice has been done'.[84] Secondly, there appears to be a close relationship between restorative and rehabilitative theories. Like rehabilitative theories, restorative theories hope that punishment will change the offender, reconciling him with the community and its norms. The distinction seems in part to be why this is done. For example, paternalistic theories of punishment emphasise that punishment is in the interests of the offender, and justify punishment on that basis.[85] The aim is to persuade the offender to reform himself, in his own interests. Rehabilitative theories, by contrast, justify punishment on the basis of the interests to society of having the offender reformed. Restorative bases for punishment may also avoid the stigma usually associated with crime. Braithwaite, for example, draws a distinction between stigmatisation, which 'means treating criminals as evil people who have done evil acts', and reintegrative shaming, which 'means disapproving of the evil of the deed while treating the person as essentially good'.[86] This may be attractive where the defendant's conduct lacks any immoral character.

Restorative theories can be explained from the point of view of compensating the victim, rather than restoring equilibrium between the perpetrator and other members of society. Compensation orders are a means of ensuring that an offender pays a sum of money to his victim. They have

---

[82] The maximum penalty for breaching the General Product Safety Regulations is three months' imprisonment.
[83] Ashworth, *Principles of Criminal Law*, p. 17.
[84] J. Braithwaite, 'Restorative Justice', in J. Braithwaite (ed.), *Regulation, Crime, Freedom* (Aldershot, Dartmouth, and Ashgale, 2000), p. 324.
[85] Morris, 'A Paternalistic Theory of Punishment'.
[86] Braithwaite, 'Restorative Justice'.

been described as 'a convenient and rapid means of avoiding the expense of civil litigation when the criminal clearly has the means which would enable compensation to be paid'.[87] Compensation orders can therefore be seen as an effective alternative to civil litigation. However, they can also be justified on grounds of punishment. The offender has to pay a sum of money in a similar way to being fined, but the money finds its way to the victim rather than the State. It is unclear whether compensation orders should be seen as a form of punishment. Clarkson and Keating point to the case of *Miller* where the court made a compensation order 'to remind the offender of the evil he has done',[88] but conclude that the Court of Appeal has generally not viewed them as a punishment, but rather as a means of meeting the victim's needs.[89] However, they are certainly a penal order in law.

What this analysis of punishment rationales shows us is that 'the quest to identify a coherent theory of punishment is multi-faceted and multi-layered'.[90] Hart recognised that for any account of punishment to be acceptable, there had to be compromise between distinct and partly conflicting principles.[91] Because much punishment theory is centred upon individual offenders and *mens rea* offences, it sits slightly uneasily with laws aimed largely at corporations. Nevertheless, these theories are important to a discussion of consumer law. First, English law has tended not to differentiate between types of defendant, and corporate criminal liability is to a large extent based on notions of individual liability. Secondly, one theme in this work is that we need to treat consumer protection offences seriously. One way of doing this is to think about the effects that criminal sanctions have on businesses and to develop the laws so that the consumer protection objectives of criminal law are met. Punishment theories may help us to think about what criminal law can do as well as what it should be doing.

Regulatory crime and consumer law

So far, we have assumed that there is something homogeneous about criminal law. At a formal level, this is no doubt the case. However, a distinction is often drawn between two different types of crime. On the one hand there is 'real crime', which consists of offences which are sometimes referred to as *mala in se* or 'sins with legal definitions'. The most obvious

---

[87] *Inwood* (1974) 60 Cr App R 70 at 73 *per* Lord Scarman.
[88] [1976] Crim LR 694.
[89] Clarkson and Keating, *Criminal Law*, p. 88.
[90] Wells, *Corporations and Criminal Responsibility*, p. 19.
[91] H. L. A. Hart, *Punishment and Responsibility* (Oxford, Oxford University Press, 1968).

examples include murder, rape, and theft. 'Real crime' covers that which the public generally recognises as being criminal. On the other hand, there is 'quasi crime', which is made up of offences *mala prohibita*. In a famous extract, Wright J identified a class of acts 'which are not criminal in any real sense, but are acts which, in the public interest, are prohibited under a penalty'.[92] Another term used for the latter type of offence is that of 'regulatory crime', and it is that expression which will be adopted in this chapter. Although these offences are criminal in a formal sense, they do not bear many similarities to 'real crime'. As Ashworth comments:

there are many offences for which criminal liability is merely imposed by Parliament as a practical means of controlling an activity, without implying the element of social condemnation characteristic of the major or traditional crimes . . . the only feature which distinguishes some of these minor offences from civil wrongs, like breach of contract and liability in tort, is the decision by Parliament that they shall be attended by criminal procedures and triable in criminal courts.[93]

Enormous difficulties are presented in trying to categorise criminal law in this way, but attempts have been made to identify the characteristics of regulatory crime in order to explain precisely how it differs from real crime. Ramsay identifies three main characteristics of regulatory crime:

(i) Over-inclusive statutory standards enforced by sanctions of strict criminal liability, generally tempered by certain statutory defences. The primary sanction is a fine rather than imprisonment.

(ii) A specialised bureaucracy is under a duty to enforce the Act . . . This will, in practice, involve the exercise of discretion by the agency in the implementation and enforcement of standards.

(iii) The courts involved in day-to-day implementation of the Act are the lay bench of the magistrates' courts, although the higher courts also play a significant role in developing the text of the Act.[94]

Some of the characteristics mentioned above distinguish regulatory offences from some 'real crimes'. Real crimes will generally be enforced by the police rather than regulatory agencies. They will often be heard in the Crown Court rather than the magistrates' court. Real crimes will also generally not impose strict liability. However, the distinction between the two categories is not as clear as it might first appear to be. Some very serious offences are sometimes investigated by regulatory agencies, including deaths at work and environmental offences. The magistrates' court hears a large number of real criminal offences which are triable

[92] *Sherras v. De Rutzen* [1895] 1 QB 918 at 922.
[93] Ashworth, *Principles of Criminal Law*, p. 1.
[94] Ramsay, *Consumer Protection*, p. 183.

either way, such as theft. Finally, there are both real offences of strict liability,[95] and offences which appear to be regulatory which require *mens rea*.[96] The distinction, therefore, is not always clear. Having said this, it does not mean that we cannot make a reasonable attempt to give a flavour of offences which will generally be regarded as regulatory. To this end, Ramsay's categorisation is useful.

There are other characteristics of regulatory offences which are not mentioned in Ramsay's classification. Perhaps the main distinction between regulatory crime and real crime concerns the attitude which we generally have to them, and the stigma that they generate. The extent to which regulatory offences carry stigma is important. First, if regulatory offences do not carry stigma, this is an important way in which they can be distinguished from real crime. Secondly, it legitimises the use of strict liability, as it is much easier to justify strict liability offences if they carry little stigma. Thirdly, if they carry little or no stigma, the deterrent effects of conviction are very much reduced. It is sometimes said that the deterrent effect of a conviction is in the bad publicity that it generates, rather than the actual sanction imposed (which will generally be no more than a fine). If a conviction has no stigma attached, the conviction may be of little deterrence.

It seems unlikely that regulatory offences carry the same stigma as real crimes. This is particularly so among those who realise that regulatory offences may be committed accidentally, and do not necessarily involve any intention or other positive fault requirement. However, it is not clear whether all consumers make the distinction between real and regulatory crimes. If our impression is that criminal law exists to punish morally wrong behaviour, then we may assume that conviction means that a person (in particular a business) has engaged in some form of immoral behaviour. If this is so, then we need either to ensure that the ambit of criminal liability is carefully restricted or to ensure that the distinction between different kinds of offences is understood.

Another characteristic of the regulatory offence is that it is often committed by a business, frequently a corporation. It is clear that the development of criminal law, and the traditional paradigms of criminal liability, rested on the idea of a human defendant possessing *mens rea*. If the criminal law was to be used to regulate businesses, this model was not entirely appropriate. The corporation, in particular, has 'no soul to be damned, no body to be kicked',[97] and could not be a potential defendant

---

[95] For example possessing a firearm without a certificate under s.1 of the Firearms Act 1968 with a maximum penalty of three years' imprisonment. See *Howells* [1977] QB 14.

[96] For example s.14(1) of the Trade Descriptions Act 1968.

[97] This is attributed to the second Baron Thurlow.

without a re-examination of traditional doctrine. Furthermore, even where the defendant is a human being rather than an artificial legal person, the requirement of proving *mens rea* could be seen as so cumbersome as to make the criminal law an inappropriate technique for ensuring protection of the public. In order to combat these difficulties, the courts have developed doctrines which are now firmly embedded in the criminal law. These techniques are among the characteristics of the 'regulatory offence'. The first, as mentioned by Ramsay, is strict liability, which ensures that defendants can be convicted of criminal offences without proof of *mens rea*. Although strict liability offences have existed for many years,[98] their development has been particularly significant in the regulatory sphere in recent times.[99] Secondly, they impose vicarious liability which ensures that employers can be criminally responsible for the strict liability crimes of their employees and, in limited circumstances, for offences requiring proof of *mens rea*. Thirdly, they sometimes invoke principles of corporate criminal liability which allow *mens rea* to be established against corporations, and so enable those corporations to be convicted of criminal offences which require proof of *mens rea*.[100] Although there is some doubt as to whether it is correct to refer to offences which require *mens rea* as being regulatory, this terminology appears to be appropriate in areas such as consumer protection. In *Wings* v. *Ellis*, Lord Scarman described the Trade Descriptions Act 1968 as 'not a truly criminal statute', even though he was dealing with s. 14(1)(a), an offence which required proof of *mens rea*.[101] There is, however, still uncertainty about the extent of these doctrines, and the law surrounding them can be seen to be both confused and inadequate. The next chapter examines the doctrines of strict, corporate, and vicarious liability, with particular reference to consumer protection offences. It will be argued that the law on these topics requires attention if consumers are to be adequately protected, and if defendants are to have a clear picture of their obligations under the criminal law.

Conclusion

The criminal law plays a variety of roles in society. Perhaps chief among these is the protection of the public from anti-social conduct. Criminal sanctions seek to achieve this protection in a number of ways. First, they may deter offenders from re-offending, and potential offenders from

---

[98] The first example of the courts imposing strict liability is often said to be *Woodrow* (1846) 15 M&W 404 where the defendant was convicted of having adulterated tobacco in his possession even though he did not know that it was adulterated.

[99] See generally L. Leigh, *Strict and Vicarious Liability* (London, Sweet and Maxwell, 1982).

[100] See generally Wells, *Corporations and Criminal Responsibility*.

[101] [1985] AC 272 at 293.

offending in the first place. This is traditionally seen to be achieved through punishment. However, much recent scholarship has emphasised the role of criminal sanctions in communicating societal disapproval of certain types of conduct. By labelling conduct as criminal, and punishing where that conduct is undertaken, this message about the unacceptability of the conduct is reinforced. This should have a number of desirable effects. First, it may deter offences by creating a norm against the behaviour in question, something that offenders will not contravene through fear of disapproval. Secondly, it may lead to a change in the offender. Unlike rehabilitation, which aims to force change, this approach tries to persuade offenders to change themselves.[102] Another aim of the criminal law is to ensure that offenders get their just deserts by being punished for the wrong they have done. This requires sanctions which have an impact on the offender proportionate to the wrong done. It seems unlikely that the sentences available under some consumer protection statutes will enable that to be done. Particular difficulties are presented here by the fact that many defendants are corporations. English law has, at present, inadequate powers to hold corporations, and their senior officers, to account. This point is examined further in the next chapter.

The core principles set out by Ashworth provide a helpful framework to consider when conduct is sufficiently anti-social that it should be criminalised. Although it is difficult to disagree with many of the assertions Ashworth makes, it has been argued that criminalising matters which may appear to be minor has its advantages. The use of due diligence offences should help to ensure that those who are without fault should be acquitted, and there are mechanisms in place to guard against inconsistent enforcement. This does not mean that the current state of the criminal law is a matter for complacency. However, we should be wary of removing from the criminal law's scope offences which aim at protecting consumers from trading malpractice.

[102] Duff and Garland, *A Reader on Punishment*, p. 15.

4   The use of the criminal law

Introduction

In the previous chapter, we examined some important questions about when something should be classed as criminal, and about what the criminal law, and punishment under it, are trying to achieve. We also looked at whether it is appropriate to try to identify a separate branch of the criminal law, known as regulatory crime. To understand the role of criminal law in protecting the consumer it is important to move on and look at the mechanisms that have been developed, primarily by the courts, to ensure that criminal offences can be used effectively to protect consumers and, in particular, to control businesses. There are three prime concepts of relevance here: strict liability, vicarious liability, and corporate liability. As will become apparent, the three are interlinked, in particular by the existence of due diligence defences. By examining these concepts, we can identify weaknesses in the structure of the criminal law, particularly where it is used against corporations. It will be argued that reform of the concepts of corporate and vicarious liability needs to be addressed if the law is to provide an appropriate degree of protection for consumers.

Strict liability

Defining strict liability

Strict liability is not the same as absolute liability, although the expressions have sometimes been used interchangeably. In *Sweet* v. *Parsley*, for example, Lord Reid used the phrase 'absolute liability' to mean that which would usually be called strict liability.[1] There is no definitive explanation of the term strict liability, but it has been stated that '(c)rimes which do not require intention, recklessness or even negligence as to one or more

---

[1] [1970] AC 132 at p. 148.

elements in the actus reus are known as offences of strict liability'.[2] This definition distinguishes strict liability, where *mens rea* may still be necessary as to part of the *actus reus*, from absolute liability, which does not require proof of *mens rea*, or even volition.[3] Absolute liability is not found in consumer protection statutes, which, it is assumed, will always require some degree of volition.[4] If offences should be regarded as imposing strict liability where the prosecution does not have to prove *mens rea* as to part of the *actus reus*, this means that offences which require some *mens rea* may be properly described as strict liability. This approach is not always followed. For example, s.14 of the Trade Descriptions Act has been described as semi-strict liability, and there are numerous offences which do not require full *mens rea* which are nevertheless viewed as *mens rea* rather than strict liability offences.[5] It is also clear that offences may still be of strict liability if they are subject to a statutory defence. This is particularly important in the consumer protection area where most are subject to due diligence defences.

Identifying strict liability offences

The courts have found it surprisingly difficult to identify the principles by which they decide that statutory provisions impose strict criminal liability. The first point to note is that a section may still require proof of mens rea even if that section makes no mention of it. In *Sweet* v. *Parsley* Lord Reid stated: 'whenever a section is silent as to mens rea there is a presumption that, in order to give effect to the will of Parliament, we must read in words appropriate to require mens rea'.[6] Here, the House of Lords upheld the presumption in favour of mens rea, and emphasised the fundamental principle that Parliament 'did not intend to make criminals of persons who were in no way blameworthy in what they did'.[7] Their lordships did recognise, however, that some offences were intended to be of strict liability. Lord Pearce, for example, stated that the factors which may show Parliament's intention to create strict liability are: 'the nature of

---

[2] J. C. Smith, *Smith and Hogan Criminal Law* (9th edn, London, Butterworths, 1999), p. 97. This is a very wide definition of the term and would include, for example, s.47 of the Offences Against the Person Act 1861, an offence that is generally seen as one of *mens rea*.

[3] See *Winzar* v. *Chief Constable of Kent* (1983) The Times 28 March.

[4] Although this has not specifically been put to the test.

[5] Contrast *Wings* v. *Ellis* [1985] AC 272 with *Spratt* [1991] 2 All ER 210.

[6] *Sweet* v. *Parsley* 148. The case has been strengthened by the recent decision of the House of Lords in *B* v *DPP* [2000] 1 All ER 833 which affirms the presumption in favour of *mens rea*.

[7] Ibid.

the crime, the punishment, the absence of social obloquy, the particular mischief and the field of activity in which it occurs, and the wording of the particular section and its context'.[8]

These remarks require some explanation. First, the nature of the crime, the field of activity, and the particular mischief are relevant as Parliament is more likely to impose strict liability where conduct relates to a 'matter of public concern'. Although it is difficult to envisage any criminal offence which does not involve a matter of such concern, it seems that threats to public safety, the environment, and the economic interests of the public are the types of concerns in question.[9] This will include consumer protection. The expression 'nature of the crime' might also take into account the nature of the defendant. Defendants in regulatory offences will usually, although not necessarily, be those acting in the course of a trade or business. Such defendants may be particularly suitable candidates for the imposition of strict criminal liability for a number of reasons. First, they are very often well placed to pay the penalty, which will usually be a fine. Secondly, they participate in a potentially hazardous activity by choice. In the words of Lord Pearce: 'those who undertake various industrial and other activities, especially where these affect the life and health of the citizen, may find themselves liable to statutory punishment regardless of knowledge or intent'.[10] Thirdly, they take the benefit of that activity, and ought therefore to bear the loss when mistakes are made.

The 'absence of social obloquy' refers to the contention that strict liability offences lack the stigma of 'real' crimes. This is a matter of some difficulty. Strict liability offences should contain some stigma if they are to be effective, as the stigma attached to conviction is one factor which helps offences act as a deterrent, particularly against businesses. It was argued by the Law Commission that 'the publicity attendant upon the prosecution of companies has a strong deterrent effect . . . and it is socially desirable to have the company's name before the public'.[11] If publicity is to have this effect, the offence must carry some stigma, or else the public may think nothing of it. It is perhaps better to say that strict liability may not carry the *same* stigma as more traditional crimes.

'The punishment' has traditionally been seen to be a factor as the courts are more willing to impose strict criminal liability where the available

---

[8] Ibid. at p. 156.
[9] See Smith, *Smith and Hogan Criminal Law*, ch. 6.
[10] *Sweet* v. *Parsley* at 156. It should be noted that offences which protect consumers' economic interests are likely to impose strict liability as well as those concerned with health and safety.
[11] Law Commission Working Paper No. 44, *Criminal Liability of Corporations* (London, 1972), para. 48.

punishment is merely a fine. By the same token, where imprisonment is an option, the offence is more likely to be interpreted as requiring proof of *mens rea*.[12] However, this will not always be the case. In *Gammon* v. *Attorney General of Hong Kong*, the Privy Council decided that although a potential sanction of three years' imprisonment and a $250,000 fine were evidence against the offence imposing strict liability, they were not conclusive. Lord Scarman said: 'there is nothing inconsistent with the purpose of the ordinance in imposing severe penalties for offences of strict liability. The legislature could reasonably have intended severity to be a significant deterrent, bearing in mind the risks to public safety arising from some contraventions of the ordinance.'[13]

When reference is made to the 'wording of the section and its context', it is important to realise that words may have different meanings in different statutes, and that the section being examined must be viewed in the context of other sections in the same statute.[14] 'Context' includes the context of the section within the statute in question. The courts will look at other sections within the same statute to see if they require *mens rea* and, if they do, they are likely to conclude that the section in question is one of strict liability.[15] An example of this approach is shown by *Cundy* v. *Le Cocq*.[16] Here, the defendant was convicted of selling intoxicating liquor to a person who was drunk under s.13 of the Licensing Act 1872, despite the fact that he neither knew that the customer was drunk, nor was negligent as to that fact. The Divisional Court examined other sections of the Act and was persuaded by the presence of the word 'knowingly' in those sections that the section in question imposed strict liability. Again, this is not conclusive.[17] The existence of statutory defences is another important factor, as the courts appear far more willing to impose strict liability if the statute provides some avenue of escape for a defendant. In the case of *Wings Ltd* v. *Ellis*[18] Lord Hailsham observed that a defence of due diligence was available to defendants charged under s.14(1)(a) of the Trade Descriptions Act, which their lordships concluded was an offence of 'semi-strict' liability.

---

[12] This is made clear in *Sweet* v. *Parsley* where the existence of imprisonment appears to have been an important factor.

[13] [1985] AC 1 at p. 17. It has even been stated that some offences which carry a life sentence can be offences of strict liability (s.5 of the Sexual Offences Act 1956 which prohibits intercourse with a girl under thirteen is perhaps the best example). This should now be viewed in the light of *B* v. *DPP*.

[14] See Smith, *Smith and Hogan Criminal Law*, pp. 102–5.

[15] The doctrine of *expressio unius exclusio alterius*.

[16] (1884) 13 QBD 207.

[17] See by contrast *Sherras* v. *De Rutzen* [1895] 1 QB 918.

[18] [1985] AC 272.

The observations of Lord Pearce do not represent the final word on when the courts will interpret a section as imposing strict liability. Whether the imposition of strict liability will promote the enforcement of the law is another factor. In the case of *Reynolds* v. *GH Austin*, Devlin J said: 'where the punishment of an individual will not promote the observance of the law either by that individual or by others whose conduct he may reasonably be expected to influence then, in the absence of clear and express words, such punishment is not intended'.[19] Defences may play an important role here, as they seek to ensure that there is an incentive for the defendant both to take all reasonable precautions and due diligence, and to be seen to do so. It is clear that judges take notice of the management systems which defendants, particularly large corporate defendants, have in place, and it seems that the courts will often accept claims of having satisfied statutory defences when a paper system is in place.[20]

There is no doubt that the majority of consumer protection offences impose strict liability.[21] When discussing the Trade Descriptions Act in *Wings Ltd* v. *Ellis*, Lord Scarman stated that the Act: 'is not a truly criminal statute. Its purpose is not the enforcement of the criminal law but the maintenance of trading standards. Trading standards not criminal behaviour are its concern.'[22] Whether trading standards and crime are in some way mutually exclusive has been questioned,[23] and the distinction is probably not as stark as Lord Scarman appears to envisage. Nevertheless, consumer protection is a typical area for the courts to impose strict liability. As well as lacking the stigma of 'real crime' it involves a 'matter of public concern' in which defendants choose to participate. The usual penalty for infringement is the fine (although imprisonment is available under some statutes), and consumer protection offences generally contain statutory defences which should help to promote the enforcement of the law.

Vicarious liability

Strict liability should be distinguished from vicarious liability, even though in most cases vicarious liability will only be imposed where the

---

[19] [1951] 2 KB 135 at 150.

[20] See *Tesco Supermarkets Ltd* v. *Nattrass* [1972] AC 153.

[21] Exceptions include s.14(1)(a) and (b) of the Trade Descriptions Act 1968 and regulation 9 of the General Product Safety Regulations 1994.

[22] [1985] AC 272 at 293.

[23] See G. G. Howells and S. Weatherill, *Consumer Protection Law* (Aldershot, Dartmouth and Ashgale, 1995) at p. 416.

statute in question creates an offence of strict liability.[24] Under the doctrine of vicarious liability the criminal offence of one person can be attributed to another, usually the former's employer. In the law of tort the employer is liable for the torts of employees committed within the course of employment.[25] The general rule in the criminal law is that employers are not responsible for the crimes of their employees. This was demonstrated as long ago as 1730 by the case of *Huggins*, where Raymond CJ stated: 'in criminal cases the principal is not answerable for the act of the deputy as he is in civil cases; they must each answer for their own acts, and stand or fall by their own behaviour'.[26] However, it became apparent that for reasons of policy, there was a need for some form of vicarious criminal liability. In the area of regulatory offences at least, the effective enforcement of protective legislation would be almost impossible without the imposition of some form of vicarious liability. Perhaps the clearest test of vicarious liability is that propounded by Atkin J in *Mousell Brothers* v. *London and North Western Railway Company*:

> while prima facie a principal is not to be made criminally responsible for the acts of his servants, yet the legislature may prohibit an act or enforce a duty in such words as to make the prohibition or the duty absolute; in which case the principal is liable if the act is in fact done by his servants. To ascertain whether a particular Act of Parliament has that effect or not regard must be had to the object of the statute, the nature of the duty laid down, the person upon whom it is imposed, the person by whom it would in ordinary circumstances be performed, and the person upon whom the penalty is imposed.[27]

It is clear that an employer can be made vicariously liable for the criminal acts of an employee by explicit wording in a statute. A recent example in the consumer protection field is found in s.1(1) of the Property Misdescriptions Act 1991 which states: '[w]here a false or misleading statement about a prescribed matter is made in the course of an estate agency business or a property development business, otherwise than in providing conveyancing services, *the person by whom the business is carried on* [my italics] shall be guilty of an offence under this section'. However, such examples are rare, and it is far more common for vicarious liability to arise by construction. There are two such ways in which an employer can be vicariously liable for the criminal acts of an employee. The first is by a process of 'extensive construction' and the second by the doctrine of delegation. Extensive construction involves saying that the act of one person

---

[24] The exception being where the doctrine of delegation applies. See below.
[25] See, for example, *Collins* v. *Hertfordshire County Council* [1947] KB 598.
[26] (1730) 2 Stra at 885.
[27] [1917] 2 KB 836.

(usually the employee) is also the act of another (usually the employer). There are few difficulties in saying that the employer has, for example, supplied goods or described a product when that has been done by his employee. The scope of extensive construction is, however, limited in two ways. First it is restricted by the use of statutory due diligence defences, and secondly it does not apply to offences which require proof of *mens rea*. These points require closer examination.

Vicarious liability and due diligence defences

Due diligence defences are found in virtually all consumer protection statutes.[28] They have a long history, and are designed to minimise the potential harshness of strict liability, distinguishing between those who are at fault and those who are not. In the words of one leading text 'the accused should have a defence where prevailing notions of natural justice suggest that it would be wholly unfair to fasten the discredit of a criminal conviction' on a trader who is morally innocent'.[29] They are also important in setting the limits of vicarious and corporate liability by establishing onto whom liability can be passed under regulatory statutes. An example of a due diligence defence is s.24(1) of the Trade Descriptions Act 1968. This states:

In any proceedings for an offence under this Act it shall ... be a defence for the person charged to prove – (a) that the commission of the offence was due to a mistake or to reliance on information supplied to him or to the act or default of another person, an accident or some other cause beyond his control; and (b) that he took all reasonable precautions and exercised all due diligence to avoid the commission of the offence by himself or any other person under his control.

The burden of proving the defence is on the defendant, something that is clear both from case law[30] and statute.[31] This reflects the practical difficulty that would face the prosecution were it to have to negative the defence. However, the standard of proof is that of the balance of probabilities rather than beyond reasonable doubt. This was seen to provide a reasonable balance between the interests of effective law enforcement and the interests of the trader. In the words of Gwyneth Dunwoody at

---

[28] See for example s.24(1) of the Trade Descriptions Act 1968, s.39 of the Consumer Protection Act 1987, and s.21 of the Food Safety Act 1990.

[29] C. J. Miller, B. W. Harvey, and D. L. Parry, *Consumer and Trading Law: Text, Cases and Materials* (Oxford, Oxford University Press, 1998), p. 709.

[30] *Amos* v. *Melcon (Frozen Foods) Ltd* (1985) 149 JP 712.

[31] Magistrates' Courts Act 1980 s.101. See also *Hunt* [1987] AC 352 in relation to offences tried on indictment.

the time of the Bill's passage 'if a person is unable to establish one of the defences I cannot think he deserves much sympathy'.[32] The 'two limb' defence found in the 1968 Act has been replaced in more recent statutes by a one limb defence. For example, s.39 of the Consumer Protection Act 1987 states: 'subject to the following provisions of this section, in proceedings against any person for an offence to which this section applies it shall be a defence for that person to show that he took all reasonable steps and exercised all due diligence to avoid committing the offence'. It would be wrong to make too much of this distinction. It may be 'no more than the recognition of the fact that the other limb was so easy to satisfy by a defendant that it had no real content'.[33] In fact, it may be that (a) is logically implied by (b), and therefore (a) is superfluous.

There was little doubt that under a due diligence defence a defendant could pass the blame onto an errant supplier or manufacturer, provided the defendant had done all he reasonably could to avoid the commission of the offence.[34] A more difficult question was whether a defendant corporation could escape responsibility by passing the blame onto one of its employees. Vicarious liability might be thought of as implying that the employer takes full responsibility for offences committed in the course of employment regardless of any fault on the part of the employer, and that, therefore, there was no room for the employer to distance itself from the acts of the employee. The issue arose in the case of *Tesco Supermarkets Ltd v. Nattrass*.[35] Here, a branch of Tesco displayed a poster which offered money off washing powder. A consumer was charged a higher price when the branch ran out of packets bearing the reduced price. This had occurred because of the store manager failing adequately to check the work of his assistant. Tesco was charged with a pricing offence under the now repealed s.11(2) of the Trade Descriptions Act 1968. Tesco argued that the commission of the offence was due to the act or default of 'another person' (the shop manager). The House of Lords accepted that a store manager carries out orders from above and so is not the embodiment of the corporation. They therefore held that, in the words of Lord Diplock: 'If the principal has taken all reasonable precautions in the selection and training of servants to perform supervisory duties and has laid down an effective system of supervision and used all due diligence to see that it is observed, he is entitled to rely on a default by a superior servant in his

---

supervisory duties as a defence under s.24(1).'[36] This decision has been subjected to criticism.[37] In particular, there has been concern that courts are too willing to accept that the defence is satisfied. Leigh commented when discussing the imposition of vicarious liability that 'if the master were permitted to escape because the fault were that of the servant, an easy excuse would have been created'.[38] Lord Widgery CJ similarly commented that unless care is taken 'we may find the administration of this Act sliding down to the sort of slipshod level at which all a defendant has to do is say in general terms that the default must have been due to something in the shop, one of the girls or some expression like that, and thereby satisfy the onus cast upon him'.[39]

One of the principal concerns with the decision in *Tesco* v. *Nattrass* is that it draws a sharp distinction between those employees who form the directing mind and will of the company, and those who do not. From the point of view of the due diligence defence, this means that if an employee who is not part of the directing mind and will is at fault and lacked due diligence, his employer may still plead the defence. In the case of a large corporation such as Tesco, the question will be whether Tesco's directing mind and will has taken all reasonable precautions and exercised due diligence. This will be answered by looking at the scheme that is in place to supervise, select, and monitor more junior staff. It is thus relatively easy for the company to distance itself from the acts of its employees. As will be seen later, this analysis also has implications for the extent to which companies can be held responsible for offences which require *mens rea*, and which are committed by their employees.

Vicarious liability, mens rea, and delegation

The second limitation on the use of extensive construction is that it does not apply to offences which require proof of *mens rea*. Although the acts of an employee can be attributed to an employer, the employee's *mens rea* generally cannot be. The exception to this is where the doctrine of delegation applies. By this doctrine, where an employer has delegated his duties to one of his employees and the employee does the prohibited act with the requisite *mens rea*, the employer may be convicted of the offence.[40] The doctrine has so far only been used in the Licensing Acts, and is necessary there because of the particular problems which those

---

[36] Ibid at p. 198.
[37] See R. J. Bragg, *Trade Descriptions* (Oxford, Clarendon Press, 1991) at p. 146.
[38] L. Leigh, *Strict and Vicarious Liability* (London, Sweet and Maxwell, 1982).
[39] (1976) 140 JP 306 at 310.
[40] See *Vane* v. *Yiannopoullos* [1964] 2 QB 739.

statutes raise. Under the Licensing Acts, only licensees could be prosecuted, because the wording of the provisions placed duties firmly upon them. However, they frequently did not possess the necessary *mens rea* for the offence, for example, because they were not present at the time of the contravention. The courts' solution was to say that where the licensee delegated authority to an employee and the employee did the prohibited act with the appropriate *mens rea*, the licensee could be convicted of the offence.[41] One eminent commentator described the doctrine as 'judicial make believe [which] does not deserve to be dignified by the name of "the delegation principle"'.[42] It remains unclear whether the doctrine is applicable where the employee is a potential defendant in his own right.[43] It is assumed that the doctrine applies only to the licensing cases and so it is not proposed to examine it in any more detail here.[44]

Corporate liability

In many consumer protection statutes the defendant will be a corporation, typically a limited company. For the purposes of the criminal law, a distinction can be drawn between the vicarious liability of corporations, and the liability of corporations for their own acts.[45] It has long been accepted that corporations can be responsible for strict liability offences when the act in question was performed by an employee. In this way they are no different from a human employer. The term 'corporate liability' is more commonly used to refer to corporations' liability for their own acts and their own *mens rea*, and it is in this sense that the term is used here. To enable *mens rea* to be proved against corporations, the law has developed the doctrine of identification. The doctrine has been an important part of English law, but there are indications that the courts are applying a new approach to corporate crime, which may call the continued use of the doctrine into question.[46] It is not clear, however,

---

[41] Ibid.

[42] P. R. Glazebrook, 'Situational Liability' in P. R. Glazebrook (ed.), *Reshaping the Criminal Law* (London, Stevens, 1978), p. 113.

[43] *Howker* v. *Robinson* [1973] QB 178 suggests that it is, although there are difficulties with the reasoning in this case. See P. J. Pace, 'Delegation – A Doctrine in Search of a Definition' [1982] Crim LR 627.

[44] For a detailed examination of the issues see Pace, 'Delegation'.

[45] For a detailed examination of the criminal liability of corporations see C. Wells, *Corporations and Criminal Responsibility* (Oxford, Oxford University Press, 1993).

[46] See, for example, P. Cartwright, 'Corporate Fault and Consumer Protection: A New Approach for the UK' (1998) 21 *Journal of Consumer Policy* 71; C. M. V. Clarkson, 'Kicking Corporate Bodies and Damning their Souls' (1996) 59 MLR 557; J. Gobert, 'Corporate Criminality: New Crimes for the Times' [1994] Crim LR 722 and 'Corporate Criminality: Four Models of Fault' (1994) 14(3) Legal Studies 393; G.R. Sullivan,

whether this new approach is of general application and so will be used in relation to regulatory consumer protection statutes. This is examined later.

Since 1944 it has been clear that corporations can be convicted of almost any offence by use of the doctrine of identification.[47] The doctrine recognises that there are individuals in any corporation, sometimes called 'controlling officers', who are the embodiment of that corporation, and whose acts and thoughts are the acts and thoughts of the corporation. The point was made graphically by Lord Denning:

> A company may in many ways be likened to a human body. It has a brain and nerve centre which controls what it does. It also has hands which hold the tools and act in accordance with directions from the centre. Some of the people in the company are mere servants and agents who are nothing more than hands to do the work and cannot be said to represent the mind or will. Others are directors and managers who represent the directing mind and will of the company, and control what it does. The state of mind of these managers is the state of mind of the company and is treated by the law as such.[48]

By using the doctrine of identification, the law is able to impute *mens rea* to a corporation. For example, s.14 of the Trade Descriptions Act 1968 requires proof of either knowledge or recklessness on the part of the defendant. Where the defendant is a corporation, knowledge or recklessness traditionally had to be proved on the part of someone who was senior in the corporation, and so could be said to represent its 'directing mind and will'. Identifying who falls under this is problematic. It is clear that if someone is to be part of the directing mind, it is his role in the organisation and not his title which is crucial. In *Tesco* v. *Nattrass*, Lord Reid referred to 'the board of directors, the managing director and perhaps other superior officers of a company [who] carry out the functions of management and speak and act as the company'.[49] Viscount Dilhorne mentioned those 'in actual control of the operations of a company or part of them'[50] and Lord Diplock identified 'those natural persons who by the memorandum and articles of association or as a result of action taken by

---

'The Attribution of Culpability to Limited Companies' (1996) 55 CLJ 515; C. Wells, 'Corporate Liability and Consumer Protection: Tesco v. Nattrass Revisited' (1994) 57 MLR 817 and 'A Quiet Revolution in Corporate Liability for Crime' (1995) 145 NLJ 1326.

[47] See for example *DPP* v. *Kent and Sussex Contractors* [1944] 1 KB 146. Exceptions are offences which by their nature can only be committed by human beings such as rape and incest, and offences which carry a mandatory sentence of imprisonment such as murder.

[48] *HL Bolton (Engineering) Co. Ltd* v. *TJ Graham & Sons Ltd* [1957] 1 QB 159 at 172.

[49] [1972] AC 153 at 171.

[50] Ibid. at 187.

the directors or by the company in general meeting . . . are entrusted with the exercise of the powers of the company'.[51]

The doctrine of identification is particularly problematic in two cases. First, the decision in *Tesco* v. *Nattrass* makes it relatively easy for a company to blame an employee as the person responsible for the commission of an offence, and to avoid liability itself by arguing that it has taken all reasonable precautions and exercised all due diligence at a high level. Secondly, it makes it extremely difficult for companies to be convicted of *mens rea* offences, because the class of persons who constitute the directing mind and will of the company is so small. Many commentators have been critical of the doctrine. Sullivan argues that '[t]here nowhere exists a convincing defence of identification, either as a theory or in terms of its practical effects',[52] Clarkson that 'it simply does not reflect modern corporate practice, particularly in larger companies',[53] Gobert that it 'works best in cases where it is needed least and works least in cases where it is needed most',[54] and Wells that it 'can result in no-one being liable, or improperly reflect the limits of moral responsibility'.[55] There are several alternative approaches, as will be seen shortly, which address some of these criticisms. However, before looking at alternative approaches to the doctrine of identification it should be noted that a series of recent decisions has cast doubt on the traditional orthodoxy of how the doctrine operates.[56] This new approach has two main implications which are of benefit for the enforcement of consumer protection offences. First, it may make it more difficult for companies to escape liability under statutory defences by arguing that an employee was 'another person' and that the employer had taken all reasonable precautions and exercised all due diligence. Secondly, it means that a company may be guilty of offences requiring proof of *mens rea* without identifying *mens rea* on the part of someone who is part of the directing mind and will of the company. As a result, these cases have ramifications, both for offences which require proof of *mens rea*, and those which are of strict liability, but subject to a statutory defence. It is worth examining these cases in some detail, as they reveal a more realistic and desirable approach towards imposing liability on corporations for the wrongs of their employees. However, as will be argued later, they still raise problems for the effective prosecution of offences against corporations.

[51] Ibid. at 200.
[52] Sullivan, 'The Attribution of Culpability', p. 540.
[53] Clarkson, 'Kicking Corporate Bodies', p. 561.
[54] Gobert, 'Four Models of Fault', p. 401.
[55] Wells, 'Corporate Liability and Consumer Protection', p. 820.
[56] See Cartwright, 'Corporate Fault and Consumer Protection', p. 71.

The new approach to identification

The new approach and defences. In *Tesco Stores Ltd* v. *Brent LBC,* Tesco was charged under the Video Recordings Act 1984 with supplying a video to a person under the age stated on the classification certificate.[57] The offence imposed strict liability, and the transaction was carried out by one of Tesco's employees. Section 11(2)(b) of the Act provided that it was a defence for the defendant to show that he neither knew, nor had reasonable grounds to believe, that the purchaser was under eighteen. It was found that the employee who supplied the video did have reasonable grounds to believe that the purchaser was under eighteen. The question at issue was whether the knowledge or belief of the employee could be attributed to the defendant (Tesco) for the purposes of the statutory defence. On the basis of *Tesco* v. *Nattrass*, one would assume that the knowledge or belief in question would have to be that of someone who constituted the directing mind and will of the corporation. The defence referred to the knowledge or belief of 'the accused', and the accused was Tesco. Just as Tesco could claim that their manager was 'another person' in *Nattrass*, and not someone whose acts and thoughts are those of the company, one would have thought that they could now claim that a junior employee's acts and thoughts are not those of the company. However, although Staughton LJ accepted that 'what mattered in terms of s.11(2)(b) was whether the accused (Tesco Stores Ltd) neither knew nor had reasonable grounds to believe that Stuart [the purchaser] was under 18', he concluded that 'it is her [the shop assistant's] knowledge or reasonable grounds that are relevant. Were it otherwise, the statute would be wholly ineffective in the case of a large company.'[58]

It is clear, as Staughton LJ noted, that if the wording of the section were to mean that the corporation could escape liability where one of its senior officers neither knew nor had reasonable grounds to believe that the purchaser was under eighteen, such a corporation could never be convicted, as no-one in that class could ever know or believe the buyer's age. Indeed, they would not even know of the existence of the buyer. As Wells argues, the court's task was made easier by the different wording, 'with its emphasis on knowledge of a circumstance rather than diligence in avoiding a result'.[59] However, the decision contrasts sharply with that in *Nattrass*. Card has argued that the Divisional Court's approach 'must be wrong', pointing out that 'the employee was not the accused; the corporation was, and the employee was too junior for her state of mind to

---

[57] [1993] 1 WLR 1037.
[58] Ibid. at 1042.
[59] Wells, 'Corporate Liability and Consumer Protection' at p. 819.

be the corporation's'.[60] This view has been echoed by Sir John Smith, who argues that the case of *Brent* was indistinguishable from that of *Nattrass* and therefore wrongly decided.[61]

Tesco v. *Brent* concerns an unusually worded defence. Would a similar approach be appropriate for cases which involve due diligence defences? The situation may arise where a corporation is charged with an offence and can show that its senior management has set up a generally effective scheme of supervision and control, but which has broken down at an operational level. A similar point arose in the case of *R* v. *British Steel plc*.[62] Here, some sub-contractors working for British Steel failed to secure a platform properly. The platform collapsed when one man stood on it, and he fell onto another man below, killing him. British Steel were charged with an offence under the Health and Safety at Work Act 1974. Section 3(1) of that Act states that '[i]t shall be the duty of every employer to conduct his undertaking in such a way as to ensure, so far as is reasonably practicable, that persons not in his employment who may be affected thereby are not thereby exposed to risks to their health and safety'. It was accepted that British Steel had to prove that it was not reasonably practicable to do more than was in fact done. The Court of Appeal decided that *Tesco* v. *Nattrass* '[did] not provide the answer'.[63] They rejected the argument put forward by counsel for British Steel that s.3(1) permitted an employer to escape criminal liability if the company had taken all reasonable care at the level of its 'directing mind'. Steyn J argued that it would 'drive a juggernaut through the legislative scheme if corporate employers could avoid criminal liability where the potentially harmful event is committed by someone who is not the directing mind of the company'.[64]

There is difficulty in reconciling this decision with traditional conceptions of corporate criminality, just as there had been in *Brent*. Under the Health and Safety at Work Act, the obligation is placed on the employer to take all such precautions as are reasonably practicable. Although this is not the same as having to take all reasonable precautions and exercise all due diligence, the wordings of the defences are similar. The cases of *British Steel* and *Brent* may suggest that the courts are increasingly reluctant to allow corporate employers to distance themselves from their employees for the purposes of statutory defences. Although the wording

---

[60] R. Card, *Card, Cross and Jones Criminal Law* (13th edn, London, Butterworths, 1995, para. 24.55).
[61] Sir J. C. Smith, casenote on *Tesco* v. *Brent* (1993) Crim LR 624.
[62] [1995] 1 WLR 1356.
[63] Ibid. at 1361 *per* Steyn LJ.
[64] Ibid. at 1362–3.

of the defence in *Brent* was quite different from that in *Nattrass*, the decision in *Brent* is significant in its rejection of the idea that *only* the knowledge of the senior officers can be that of the company. This reasoning could be seen as being taken a step further in *British Steel*, where it was applied to a defence which was similar to a due diligence defence, and which clearly was concerned with the steps taken by the company itself. Due diligence defences are designed to avoid 'penalising an employer or principal who has done everything that he can be reasonably expected to do'.[65] It might be thought that, following *Brent*, when a corporate employer is charged with an offence under the Trade Descriptions Act and pleads a defence under s.24(1), the court will be concerned, not just with the actions of those who form the corporation's directing mind and will, but with the actions of the employee whose acts gave rise to the offence. If the employee has failed to exercise all reasonable precautions and all due diligence, perhaps the company's defence will have to fail. Indeed it is the opinion of one eminent commentator that trading standards officers might conclude that 'the ghost of *Tesco* v. *Nattrass* [which] still stalks their offices . . . has now been laid'.[66]

However, it is not certain that the courts will take this approach. Until they are required to look specifically at the use of the new approach in a case concerning a due diligence defence, the law will remain in a state of uncertainty. In *Meridian Global Funds Management Asia Ltd* v. *Securities Commission*,[67] Lord Hoffmann argued that questions of statutory corporate and vicarious liability are ultimately questions of construction, and this may mean that *Nattrass* will be followed in future cases concerning due diligence defences. Indeed, none of the new approach cases specifically overrules *Tesco* v. *Nattrass*. *Tesco* v. *Brent* and *British Steel* saw *Nattrass* as being different because of the wording of the statutes in question.[68] Moreover, despite its shortcomings, the decision in *Tesco* v. *Nattrass* has the merit of enabling companies to be judged on the decisions which their senior officers take, and therefore ensures that companies, through their senior management, have an incentive to take all reasonable steps to avoid offences being committed. Any form of absolute liability might remove this incentive. If the company is told that no matter how good its system of supervision and control is it will be convicted if one of its employees makes an error, it may be inclined to abandon its system or, at the very least, spend fewer resources to support it. Lord Diplock emphasised that

---

[65] *Tesco* v. *Nattrass per* Lord Diplock at p. 198.
[66] Wells, 'Corporate Liability and Consumer Protection' at p. 819.
[67] [1995] 2 AC 500.
[68] The specific reference to the case in *Meridian*'s decision may indicate the Privy Council's approval of that decision.

while there was a 'rational and moral justification' for imposing strict liability in regulatory offences such as consumer protection, this 'does not extend to penalising an employer or principal who has done everything that he can reasonably be expected to do by supervision or inspection, by improvement of his business methods or by exhorting those whom he may be expected to control or influence, to prevent the commission of the offence'.[69]

Despite the attractions of the reasoning in *Nattrass*, it is submitted that the courts are correct to move away from that reasoning in regulatory offences. The employer tends to benefit when consumer protection offences are committed. The employer controls the employee by the contract of employment. Because of this, there are good reasons for imposing strict sanctions on the employer. One difficulty with *Nattrass* is that an employer who takes responsibility for the wrong of an employee will be at a disadvantage compared with one who is unwilling to take the blame. This creates a misleading picture of the extent to which statutes are being contravened.[70] Furthermore, if the prosecution of the corporation is unsuccessful, there must be a danger that action will be taken against the employee whose act has given rise to the offence. Although the evidence suggests that most prosecutors are reluctant to take action against employees, particularly those who are relatively junior, it remains a possibility.[71] It would be unfortunate if employees began to be prosecuted because of the difficulties of prosecuting their corporate employers. In the words of Cranston, employees are: ' captives of promotional practices adopted by their employers and it is quite unfair to lay the blame at their feet'.[72]

Indeed, it is not certain that employees were originally seen as potential defendants under statutes such as the 1968 Act. The Act has always been viewed as being primarily aimed at controlling businesses, and it is rare in practice for employees to be prosecuted unless they are very senior. The concern at the prosecution of more junior employees is shown by the approach taken by Parliament in Parts II and III of the Consumer Protection Act 1987. The 1987 Act specifically states that a defendant must be acting in the course of any business 'of his' before he can be prosecuted. Lord Beaverbrook, a spokesman for the Government, stated at the time when the Bill which became the 1987 Act was being debated that

---

[69] *Tesco* v. *Nattrass* [1972] AC 153 at 194.
[70] See *Review of the Trade Descriptions Act 1968* Cmnd 6628 para. 54.
[71] P. Cartwright, 'Defendants in Consumer Protection Statutes: A Search for Consistency' (1996) 59 MLR 225.
[72] C. Scott and J. Black, *Cranston's Consumers and the Law* (3rd edn, London, Butterworths, 2000) p. 325.

'we have included the words "of his" to ensure that individual employees will not be prosecuted'.[73] It seems likely that UK consumer protection legislation in the future will follow this approach.[74]

It may be that *Tesco v. Nattrass* is still valid law, but will be limited in future to statutes which have a due diligence defence. This would be a valid interpretation of the decision in *Meridian*. But the decision in *British Steel* is only a small step from saying that forms of the due diligence defence may no longer be interpreted in the light of *Nattrass*. Even if *Nattrass* is a valid authority on the question of s.24 its authority is surely much reduced. This will be welcomed by those who are charged with enforcing consumer protection legislation. If we are now to see the employee as part of the corporation, it will be much more difficult for a corporate employer to pass the blame onto its employee.

The new approach and offences of mens rea. As mentioned above, it has long been accepted that corporations can be convicted of offences requiring proof of *mens rea* provided *mens rea* can be shown on the part of someone who is the corporation's 'directing mind and will'. This has, however, been called into question by a number of recent decisions. These decisions, described by one commentator as a 'quiet revolution',[75] have important implications for the enforcement of consumer protection legislation.

The main case to examine in relation to *mens rea* offences is that of *Meridian Global Funds Management Asia Ltd* v. *Securities Commission*.[76] Here, two officers of an investment management company used funds managed by the company to acquire shares in a New Zealand company. Section 20 of the New Zealand Securities Amendment Act 1988 provided a duty of disclosure. The question was whether the company 'knew' that it had acquired the shareholding. The Privy Council reviewed the law and said that whether the employees' acts and knowledge were those of the company was a question of construction 'rather than metaphysics'.[77] They added that 'the company knows that it has become a substantial security holder when that is known to the person who had authority to do the deal'.[78] Otherwise, they believed, the policy of the Act would be defeated. The court was eager to emphasise that they were not suggesting that when an employee does an authorised act with knowledge, the

---

[73] HL Debs (5th series) vol. 485 col. 1143.
[74] See, for example, the General Product Safety Regulations 1994.
[75] Wells, 'A Quiet Revolution'.
[76] [1995] 2 AC 500.
[77] Ibid. at 511.
[78] Ibid.

company will *always* be found to have done the act with that knowledge. According to Lord Hoffmann:

> It is a question of construction in each case as to whether the particular rule requires that the knowledge that an act has been done, or the state of mind with which it was done, should be attributed to the company... Each [decision] is an example of an attribution rule for a particular purpose, tailored as it must be to the terms and policies of the substantive rule.[79]

This decision leaves the law in a state of uncertainty. It seems, following *Meridian*, that there is no general theory of how to attribute states of culpability to companies.[80] This approach has its attractions. It was described by Sealy as bringing 'a welcome degree of flexibility into a difficult area of law'.[81] But this flexibility, inevitably, has come at the expense of certainty. For example, s.14(1) of the Trade Descriptions Act 1968 is a rare example of a consumer protection offence which requires proof of *mens rea*. It states: 'It shall be an offence for any person in the course of any trade or business (a) to make a statement which he knows to be false or (b) recklessly to make a statement which is false as to any of the following matters'. The section then lists the matters in question, which relate to services, accommodation, and facilities. It was always thought clear that if a corporate defendant was to be convicted under this section, the requisite *mens rea* must be shown on the part of someone who constitutes the defendant's directing mind and will. It is now open to the prosecution to argue that the *mens rea* of a relatively junior employee should be attributed to his employer. Lord Hoffmann in *Meridian* stated that when deciding whether a person's 'act (or knowledge or state of mind)' was that of the company, the court should apply 'the usual canons of interpretation, taking into account the language of the rule (if it is a statute) and its content and policy'. It could certainly be argued that the language, content and policy of s.14 would be entirely consistent with a finding that the *mens rea* of a relatively junior employee is that of his corporate employer. The wording of the section would allow this approach and it would be consistent with legislative intent to protect consumers from wrongs done in the course of business. It has been said that the Trade Descriptions Act 'is not a truly criminal statute. Its purpose is not the enforcement of the criminal law but the maintenance of trading standards.'[82] If this is so, it may be a perfect example of how the new approach could be used,

---

[79] Ibid. at 511–12.
[80] This is the view of Sullivan, 'The Attribution of Culpability'.
[81] L. Sealy, 'The Corporate Ego and Agency Untwined' (1995) 54 CLJ 507 at p. 508.
[82] *Wings* v. *Ellis* [1985] AC 272 *per* Lord Scarman at p. 293.

furthering the prime aim of the statute by making convictions far easier to achieve.

The 'new approach' has significant implications for the ability of enforcement officers, such as trading standards officers, to secure the conviction of corporations for regulatory offences. First, it may make it more difficult for corporations to escape liability by blaming their employees. Secondly, it may make it easier for the prosecution to prosecute corporations for offences requiring *mens rea* by enabling the *mens rea* of employees to be attributed to their corporate employers where this was previously impossible. But it is troubling that we are left with a series of cases which do not provide a definite answer to important issues of corporate and vicarious liability. The cases have resulted from drafting which makes the purpose of legislation difficult to achieve. It might be appropriate to remember the words of Lord Donovan, that 'if a decision that "knowingly" means "knowingly" will make the provision difficult to enforce, the remedy lies with the legislature'.[83]

Alternative approaches to corporate liability

The new approach examined above has advantages over the traditional identification principle. Chief among these is that it casts the net wider when considering whose act or state of mind can be the act and state of mind of the company. As a result, it provides an incentive for companies to control the conduct of employees by making the company responsible for that conduct. However, the new approach retains a focus on identifying an individual within the company who can be said to be at fault, and to possess, where appropriate, the *mens rea* for the offence in question. Fault still has to be located within individuals.

Another approach to corporate liability, which would still focus primarily on the actions of individuals, but would allow the fault of a larger number of people to be considered, is the doctrine of aggregation. Under this approach, the acts and mental states of more than one individual can be combined in order to establish the elements of the crime.[84] Such an approach has been used in the United States. In *United States* v. *Bank of New England* the court had to decide what was meant by 'knowledge' of a bank for the purposes of reporting currency transactions. The court stated that 'if employee A knows one facet of the currency reporting requirement, and B knows another facet of it, and C a third facet of it, the

---

[83] *Vane* v. *Yiannopoulos* [1964] 3 All ER 820.
[84] Gobert, 'Four Models of Fault' at pp. 395 and 403–7.

bank knows them all'.[85] This approach was rejected in the English courts in the case of *R* v. *HM Coroner for East Kent ex p Spooner*[86] on the grounds that '[a] case against a personal defendant cannot be fortified by evidence against another defendant'.[87] However, this is no reason for finding that a case against a corporation cannot be established by evidence against several individuals within that corporation. Gobert explains the use of the doctrine in the context of the Clapham Rail crash:

The Clapham Rail crash would not have occurred if British Rail had paid closer attention to whether its safety regulations were being adhered to. Nor would it have occurred if the technician and his supervisor had been more diligent. It was the combination of these actions and inactions which proved lethal. Rather than setting off these failings against one another, however, it would seem more appropriate to add them together in order to capture the true extent of the company's fault.[88]

As a corporation is a collection of individuals with different responsibilities, there may be some attraction to the idea of collecting together the knowledge of those individuals and holding them to be the knowledge of the corporation. Where a corporation commits an offence, it will often result from a number of faults in different areas. The initial policy may be misconceived, or it may be wrongly implemented. Aggregation allows the combination of these faults, to establish both *actus reus* and *mens rea*. Nevertheless, there are strong arguments against the aggregation doctrine. Clarkson argues that it does not reflect the reality of corporate decision-making, by failing to take account of companies' organisational structures, procedural rules, and policies.[89] In addition, the individuals whose fault is combined to become the fault of the company will be closely associated with any conviction of the company that results. Where the offence is a serious one, there may be a perception that they are guilty of that offence, even though their individual contributions may have been minimal.[90] The final concern is that, far from streamlining trials by removing the requirement to find full *mens rea* on the part of an individual, aggregation might lengthen and complicate the trial process, encouraging the prosecution to seek out as many examples of minor fault

---

[85] 821 F2d 844 at 855.
[86] (1989) 88 Cr App R 10.
[87] Ibid. at 17.
[88] Gobert, 'Four Models of Fault', pp. 403–4.
[89] Clarkson, 'Kicking Corporate Bodies', pp. 568–9.
[90] In the words of Sullivan, '[t]hey will fall under the shadow of a serious offence (with possible disciplinary, employment and pension-right consequences) without the necessary culpability being established against them' ('The Attribution of Culpability', p. 529).

as they can in order to persuade the jury that the combination of them satisfies the *mens rea* required for the offence.[91] It seems highly unlikely that the aggregation doctrine will find much favour with the courts or the legislature.

Like the identification principle, the aggregation principle is based on the idea that there must be individuals within the company whose acts and mental states can be attributed to the company.[92] The theory 'is underpinned by the assumption that a corporation is a real person, absorbing over time and space the totality of the faults of all those other persons associated with it'.[93] Perhaps a better approach would be to attempt to locate fault within the company itself.[94] There are two possible approaches here. The first is 'reactive fault', and the second 'corporate fault'.

'Reactive fault' is associated with the work of Fisse and Braithwaite. Under this approach, if a company commits the *actus reus* of an offence the court then investigates the steps taken by the company to address the matters which led to the offence. An 'unreasonable corporate failure to devise and undertake satisfactory preventative or corrective measures in response to the commission of the *actus reus* of an offence' will lead to conviction.[95] The court is concerned, therefore, with the steps taken subsequent to the causing of the harm rather than any fault that existed at the time of, or prior to, that harm. Although there may appear to be an attraction in punishing a company for its failure to address its shortcomings, particularly in the light of specific harm caused, there are difficulties with this proposal. Two are identified by Sullivan.[96] First, he questions whether the culpability proposed has to be comparable in turpitude to that which would ordinarily be required for the offence. For example, if the offence is manslaughter, need the prosecution show that the 'unreasonable corporate failure' amounted to gross negligence? The answer appears to be no. If this is so, there is an obvious concern about fair labelling.[97] Secondly, he asks if it is possible to establish corporate culpability commensurate with that normally required for the offence where no individual can be found to have shown such culpability. The

---

[91] Ibid. p. 529.
[92] Gobert, 'Four Models of Fault', p. 407.
[93] Sullivan, 'The Attribution of Culpability', p. 528.
[94] Although it should be pointed out that Sullivan also regards the aggregation theory as 'an attempt to capture and express a truly corporate guilt' ('The Attribution of Culpability', p. 527).
[95] B. Fisse and J. Braithwaite, *Corporations, Responsibility and Corporate Society* (Cambridge, Cambridge University Press, 1993), ch. 2.
[96] Sullivan, 'The Attribution of Culpability'.
[97] Ibid. at pp. 525–7.

problems with this form of liability appear significant and it is unlikely to be accepted in the UK.

Under the 'corporate fault' model of corporate criminality, the company is 'treated as a distinct organic entity whose mind is embodied in the policies it had adopted'.[98] Here, where the company's general ethos leads to a crime being committed, the company is held responsible for that crime. It is not necessary to point to an individual who has committed an offence, nor even to an individual who embodies that culpable ethos. Gobert points out that the concept of corporate intent should be as easily discernible as that of legislative intent. This would have the advantage that where an offence results from decisions taken by a number of individuals at different times it can be described as having been caused by the company, rather than the individuals who make it up. This is particularly apt where the policy that emerges from the decisions of various people does not reflect the views of any individual. A corporation, it has been said, 'marches on its elephantine way almost indifferent to its succession of riders'.[99]

Gobert concludes that a form of corporate fault model should be adopted, which makes a company criminally liable where a crime is authorised, permitted, or tolerated as a matter of company policy or *de facto* practice. Clarkson similarly argues that 'a company through its corporate policies can exhibit its own culpability'.[100] In this situation, Gobert argues, liability should be for the substantive offence which has occurred. In addition, he calls for liability for the creation of risks likely to lead to the occurrence of serious harm. If the risk materialises, he argues, liability should exist for failing to prevent the harm, rather than for the harm itself. However, he seems to go further than this to argue for liability regardless of whether or not any harm occurs. This approach is to be welcomed. The company's culpability is primarily in taking decisions which create unreasonable risks, and it is often purely a matter of chance whether harm is caused. Gobert's proposals require a re-thinking of the concept of *mens rea*. He suggests that instead of asking whether the company

---

[98] J. Gobert; 'Corporate Criminality: New Crimes for the Times' [1994] Crim LR 722 at p. 723. For an examination of this type of approach see P. French, *Collective and Corporate Responsibility* (New York, Colombia Press, 1984). Clarkson also favours such an approach, arguing that '[a] better approach [than identification] would be to effect a complete break from all attribution rules and hold companies, as such, directly criminally liable'. Clarkson, Kicking Corporate Bodies, p. 566.

[99] K. E. Boulding, *The Organizational Revolution* (New York, Harper, 1968), p. 139. Cited in B. Fisse and V. Braithwaite, 'The Allocation of Responsibility for Corporate Crime: Individualism, Collectivism and Accountability' (1988) 11 *Sydney Law Review* 468 at p. 497.

[100] Clarkson, 'Kicking Corporate Bodies', p. 570.

had traditional *mens rea*, we should ask whether the company could have taken steps to identify and avoid the occurrence of harm, whether it was reasonable for it to do so, and whether it in fact did so. In effect, instead of asking whether the company had *mens rea* we ask whether it has proved a due diligence defence. The defence would differ from that traditionally used in consumer protection statutes. 'What is envisaged here ... is [a] more broadly conceived, across the board defence which would protect a corporate defendant from liability where the company has made a conscientious and reasonable effort to prevent the substantive crime which has occurred.'[101]

The alternative models of fault considered above are of particular importance where an offence requires proof of *mens rea*. Indeed, the vast majority of the considerable academic literature on the subject is primarily concerned with the question of how best to convict companies of *mens rea* offences. However, the decision of *Tesco* v. *Nattrass* has meant that the identification doctrine, and the rules of corporate liability generally, have broader implications. In particular, they create a barrier to the conviction of companies for strict liability offences where those offences are subject to due diligence defences. It is perhaps this aspect of *Tesco* v. *Nattrass* which is of most concern to consumer lawyers.

A proposal for mens rea offences

It is submitted that where an offence imposes a requirement of mens rea, the new approach to identification illustrated by *Meridian* is to be supported. This means that corporations will take responsibility for the actions of employees which occur in the course of employment.[102] Just as vicarious liability in tort does not extend to an employee on a frolic of his own, corporations should not be forced to take responsibility for employees who act outside the course of their employment. However, where the act is done in the course of employment, the company should be liable. Requiring companies to take responsibility for the acts of their employees would bring a number of benefits. In particular, it would make it easier for the prosecution to establish guilt, and provide an incentive for companies to ensure that their employees are properly trained and supervised. Companies take the benefit of their employees' acts and this justifies their taking responsibility for those acts committed in the course of employment. On the occasions where employees act for personal benefit and

---

[101] Gobert, 'New Crimes for the Times', pp. 729–30.
[102] This, essentially, is the approach taken in the USA. See *United States* v. *Bank of New England* 821 F.2d 1000 and the cases cited in Gobert, 'New Crimes for the Times', p. 722 n. 3.

against the interests of the company it would be possible to argue that the act was not in the course of employment. Where the employee comes within the definition of the offence it should be possible to prosecute him as a defendant in his own right, although it might be appropriate to limit the possibility of doing this to the situation where the employee acts outside the course of employment and for his own ends. Furthermore, as is argued below, the prosecution of junior employees should not be possible where regulatory offences are concerned.

A proposal for regulatory offences

Most consumer protection offences impose strict liability. Where that strict liability is tempered by a due diligence defence the doctrine of identification, as interpreted in *Tesco* v. *Nattrass*, means that companies can escape liability by blaming employees whose acts have given rise to the commission of the offence. It is submitted that where strict liability offences are concerned, there is a need to create a doctrine which ensures that corporations take responsibility for their employees' actions. This could best be done by the following changes. First, we should encourage the use of strict liability for offences which are primarily aimed at corporations. In practice the vast majority of regulatory offences impose strict liability, and provisions such as s.14 of the Trade Descriptions Act 1968 are anomalies. However, a major difficulty with those offences at present is not that they are subject to due diligence defences, but that they are subject to the decision in *Tesco* v. *Nattrass*, which drives a coach and horses through the doctrine of vicarious liability. One solution would be to remove due diligence defences and turn the offences into a form of absolute liability, but it is submitted that this would be a step too far. Due diligence defences play an important role in enabling defendants to escape liability where no-one within their organisation has been at fault. The problem with the system at present is not that companies can escape liability, but that they can escape liability by blaming their employees. It is submitted that the best solution would be to allow a company to plead that it had taken all reasonable precautions and all due diligence where everyone in the company has fulfilled this requirement. If an employee is at fault then the company should take responsibility for that, even if he is outside the company's directing mind and will. Only where the fault to which the offence is attributable is outside the company should the company be able to plead the defence.

It is recognised that the changes suggested above will have a number of implications. It will mean an abolition of the doctrine of identification in the sense that we know it, both for *mens rea* offences and in the context of due diligence defences. It will make corporations responsible for all the criminal wrongs of their employees committed in the course of employment. It involves an endorsement of the concepts of strict and vicarious liability. The former, in particular, has come under strain in recent years, both from academic writers and the courts. The presumption in favour of *mens rea* (and therefore against strict liability) has been strengthened by the decision of the House of Lords in *B* v. *DPP*.[103] It is therefore important to set out the policy reasons for making corporations strictly liable for the acts of their employees. It will be argued that provided the changes above are accompanied by the restriction on the ability to prosecute junior employees, and provided that due diligence defences are always available we should not fear a regime based upon strict and vicarious liability.

In defence of strict liability

There are strong policy justifications for imposing strict and vicarious liability on defendants who commit regulatory offences against consumers, but there are also concerns about whether it is effective or just.[104] It is helpful to consider the issues of effectiveness and justice in turn, and to consider ways of obviating any major concerns that arise with the use of strict liability.

Is strict liability effective?

The main argument in favour of imposing strict liability is that it is necessary in order to ensure that the public are adequately protected. It could be argued that it would be unduly difficult to prove *mens rea* in many cases, particularly where the defendant is a corporation. Clearly it is easier for the prosecution to establish guilt if they have only to prove the commission by the defendant of the *actus reus*, and it may be that strict liability can be supported on these practical grounds.[105] However, it might be argued that although strict liability ensures that the prosecution does not have to prove *mens rea* in order to establish guilt, fault will still need to be proved if the court is to be able to impose an adequate sanction. There is a major difference between a trader who sells a product which turns out unexpectedly to be dangerous, and a trader who sells products

---

[103] [2000] 1 All ER 833.
[104] See A. Ashworth, *Principles of Criminal Law* (3rd edn, Oxford, Oxford University Press, 1999), pp. 167–76.
[105] See B. Wootton, *Crime and the Criminal Law* (2nd edn, London, Sweet and Maxwell, 1981).

which he knows to be dangerous, and one would expect the court to deal with the latter far more severely. Where the offence is committed with a degree of culpability it will remain important for the prosecution to prove some form of *mens rea* for a proper sentence to be handed down. It could be argued that if proof is admissible for one purpose, it might as well be admitted for another purpose. In the words of Dickson J, 'in sentencing, evidence of due diligence is admissible and therefore the evidence might just as well be heard when considering guilt'.[106] Nevertheless, there will still be an advantage for the prosecution in having strict liability, as they will be able to secure a conviction without proof of *mens rea* and, if necessary, can use this as a bargaining tool. As Richardson notes, 'enforcement is conducted against a background of the criminal law and the implicit threat of its invocation'.[107] From the point of view of the effectiveness of compliance strategies, therefore, strict liability brings benefits.

The second way in which strict liability is seen as effective in protecting the public is through its deterrent effect. It was argued in chapter 3 that a prime aim of the criminal law is to deter potential offenders from breaking the law, although it was accepted that the extent to which criminal sanctions deter in fact is uncertain. If the prosecution does not have to show *mens rea*, the defendant knows that it will be relatively easy to establish a case and so will take steps to avoid the commission of the offence. The defendant will not be able to hide behind the argument that he lacked *mens rea*. Where there is a greater risk of prosecution, greater efforts can be expected to be taken to avoid prosecution. There is evidence that 'the existence of strict liability does induce organisations to aim at higher and higher standards', although the evidence on this point is not conclusive.[108] Indeed, Dickson J has argued that 'there is no evidence that a higher standard of care results from absolute liability'.[109] It seems likely that strict liability will act as a deterrent most effectively when combined with a due diligence defence. If the defendant knows that he can escape liability by showing that he took all reasonable precautions and exercised all due diligence to avoid committing the offence, there is a great incentive on the defendant to have a system in place that will satisfy this requirement. This will particularly be so where the defendant is a large corporation. The courts have made it clear that they will be influenced by the paper system which the defendant has in place.[110] The

---

[106] *City of Sault Ste Marie* (1978) 85 DLR (3d) 161 at p. 172.
[107] G. Richardson, 'Strict Liability for Regulatory Crime: The Empirical Research' [1987] Crim LR 295 at p. 303.
[108] M. Smith and A. Pearson, 'The Value of Strict Liability' [1969] Crim LR 5 at 16.
[109] *City of Saulte Ste Marie* at p. 171. He is using the phrase 'absolute liability' in the sense that the term 'strict liability' is used in this book.
[110] See *Tesco* v. *Nattrass* [1972] AC 153.

risk with this approach is that it is all too easy for a defendant to appear to have satisfied the defence.[111] The defences invariably refer to *all* reasonable precautions and due diligence, meaning that if there was anything reasonable which the defendant could have done but did not do, he should be convicted. It is questionable whether the courts have followed the wording quite so strictly. Where there is no due diligence defence, there will still be some incentive on the defendant to try to avoid committing the offence, although the incentive will not be so great. Indeed, it could even be argued that the existence of a strict liability offence without a statutory defence could be counter-productive. If the defendant knows that he could be convicted regardless of his having taken all reasonable steps, he may feel that there is no point in making an effort: 'If a person is already taking every reasonable precautionary measure, is he likely to take additional measures, knowing that however much care he takes, it will not serve as a defence in the event of breach?'[112] However, this is not necessarily the case, as the taking of precautionary measures is likely to reduce the chance of the offence occurring in the first place, so there is still an incentive to take those measures. There is no doubt, however, that statutory defences are an additional incentive for the defendant to take all reasonable care.

Is strict liability just?

The existence of defences is one matter which can be used to counter the view that it is morally wrong to impose criminal sanctions on a defendant without proof of fault. Strong arguments have been made that the existence of strict liability is an affront to justice. According to Packer, 'to punish conduct without reference to the actor's state of mind is both inefficacious and unjust'.[113] However, empirical research shows that the use of discretion by enforcement agencies is important in countering any potential harshness in strict liability. The use of 'compliance strategies', in which enforcement agencies seek to ensure compliance with the law by warning and persuasion and without the need to prosecute, help to ensure that the odd accidental infraction will not be prosecuted. In the words of the Law Reform Commission of Canada, this approach 'centres upon the attainment of the broad aims of the legislation rather than sanctioning its breach'.[114] Bragg has even stated that 'in many authorities

---

[111] See *McGuire* v. *Sittingbourne Co-operative Society per* Lord Widgery CJ.

[112] *City of Sault Ste Marie* at 171 *per* Dickson J.

[113] 'Mens Rea and the Supreme Court' (1962) Sup Ct Rev 107 at p. 109. See also A. Ashworth, 'Is the Criminal Law a Lost Cause?' (2000) 116 LQR at 240.

[114] Law Reform Commission of Canada Working Paper No. 16, *Sanctioning the Corporate Offender in Criminal Responsibility for Group Action* (1976).

prosecution is seen as a last resort and, sometimes, even as an admission of failure'.[115] An annual report of the Health and Safety Executive demonstrates the approach of one important regulatory agency when it says: 'It is not our policy to prosecute for every breach of health and safety legislation which comes to our knowledge. This would be neither practical nor productive.'[116] Empirical research on the enforcement of consumer protection legislation has also shown the importance of compliance strategies.[117] Cranston studied three consumer protection departments in the UK in the mid 1970s. He examined the approach taken by enforcement officers when they discovered that provisions of the Trade Descriptions Act had been contravened. He found that of the 21,430 infringements over a six-month period, 1,003 were prosecuted, 5,885 were cautioned, and 14,542 were resolved by the giving of advice.[118]

Despite the discretion shown in practice, it might be viewed as concerning that such power is placed in the hands of the enforcement agencies. There is evidence of such agencies bringing prosecutions when justice would appear to suggest that the defendant should not be convicted, although such cases are rare, and it should be remembered that the reader of the case (and the judge) will seldom know the background to the prosecution.[119] Furthermore, because many regulatory statutes are enforced locally, there is the potential for discrepancies between different areas of the UK. Indeed, recent work by the Audit Commission has found variations in the enforcement of consumer protection offences.[120] However, as we will see in chapter 7, important steps have been taken to minimise the risks of inconsistent enforcement, and initiatives are in place to tighten this further.[121]

One argument which is sometimes advanced in support of strict liability is that it deals with offences that are not truly criminal. They are 'not criminal in any real sense but are acts which in the public interest

[115] R. J. Bragg, *Trade Descriptions* (Oxford, Clarendon Press, 1991) at p. 202.
[116] Cited in C. M. V. Clarkson and H. M. Keating, *Criminal Law: Text and Materials* (4th edn, London, Sweet and Maxwell, 1988), p. 213.
[117] See R. Cranston, *Regulating Business* (London, Macmillan, 1979). It is clear that a similar approach is taken by enforcement officers in related fields. See e.g. B. Hutter, *The Reasonable Arm of the Law?* (Oxford, Clarendon Press, 1988), W.G. Carson, 'White Collar Crime and the Enforcement of Factory Legislation' (1970) 10 Br J Criminology 383, and K. Hawkins *Environment and Enforcement* (Oxford, Clarendon Press, 1987).
[118] Cranston, *Regulating Business*.
[119] See *Smedleys* v. *Breed* [1974] AC 839 and *Wings* v. *Ellis* [1985] AC 272 and Howells and Weatherill, *Consumer Protection Law*, p. 437.
[120] *Measure for Measure: The Best Value Agenda for Trading Standards Services* (London, The Stationery Office, 1999).
[121] The Government intends to set national standards to deal with inconsistent enforcement. See OFT Press Release 24/00 (22 June 2000) and Scott and Black, *Cranston's Consumers and the Law*, p. 334.

are prohibited under a penalty'.[122] To counter this it has been pointed out that many strict liability offences deal with matters which the public would regard as serious criminal offences. Braithwaite has observed that corporate acts which have serious consequences, such as selling drugs which are known to be harmful, are rated as seriously as more traditional violent crimes, and that business crimes such as consumer fraud are rated as seriously as more traditional examples of theft.[123] Environmental offences too are likely to be regarded as serious. One argument states that it is wrong for defendants to be convicted of offences carrying a moral stigma if they lack *mens rea*, and this was forcibly advanced by their lordships in *Sweet* v. *Parsley*. However, as has already been noted, it could also be argued that it is important for regulatory offences to carry some stigma, to ensure that they provide an effective deterrent.[124] The difficulty is that the public may not always be able to distinguish when there is fault from when there is not, as that information is generally not available.[125] Furthermore, it may be of little comfort to a trader to hear that his conviction carries little stigma. He will still have been put to expense in terms of legal costs and, perhaps, disruption to his business, and will still be labelled a criminal.[126] However, a solution to this may be to increase awareness of the nature and objectives of regulatory offences. Furthermore, it is not clear that the public would necessarily assume that *mens rea* is a requirement of serious offences. For example, it is assumed that many members of the public would approve of environmental and health and safety laws which punish corporations for failing to employ necessary measures to avoid the risk of harm. Few would seek to justify the imposition of absolute liability, but there are strong arguments for supporting the imposition of liability without proof of *mens rea*.

Possible solutions to concerns about strict liability

Requiring proof of negligence. Despite the arguments which have been made in favour of strict liability, there are concerns that it may sometimes lead to injustice for the defendant. One solution is to require the prosecution to prove negligence on the part of the defendant. Some of the justifications for strict liability have emphasised that it would be

---

[122] *Sherras* v. *De Rutzen* [1895] 1 QBD 918 at 922 *per* Wright J.
[123] J. Braithwaite, 'Challenging Just Deserts: Punishing White Collar Criminals' (1982) 73 JCLC 723.
[124] According to Ashworth 'there is hardly any stigma in being convicted of... [regulatory] offences' (Ashworth, *Principles of Criminal Law*, p. 171).
[125] See D. Tench, *Towards a Middle System of Law* (London, Consumers' Association, 1981).
[126] See the comments of Dickson J in *City of Sault Ste Marie.*

wrong to allow those who are careless to escape liability.[127] In the words
of Baroness Wootton:

in the modern world as much and more damage is done by negligence, or by
indifference to the welfare or safety of others as by deliberate wickedness... the
time has come for the concept of legal guilt to be dissolved into a wider concept
of responsibility... in which there is room for negligence as well as purposeful
wrongdoing.[128]

In other cases, too, it appears that arguments which are formed in such
a way as to appear to be favouring strict liability are in fact arguments
in favour of imposing liability for negligence. If the concern is to protect
the public from 'clumsy, ignorant but nevertheless dangerous people',[129]
then imposition of responsibility for negligence may be the answer. However, there are problems with imposing criminal liability on the basis of
negligence. Williams has argued that it 'often wears the appearance of being an unrewarding exercise in moralism',[130] while Leigh has stated that
'a body of rules which required us all to be careful in all aspects of our
daily lives on pain of punishment would seem totalitarian'.[131] This may
be so, but it does not offer a conclusive argument that it should *never* be
appropriate to impose criminal responsibility on the basis of negligence.
Leigh's argument, in particular, is merely a warning that it would be inappropriate to impose laws which required us to be careful 'in all aspects
of our daily lives'. It is not an argument that laws should require us to be
careful in no aspect of our daily lives. In other words, there may be some
situations where negligence is an appropriate test for criminal liability.
This is recognised in some areas of the law. For example, road traffic law
imposes a requirement not to drive negligently or carelessly. Section 3 of
the Road Traffic Act 1988 makes it an offence to drive a motor vehicle on
a road without due care and attention, or without reasonable consideration for other persons using the road. This makes an offence of careless
driving. Driving is one activity in our daily lives where it is important to

---

[127] For discussion see Ashworth, *Principles of Criminal Law*, pp. 167–76.

[128] Wootton, *Crime and the Criminal Law*, p. 50. Cited in Ashworth, *Principles of Criminal Law*, p. 167. At other points, however, Baroness Wootton made it clear that she was advocating strict liability, saying that 'if the object of the criminal law is to prevent the occurrence of socially damaging actions, it would be absurd to turn a blind eye to those which were due to carelessness, negligence *or even accident*' (my italics).

[129] Ashworth, *Principles of Criminal Law*, p. 169. See also J. Braithwaite, *Corporate Crime in the Pharmaceutical Industry* (London, Routledge, 1984). It appears that the House of Lords in *Sweet* v. *Parsley* did not think it open to them to impose liability for negligence, although it is not clear why it should be open for them to impose a requirement of knowledge instead.

[130] G. Williams, *Textbook of Criminal Law* (2nd edn, London, Stevens and Sons, 1983).

[131] L. Leigh, 'Liability for Inadvertence: A Lordly Legacy?' (1995) 58 MLR 457 at p. 467.

encourage people to act carefully and, as Brett has argued, fear of being seen to drive carelessly encourages drivers to take more care.[132] It is clear that there will be other activities where the imposition of criminal responsibility for negligence will encourage defendants to take care. One of the problems faced by those supporting the imposition of liability for negligence is that negligence is usually contrasted with the forms of advertent *mens rea* such as knowledge or recklessness.[133] However, three points need to be addressed here. First, recklessness has been held to include inadvertent as well as advertent recklessness in most contexts. The landmark case of *Caldwell*[134] stated that recklessness includes the state of mind of 'failing to give thought to whether or not there is any . . . risk in circumstances where, if any thought were given to the matter, it would be obvious that there was'.[135] It was subsequently decided that the test of recklessness is even wider than it might appear in *Caldwell* as a person can be reckless even if, had he given thought to the danger in question, he might not have realised that danger.[136] As a result of this, there is relatively little difference between recklessness and negligence, because the defendant is being judged against the objective standard of the reasonable person. It is requiring defendants to give thought to risks and punishing them where they cause harm by not giving thought. There is one situation where someone would be negligent but not reckless. This is where the defendant adverts to the possibility of a risk but unreasonably concludes that it does not exist.[137] Such a defendant has fallen into the so-called 'Caldwell Lacuna', but would nevertheless be negligent. Despite this, it is clear that negligence and recklessness in most ways impose very similar requirements on defendants. The second point is that it is assumed sometimes that negligence is being contrasted with forms of *mens rea* because it is a type of *mens rea* itself. It is, however, arguable whether it is correct to refer to negligence and carelessness as states of mind, or *mens rea* at all. In the words of White, 'A careless man is one who does not take care; a man who does not care is called "indifferent" . . . to attribute

---

[132] P. Brett, *An Inquiry into Criminal Guilt* (London, Sweet and Maxwell, 1963), pp. 98–100.

[133] See for example the discussion by Lord Atkin in *Andrews* v. *DPP* [1937] AC 576 at 583 and G. Williams, 'Recklessness Redefined' [1982] CLJ 252.

[134] [1982] AC 341.

[135] Ibid. at 352.

[136] *Elliot* v. *C* (1983) 77 Cr App R 103. Now that the offence of reckless driving has been replaced by that of dangerous driving, *Caldwell* is no longer of significance in driving offences. It is, however, still of central importance to the offence of criminal damage and may apply to other offences.

[137] *Chief Constable of Avon* v. *Shimmen* (1987) 84 Cr App R 7. See also *Reid* (1992) 95 Cr App R 393.

carelessness ... is not to attribute an attitude or state of mind'.[138] This view was also held by Kenny when he said that there can be no: 'degrees of inadvertence when that word is used to denote a state of mind, since it means that in the man's mind there has been a complete absence of a particular thought, a nullity; and of nullity there can be no degrees'.[139] There is merit to this argument, but it does not mean that it is inappropriate to impose criminal responsibility for negligence and carelessness. As Smith and Hogan emphasise, there may be no degrees of inadvertence, but there can be degrees of fault in failing to advert.[140] The court is primarily concerned with the conduct of the defendant, rather than precisely what went on in the defendant's mind at the time of the alleged offence. The same may appear to be true of *Caldwell* recklessness which also imposes liability for inadvertence. However, as mentioned above, *Caldwell* recklessness is concerned with what went on in the defendant's mind because of the existence of the lacuna.

The third point is that objection to the imposition of criminal responsibility for negligence might be less pronounced if it were contrasted, not with knowledge, intention and recklessness, but with strict liability. The argument in this section is that the law might be more palatable if the prosecution were required to prove negligence on the part of defendants who commit offences against consumers. The imposition of a negligence requirement would have some advantages. In particular, it would obviate the much-repeated criticism that strict liability can lead to the conviction and punishment of those who are faultless. Furthermore, the burden on the prosecution would not be unduly harsh, as they would only have to show that the defendant did not reach an objective standard, something which might often be easily established.[141]

However, there are difficulties in requiring proof of negligence as an alternative to strict liability. The most obvious objection is that it would put an undesirable burden on the prosecution. Proving fault is not as easy as proving a result, and even though it is submitted that negligence is not a form of *mens rea* as such, the courts might well reason by analogy with the case where recklessness has to be proved on the part of a corporation and insist that when a corporation was the defendant, negligence would have to be proved on the part of someone who is the directing mind

---

[138] A. White, 'Carelessness, Indifference and Negligence' (1961) 24 MLR 592 at 592.

[139] C. S. Kenny, *Outlines of the Criminal Law* (19th edn, Cambridge, Cambridge University Press, 1965 by J. W. C Turner), p. 39.

[140] Smith, *Smith and Hogan Criminal Law*, p. 93. Smith argues that the more obvious the risk, the greater the fault in failing to be aware of it. This is because negligence can be seen as the 'non-attainment' of a required standard of conduct.

[141] It is conceded that this may be easier to prove in the case of an individual defendant than a corporate defendant.

and will of the corporation. Although it could be argued that at present the prosecution in effect has to prove negligence in order to counter a defendant's pleading of a no negligence defence, it is nevertheless easier for a prosecution to show that a defendant may not have taken 'all reasonable precautions and exercised all due diligence' than it is for the prosecution to prove beyond reasonable doubt that a defendant was negligent. A final point is that imposing a requirement of negligence does little to solve the problem of what the law should do about junior employees who commit offences in the course of a trade or business. It is argued below that such employees should not be strictly liable for offences committed on behalf of their employers, and it is submitted that the same is so, even if the employee is careless. Employees often suffer at the demands of their employers, and often work in a highly stressful environment, in a job for which they have been poorly trained. A requirement that they are not negligent would, it is submitted, do little to encourage them to take more care. While a requirement of proving negligence may encourage employers to take care, it seems likely that the most effective way to encourage such care is to require employers to prove their lack of negligence; in other words, to retain the due diligence defence.

Limiting prosecutions to businesses and decision-makers. Despite what has been said above in defence of imposing strict criminal liability, there is no doubt there is a risk of injustice in certain cases. One such case is where the defendant is a relatively junior employee who breaches a consumer protection statute. Many strict liability offences are committed by businesses. When a shop assistant wrongly labels a product, or a factory worker allows a substance to adulterate some food being packaged, it will normally be the individual's employer who will be prosecuted.[142] However, most regulatory offences allow for the prosecution of the employee, even if that employee performed the wrongful act accidentally. One of the major objections to strict liability is that it punishes the innocent individual as well as the innocent business.[143]

As we have seen, *Tesco v. Nattrass* distinguished between two types of employee: those who 'carry out the functions of management and speak and act as the company', and the 'subordinates [who] carry out orders from above'.[144] The importance of this from the point of view of the corporation trying to escape responsibility is shown above. *Tesco* also

---

[142] See P. Cartwright, 'Defendants in Consumer Protection Statutes: A Search for Consistency' (1996) 59 MLR 225.
[143] Ibid. at 237.
[144] [1972] AC 153 at p. 171.

makes it clear that employees can be prosecuted, either for causing their employers to commit offences,[145] or directly under provisions such as s.1 of the Trade Descriptions Act. All that has to be proved is that the offending act was performed in the course of a trade or business. Many consumer protection statutes appear to allow for the prosecution of junior employees, whether they have some sort of management function or are merely low-paid subordinate assistants.[146] This is a matter for concern. Employees have been described as being 'locked in a system where they have to carry out a company's marketing scheme; in the case of junior employees, for low wages in an uncreative environment'.[147] The policy arguments against making employees strictly liable are significant. The commission of the offence will usually benefit the employer rather than the employee, so the only incentive for employees to commit offences is likely to be to please their employers.[148] Although the imposition of criminal liability may encourage employees to take care, it is unlikely to have a significant effect to this end. Employees are often 'captives of promotional practices adopted by their employers'[149] which are adopted by their employers and prosecuting them is of little benefit.

The criticisms of prosecuting employees is generally made in the context of junior employees such as shop assistants. There may be stronger arguments for allowing the prosecution of those who perform a function of management, even if they are not part of the directing mind and will of the organisation. The manager in *Tesco* v. *Nattrass* would be included here, as would the manager in the pricing case of *Warwickshire County Council* v. *Johnson*.[150] When the latter case was heard in the Divisional Court, Popplewell J thought it bizarre that the manager of a shop should be able to escape conviction when 'it is the nature of current day retailing that corporate entities own very large numbers of individual retail outlets all over the country which are managed by employees'.[151] There is difficulty in deciding where the line should be drawn. The strongest argument is perhaps that senior executives should be prosecuted more frequently for offences committed by their corporations, particularly where the commission of the offence can be said to result directly from decisions made

---

[145] Using bypass procedures such as that contained in s.23 of the Trade Descriptions Act.
[146] It is unclear whether or not the Food Safety Act 1990 allows for the prosecution of employees. See Cartwright, 'Defendants in Consumer Protection Statutes', p. 231.
[147] Scott and Black, *Cranston's Consumers and the Law* at p. 330.
[148] There may, of course, be some cases where both benefit, for example where the employee is paid on commission.
[149] Scott and Black, *Cranston's Consumers and the Law*, p. 325.
[150] (1992) 156 JP 577.
[151] Ibid. at p. 586.

by those executives.[152] A further answer is to prevent corporations from being able to escape liability by naming employees, rather than to allow employees to be prosecuted. This was considered above.

A partial solution to problems raised by the prosecution of employees is provided by the Property Misdescriptions Act 1991. Section 1(1) of that Act states that: '[w]here a false or misleading statement about a pre-scribed matter is made in the course of an estate agency business or a property development business, otherwise than in the course of provid-ing conveyancing services, the person by whom the business was carried on shall be guilty of an offence under this section'. As noted above this expressly provides for vicarious liability. It states that where the employee makes the statement, the employer is guilty. This gets around the prob-lem of deciding whether or not to use extensive construction, and ensures that the employee is not the prime defendant. However, it is important to read this in conjunction with s.1(2) which states: '[w]here the making of the statement is due to the act or default of an employee the employee shall be guilty of an offence under this section; and the employee may be proceeded against and punished whether or not proceedings are also taken against his employer'. Therefore, the Act still provides for the em-ployee to be strictly liable. Although it requires an act or default, there is no requirement of *mens rea* on the part of the employee. This means that there will still be an incentive on enforcement agencies to take action against employees, particularly where the employer has escaped liability by successfully pleading the due diligence defence. The Trade Descrip-tions Act appears to go even further by allowing the prosecution of private individuals where those individuals cause someone acting in the course of a trade or business to commit an offence. This situation stems from the decision of the Divisional Court in *Olgeirsson* v. *Kitching*,[153] where the Di-visional Court decided that a private individual could be convicted under s.23. There are difficulties with the reasoning in this case. In particular, the Divisional Court based its decision on that in *Meah* v. *Roberts*.[154] In that case, it was decided that a pipe fitter who put caustic soda in a lemon-ade bottle in a restaurant which was consumed by a customer could be prosecuted under s.113(1) (the bypass procedure) of the Food Act 1955. McNeill J in *Olgeirsson* said of *Meah*, 'I find it cogent and indeed per-suasive authority as it mirrors almost precisely the factual decision with which this court is dealing.'[155] However, *Meah* did not decide that a

---

[152] See *United States* v *Park* 421 US 658 (1975) and the discussion in Scott and Black, *Cranston's Consumers and the Law*, pp. 325–7.
[153] [1986] 1 WLR 304.   [154] [1977] 1 WLR 1187.   [155] *Olgeirsson* v. *Kitching* p. 311.

private individual could be prosecuted. It decided that the third party did not have to act in the course of the same trade as the first-mentioned person. In the words of Wien J, the procedure applied 'whether that third party sells food or not'. Although the private individual did possess *mens rea* in this case, it is far from clear that *mens rea* is a requirement for convicting an individual under s.23. The only statute which clearly does not allow junior employees to be prosecuted is the Consumer Protection Act 1987. This limits prosecutions to a defendant who is 'acting in the course of a trade or business of his'.[156] This has been taken to mean 'any business of which the defendant is either the owner, or in which he has a controlling interest'.[157] Although liability remains strict, it is limited to businesses themselves, and those who are senior in a business.

If statutes which impose strict liability were to limit convictions to businesses and those who are senior in businesses, some of the objections to strict liability would be removed. Many of the justifications for strict liability apply more to businesses and decision-makers in businesses than they do to employees or private individuals, particularly in terms of deterrence. Whether liability should extend to employees such as store managers is debatable. It is submitted that corporations should take responsibility for the acts of their employees and that where an offence is committed by a store manager in the course of his employment then his employer should be convicted and the manager immune from prosecution.

Establishing general defences of due diligence. It is submitted that another solution to some of the difficulties with strict liability is to ensure that all regulatory statutes which impose strict criminal liability contain due diligence defences. Dickson J argued forcibly for the recognition of a class of offences: 'in which there is no necessity for the prosecution to prove the existence of mens rea'. However, 'the defendant would be allowed to exculpate himself by proving affirmatively that he was not negligent'.[158] In the case of consumer protection offences this is not a problem, as all such offences contain these defences. In other regulatory fields these may not be present, and there is a strong argument for making due diligence a general defence to strict liability offences. This is the position in a number of Commonwealth jurisdictions, and was lent some support by the House of Lords in *Sweet* v. *Parsley*. Orchard has argued that offences in Australia which appear to impose strict liability 'should be understood merely as imposing responsibility for negligence

---

[156] Sections 20(1) and 40(1).
[157] *Warwickshire County Council* v. *Johnson* [1993] 1 All ER 299 at p. 304 *per* Lord Roskill.
[158] *City of Saulte Ste Marie* (at p. 173 *per* Dickson J). Indeed, due diligence defences are sometimes referred to as 'no negligence' defences.

but emphasising that the burden of rebutting negligence by affirmative proof of reasonable mistake rests upon the defendant'.[159] However, even where statutes provide for defences of due diligence, there are difficulties in the way that these defences are used. The main concern is that the courts are too willing to accept that a defendant has satisfied the requirement of proving that he took all reasonable precautions/steps and exercised all due diligence to avoid committing the offence. It has already been noted that judicial concern has been expressed that the courts are too willing to accept that due diligence defences have been made out, and this will be difficult to remedy. The problems raised by *Tesco v. Nattrass* in allowing blame to be passed on to employees are also relevant here, and any expansion of due diligence defences would have to be carried out alongside a rethinking of the operation of corporate and vicarious liability, as is discussed above.

Conclusions

Criminal law performs a number of important functions in society, but chief among these is that of protecting the public from harm. Where the public is put at risk by an activity then the criminal law can have a role in avoiding that harm by deterring the defendant from taking risks in the course of that activity. Where the duty placed upon the defendant is absolute then there is a risk of serious injustice for the defendant, and so absolute liability is to be avoided. However, where the duty is subject to the prosecution establishing *mens rea* then there is a risk that it will be extremely difficult to enforce. This can lead to injustice for the public.[160] A balance must therefore be created.

Mens rea has a place in serious crime, and there are some offences which cannot reasonably be said to be committed without a mental element. Most of these offences can be committed by corporations.[161] Principles of corporate liability have developed in recognition of the power of such organisations in everyday life, and the desire to fit the corporation into a structure which emphasises individual liability. However, it is submitted that existing rules on corporate liability do not facilitate the prosecution of corporations for *mens rea* offences. In particular, the doctrine of identification makes it extremely difficult to prove *mens rea* against large corporations. There are several solutions to this, with perhaps the two

[159] G. Orchard, 'The Defence of Absence of Fault in Australasia and Canada', in P. Smith (ed.), *Criminal Law Essays: Essays in Honour of J. C. Smith* (London, Butterworths, 1987), p. 114.
[160] See Braithwaite, *Corporate Crime in the Pharmaceutical Industry*, ch. 9.
[161] The exceptions being rape and murder.

main ones being rethinking the rules on corporate liability for *mens rea* offences, and removing the requirement of *mens rea* offences for offences committed by corporations. It is submitted that both should be considered. In relation to the first, it is argued that corporations should be guilty of serious *mens rea* offences where *mens rea* is proved, but that it should be possible to establish *mens rea* by showing that it was possessed by any employee acting in the course of his employment. Provided the corporation can also be said to have committed the *actus reus*, the company should be guilty. Where the offence is subject to a due diligence defence, the company should not be able to escape liability by passing the blame onto an employee. Instead, it should have to show that it, and all its employees, took all reasonable precautions and exercised all due diligence to avoid committing the offence. Where the employee has *mens rea*, it is submitted that this will be virtually impossible.

As well as facilitating the prosecution of corporations for *mens rea* offences, it is important to consider liability of corporations for offences of strict liability. The traditional method by which strict liability has been imposed on corporations is through vicarious liability. The major difficulty for the prosecution has been the case of *Tesco* v. *Nattrass*, which allows a corporate defendant to escape liability by blaming a junior employee, and arguing that it has taken all reasonable precautions and taken all due diligence at a senior level. It is submitted that corporations should only be allowed to escape liability where they can show that all their employees took all reasonable precautions and exercised all due diligence. Corporate employers would therefore be truly vicariously responsible for the acts of their employees undertaken in the course of employment.

In addition to the changes supported above, it is submitted that there is a need to introduce some new offences which more directly address the decisions, attitude and internal organisation of corporations. It was mentioned above that Gobert has argued for corporations to be liable where crimes are authorised, permitted, or tolerated as a matter of company policy or *de facto* practice. There are attractions to this form of approach as it addresses the company's prime culpability directly. However, the difficulty of establishing this in practice means that it should be given only a cautious welcome at this stage.

The conclusions above relate to corporate defendants. It is submitted that they should apply equally to others who form the mind of a business, such as sole traders and partners. Junior employees, on the other hand, should not be subjected to strict liability. The arguments against prosecuting employees for strict liability offences committed in the course of their employment are compelling. It should still be possible to prosecute employees where they commit offences with *mens rea*, and are acting

outside the course of their employment, but allowing them to be prosecuted without proof of fault is surely unacceptable. The final comment
should be given to Leigh: '[i]f we have not as yet avoided subjecting the
"blameless harmdoer" to the risk of criminal conviction, we have at least
gone a long way towards reconciling his interest in individual justice with
the need to protect the public against a variety of evils associated primarily with carrying on particular trades and industries'.[162] We may have
gone a long way, but the journey is far from over.

---

[162] Leigh, *Strict and Vicarious Liability*, p. 115.

5   Consumers and safety: the protection of physical integrity

Introduction

Probably the most serious threat to consumers is to their health and safety, and few would dispute that the law has a role to play in controlling the supply of dangerous products. However, behind this broad consensus there are many areas of disagreement. First, it is unclear precisely on what basis the law should provide this protection. If we analyse the law in terms of market failure we might conclude that dangerous products should be controlled for two main reasons: first, because consumers tend to be unaware of the threats that such products pose (information failure), and secondly, because dangerous products pose threats to third parties (they create externalities). On those bases, product safety regulation can be justified from an economic perspective. However, we might go beyond this analysis and argue that even if consumers were properly informed about the risks posed by a product, and there was no risk of the product affecting third parties, the law should nevertheless forbid the supply of that product. Such a conclusion is sometimes rejected as unwarranted paternalism, but, as we saw in chapter 1, there are arguments for protecting consumers from themselves. There have been attempts to argue that where the state imposes mandatory product safety standards this may not be classified as paternalism, but as the state giving effect to citizens' wishes that someone make a judgement about safety on their behalf. The persuasiveness of this is considered below.

A second issue to consider is that of the form that product safety regulation should take. A variety of legal techniques is open to the policy-maker, all of which have inherent advantages and disadvantages. A comparison of the strengths and weaknesses of different regulatory techniques was undertaken in chapter 2, so it is not proposed to repeat that here. However, the chapter briefly considers the particular problems that choice of legal technique presents in the context of product safety.

Product safety in the UK is governed by a variety of measures, but the main legislation which controls dangerous products is contained in the General Product Safety Regulations 1994. The Regulations provide a useful illustration of many of the difficulties facing law-makers who seek to balance effective consumer protection with a thriving free market and are examined in some depth as a case study. The chapter also considers briefly the relevant provisions of the Food Safety Act 1990 and the Consumer Protection Act 1987. It will be seen that the substantive law addresses many of the difficult issues arising in this area, but sometimes lacks the sanctions necessary for it to fulfil its purpose.

Rationales for intervention to ensure consumer safety

There are a number of justifications, both economic and social, for intervening in the market to protect consumers from dangerous products. First, although the market undoubtedly has a role to play in consumer protection, and a freely functioning market should ensure that consumers have a wide choice of products, it has been argued that the market alone cannot provide adequate protection from dangerous products.[1] The limitations of the market were dealt with in detail in chapter 1, but there are factors which require particular consideration here in the context of consumer safety.

Economic justifications for intervention

There are economic arguments in favour of regulating dangerous products, based on the idea of correcting market failure. The two main ways in which markets for dangerous products may fail are through information deficits and externalities.

Information deficits. The role of information in the market was examined in chapter 1, and the use of information remedies in chapter 2. The provision of information about products will have a significant role in providing the consumer with protection. Labelling, for example, can ensure that a user knows when the use of a product is likely to lead to danger, and so can take steps to avoid that danger by taking care in using the product. As will be seen later, providing information is one way of helping to make a product reasonably safe for the purposes of mandatory standards, and the present law specifically provides a duty to provide information to enable consumers to assess the safety of a product.[2] There

---

[1] See e.g. G. G. Howells, *Consumer Product Safety* (Aldershot, Dartmouth and Ashgale, 1998), pp. 16–23, I. Ramsay, *Consumer Protection: Text and Materials*, ch. 11.
[2] See the General Product Safety Regulations reg. 8(1)(a) (below).

are areas in which products which are inherently likely to cause harm are tolerated because of the mandatory information which is supplied with them. The most obvious example is tobacco, which can only be sold if it is accompanied by a health warning. As well as enabling consumers to take care in using products, information can also protect consumers by helping them to avoid products which may be of particular risk to them, for example, food containing nuts.

However, there are problems with relying on information to ensure consumer safety. It is widely recognised that markets do not supply optimal information about the risks posed by products for a number of reasons. First, where the consumer may not be a repeat player there is a risk that 'fly by night' operators will avoid being held to account by litigation or through normal market processes. Secondly, the market provides a strong incentive for producers to avoid drawing attention to possible dangers in a product, and evidence suggests that rival traders will also frequently be reluctant to draw attention to the safety record of their competitors.[3] Furthermore, even if all the relevant information were given to the consumer, that information is likely to be complex and difficult for many consumers to act upon. Consumers suffer from 'bounded rationality', which means that they are only able to receive, store, and process a limited amount of information.[4] This is particularly so in areas such as nutritional information and food additives, where information may be complex. Achieving any meaningful level of 'optimal information' proves elusive. Finally, information will generally not tackle the risks created by externalities. This is now examined.

Externalities. Externalities raise problems which free markets, and information remedies, cannot adequately solve. In chapter 1, we examined the argument that if consumers had perfect information about the characteristics of products and behaved rationally in accordance with their preferences, then the only reason for intervention would be because of the risks to third parties, known as 'externalities' or 'spillovers'.[5] Free market theory may tell us that if a consumer chooses to purchase a dangerous motor car because it is cheap, and she has all the relevant information, that should be her choice, but recognises that the risks posed to third parties such as other road users and pedestrians take the implications of the

---

[3] See ch. 1 and *Consumer Detriment under Conditions of Imperfect Information* (OFT Research Paper 11, August 1997), p. 38.

[4] See H. A. Simon, *Administrative Behaviour* (1975), at pp. 39–41 and generally H. A. Simon, *Models of Bounded Rationality* (Cambridge, Mass., MIT Press, 1982).

[5] See A. I. Ogus, *Regulation: Legal Form and Economic Theory* (Oxford, Clarendon Press, 1994), at pp. 190–205.

sale beyond the interests of buyer and seller. Consumer safety provides
the most striking illustration of the importance of regulating to protect
third parties because of the number of potential victims of dangerous
products, and the costs associated with any injury they are caused. There
have been attempts to argue that third party effects can be internalised
through the private law, but they remain unconvincing.[6] Furthermore,
when judged against the social justifications for intervention considered
below, the limitations of the market, and of private law, are particularly
apparent.

The existence of market failure through information deficits and externalities does not mean that regulation should always be used as a means
of correction. If we base our justification for regulation on economic
grounds we should be confident that the regime we use is less costly than
an absence of regulation. The cost to society in purely financial terms of
a dangerous product may be significant, and in some cases it may be that
it is cheaper to regulate than to pay the economic price of sorting out
the consequences of having dangerous goods on the market. According
to research by the Pearson Commission, over the period 1971 to 1976,
the cost of compensation to injured persons at 1977 currency values was
£421 million per annum in social security and £202 million per annum in
tort.[7] Sunstein argues that some forms of safety regulation pay for themselves, for example those relating to car-safety standards.[8] We may simply
decide to regulate where the economic benefits of regulation outweigh the
economic costs.[9] In other cases, the expense of correcting market failure,
for example, information failure, may outweigh the economic benefits. In
such circumstances, it may be better to eschew regulation and recognise
that market failure will always exist. However, this approach ignores the
social benefits of regulation, which are considered below.

Social justifications for intervention

Paternalism and politics. When consumer safety is at issue, concern may go wider than correcting market failure. It may be viewed as
inappropriate to use an economic approach when there is a threat to physical integrity, health and safety being perceived as matters which should

---

[6] But see G. Calabresi and A. Melamed, 'Property Rules, Liability Rules and Inalienability:
One View of the Cathedral' (1972) 85 Harvard LR 1089.

[7] *Report of the Royal Commission on Civil Liability and Compensation for Personal Injury,*
Cmnd 7054, 1978, vol.II, table 158.

[8] C. Sunstein, *Free Markets and Social Justice* (New York, Oxford University Press, 1997),
p. 272. See also W. K. Viscusi, *Fatal Tradeoffs: Public and Private Responsibilities for Risk*
(New York, Oxford University Press, 1992).

[9] Ramsay, *Consumer Protection,* p. 471.

not be subjected to a rigid cost-benefit analysis, particularly where matters of life and death are at issue.[10] There are both practical and ethical difficulties with using a purely economic approach to product safety. From a practical point of view, we have to decide how to value life and limb, a matter which has long been difficult and contentious. From an ethical perspective we might say that health and safety are too important to be given a monetary value. As a result of this approach, it has been argued that the main value which influences consumer safety legislation is not efficiency but autonomy.[11] In the words of Michael Pertschuk: 'we will not concede that the economist's useful, but imperfect, tool of cost-benefit analysis dictates policy judgements on what is right and wrong'.[12]

Consumer safety is one area where there may be particular pressure for a paternalistic approach to regulation to be taken. Even on a strict interpretation of paternalism,[13] the Legislature may argue that individuals do not adequately protect themselves, particularly when faced with products which provide short-term pleasure but long-term risks. There is ample evidence that consumers are irrational when it comes to assessing matters such as risk. For example, they tend to overestimate remote risks with serious consequences, and underestimate risks over which they feel they have some control.[14] It may be better for experts to determine what is in individuals' best interests rather than the individuals themselves. In the words of Maniet, 'the consumer, even if we assume that he is rational and well informed – which is not true in an imperfect market – should not be left free to decide how much safety he wants to buy and how much he is ready to pay for it'.[15] A similar approach is taken by Howells, who argues that 'protection of life is too important to simply be left to the market . . . where life and limb are at stake the consumer understandably favours prevention to reparation', although Howells' language

---

[10] See P. Asch, *Consumer Safety Regulation: Putting a Price on Life and Limb* (Oxford, Oxford University Press, 1988).

[11] See M. Sagoff, 'On Markets for Risk' (1982) 41 MLR 755, and the discussion in Ramsay, *Consumer Protection*, pp. 471–2.

[12] M. Pertschuk, *Revolt Against Regulation* (Berkeley, University of California Press, 1982) at p. 138.

[13] See G. Dworkin, 'Paternalism' in R. Wasserstrom (ed.), *Morality and the Law* (Belmont, Calif., Wadsworth Publishing 1971), p. 108 and Ogus, *Regulation*, pp. 51–3 for a discussion.

[14] See O. Svenson, 'Are We Less Risky and More Skilful Than Our Fellow Drivers?' (1981) 47 *Acta Psychologica* 143 and the discussion in Howells, *Consumer Product Safety*, pp. 21–2.

[15] F. Maniet, 'The Safety of Consumer Goods and Services' in F. Maniet and B. Dunaj (eds.), *The Implementation Process of EU Directives on Product Safety, Product Liability and Unfair Contract Terms* (Louvain la Neuve, Centre de Droit de la Consommation, 1994) at p. 87.

emphasises the issue of choice to a much greater extent.[16] The arguments in favour of regulation to protect physical safety rather than relying on the market are clearly strong. The point is put quite nicely by Leff in the following terms: 'If one buys an automobile whose steering wheel is given to casual driver evisceration, one *will* learn. "I'm not going to buy *that* model again" you say, trying neatly to refold and repack the last 17 feet of disheveled intestine. "If those guys at Pterodactyl Motors aren't going to level with me, that's the last they see of any of *my* money."'[17]

As was mentioned in chapter 1, there have even been attempts to square paternalism with notions of individual choice, by arguing that individuals, knowing that they will face choices that they cannot resist, ask others to make rational decisions about what is in their best interests on their behalf.[18] Howells takes a similar view. He argues that while it is natural for 'man to want to protect his self-interest', this can best be done by delegating the task of representing these interests to trusted institutions. He asks for 'a certain humility about one's own abilities to look after one's own interests in an increasingly complicated environment'.[19] The advantage of Howells' approach over a strict interpretation of paternalism is that it is consistent with free market rhetoric in that it accepts that it is the consumer who decides how the level of safety to which he is exposed is to be set; it is just that the consumer chooses to delegate the details to those who know best. Viewed this way, the distinction between a free market approach and a paternalistic approach becomes less obvious.

There may be difficulties with the theoretical basis for paternalism and with its relationship to free market ideas, but there can be little doubt that it is influential. Paternalistic influences on political decision-making may be considerable, particularly where the media draws attention to an emotive subject. Ramsay, for example, highlights the reaction of the Government in the UK to the supplying of erasers which looked and smelt like food and were aimed at children. He argues that this demonstrates the emotive nature of many safety issues, which are picked up by governments and lead to speedy and perhaps ill-considered responses.[20] Such responses may, of course, be beneficial from the point of view of political capital, with the public eager to see that the government is 'doing something'.

---

[16] Howells, *Consumer Product Safety*, p. 16.
[17] A. A. Leff, 'The Pontiac Prospectus' (1974) Consum LJ 25 at p. 34.
[18] G. Loomes and R. Sugden, 'Regret Theory: An Alternative Theory of Rational Choice under Uncertainty' (1982) 92 Econ J 805. See also T. Schelling, *Choice and Consequence* (Cambridge, Mass., Harvard University Press, 1984).
[19] Howells, *Consumer Product Safety*, p. 17.
[20] Ramsay, *Consumer Protection*, pp. 478–89.

Distributive justice. There can be little doubt that raising safety standards may mean raising costs of products. Ultimately, a decision has to be made about how much we are willing to pay for improvements in safety. One factor to bear in mind is the distributive effect of product safety regulation. For example, disclosing information in a way which only one sector of the population will be able to understand will only benefit that sector. Disclosing information which the vast majority of the population knows anyway will benefit only a few. In both cases the costs of disclosure will be passed on equally to all consumers. It is therefore important that a decision is made about how much regulation will cost, and who will benefit. There may be good social reasons for benefiting the most vulnerable, and this might justify requiring the disclosure of information which many consumers would already know. However, information may be at its least effective where vulnerable consumers are concerned.[21] As a result, mandatory safety standards may be seen as an appropriate tool to achieve distributive justice. However, as we will see below, mandatory safety standards may sometimes have a degenerative effect where the poorest and most vulnerable consumers are concerned. The rationale of ensuring distributive justice is relatively clear, but the means by which that can be achieved has been the subject of much debate.

Product safety and techniques for intervention

Several techniques are available to protect consumers from dangerous products, and there are different ways of categorising these techniques. We can distinguish, for example, between pre-market controls such as prior approval or minimum product safety standards, and post-market controls, or enforcement powers.[22] Post-market controls are dealt with in this book in chapter 7. It is worth saying a few words about the characteristics of the available legal techniques and assessing their advantages and disadvantages, although a more detailed examination was undertaken in chapter 2. Furthermore, it should be recognised that this is only a rough categorisation, and that the dividing line between different techniques is not always clear. For example, when deciding to approve a product, the regulator may dictate that mandatory standards be invoked, and one type of standard may concern the type of information that is supplied. Nevertheless, the categorisation provides a framework within which to judge the approaches that are available.

---

[21] See K. McNeil, J. Nevin, D. Trubek, and R. Miller, 'Market Discrimination Against the Poor and the Impact of Consumer Disclosure Law: The Used Car Industry' (1979) 13 *Law and Society Review* 695.
[22] See Howells, *Consumer Product Safety*, ch. 1.

Prior approval

In the context of product safety, prior approval, sometimes called screening, authorisation, or licensing, requires that the product in question be formally approved, for example by a regulatory agency, before it can be marketed. The most obvious area where this approach is used is that of medicines. The main concerns with such a system are that it is time consuming, expensive, and can be used as a technique for creating an anti-competitive barrier to entering a particular market. The time lag between when a product is produced and when it can get approval can lead to welfare losses, such as those of a patient who is refused a new and effective drug. Sunstein argues that 'by delaying the entry of beneficial drugs into the market, the FDA [Food and Drugs Administration in the USA] has, in many settings, dramatically increased risks to life and health'.[23] The expense of prior approval can have a number of deleterious effects upon consumers. First, it will tend to increase the price of the product, which may take it out of the reach of consumers and, in the case of medicines, even health authorities. Secondly, the research and development costs may be so high that when they are coupled with the uncertainty of whether the drug will be approved, firms are discouraged from undertaking that investment. This may lead to fewer new products and also the market being dominated by a small number of firms. This may, of course, have competition implications. An additional concern with prior approval is that it may lead to less than rational decision-making on the part of those administering the system. Again, medicines provide a useful illustration. Where a regulator is deciding whether or not a drug can be placed on the market there are two types of mistake that may be made. First, an unsafe drug may be certified as safe, and secondly, a safe drug may be certified as unsafe. The first mistake is far more visible than the second, and far more likely to lead to recriminations being made against the regulator. As a result there may be an incentive upon regulators to be over-cautious in allowing new drugs on to the market.[24]

Despite these concerns, there are undoubtedly many advantages to prior approval schemes. Where products pose potentially huge risk when unsafe it might be seen as desirable to control those very closely. Medicines provide an obvious illustration of this. The type of harm (death) that could result and the numbers of people potentially affected by dangerous drugs being placed on the market may justify the close supervision under

---

[23] Sunstein, *Free Markets and Social Justice*, p. 276.
[24] See R. Parish, 'Consumer Protection and the Ideology of Consumer Protectionists' in A.J. Duggan and L. W. Darvall (eds.), *Consumer Protection Law and Theory* (Sydney, The Law Book Company, 1980), p. 229 at p. 231.

which they are placed. It should be remembered that the harm posed by dangerous products will frequently be in the form of externalities. A dangerous drug or car will pose risks not only to those who choose to subject themselves to those risks in an informed manner, but also to passengers in cars, pedestrians, and patients. Information remedies, which may help certain classes of potential victim, may be ineffective where externalities occur. Ogus argues that in areas such as MOTs (a form of prior approval) the risk to the driver is far greater than to other road users and that as this could be dealt with, to some extent at least, by an information remedy such as certification, the main justification for such prior approval is paternalism.[25] Although paternalism will be an influential factor upon prior approval regimes it is submitted that the market failures caused by externalities are so great in these areas of product safety that they justify intervention without the need to refer to paternalism.

Standards

The approach taken by the UK and other states within the European Community (EC) is that of imposing mandatory product standards. The different types of standard all have their advantages and disadvantages. One common distinction to make is between the 'old approach' and the 'new approach'. Under the former, detailed technical standards were devised which specified the precise specifications that producers were obliged to follow. Such standards are usually referred to as specification standards. The main advantage of specification standards concerns the cost of enforcement, as it is relatively easy to see if a product meets the standard in question. This is of benefit to regulators, but also can be attractive for producers as there is certainty about the standards they should meet. However, specification standards suffer from some significant disadvantages. First, they restrict innovation by limiting the scope for manufacturers to produce more efficient and effective products. By being excessively prescriptive they provide little incentive for producers to find better ways of meeting their goals. Secondly, evidence has shown the standard-setting approach to be time-consuming because of the procedures that generally have to be followed. It frequently takes a long time for a new specification standard to be accepted. Thirdly, from a practical point of view, it is impossible to devise detailed standards for all products. Any attempt to do so is likely to lead to complex and convoluted standards which may be over- and under-inclusive in different areas. Fourthly, the reality of specification standards is that they tend to become

---

[25] Ogus, *Regulation*, p. 218.

outdated very quickly, and therefore have difficulty in keeping up with technological advances.[26] Finally, there are question-marks over the legitimacy of such an approach from the point of view of democracy, as there is often limited transparency and accountability in decision-making.[27]

A solution to some of these concerns is to use performance standards. Performance standards identify the regulatory goals that must be met rather than the technique by which they are met, and provide a number of advantages. Chief among these is that they allow producers considerable flexibility in how they meet regulatory goals. They address the central objective of regulation directly by focusing upon the end result that must be achieved. As a result, producers are under an incentive to find more efficient and effective ways of meeting regulatory goals. With this approach, legislation sets out the standard of performance that a product is required to meet, but the manufacturer has a choice about how to meet that standard. The burden of design is, to a large extent, transferred from the standard-setter to the manufacturer, and the manufacturer is thus given the flexibility to innovate, while still being required to produce a product that meets given standards. The approach of the UK since 1987 has been to say that products must be reasonably safe, thus employing an objective but flexible performance standard.[28] This approach is now used by the EC, and is contained in the General Product Safety Regulations 1994. These are considered in some detail below.

There is an obvious difficulty in deciding which form of standard to adopt, and the advantages and disadvantages have to be weighed up. The advent of the General Product Safety Regulations has meant that specific standards are still important, but that all other products must meet a general objective test of safety. The difficulties in deciding upon what is the optimal level of safety are considered below, where the Regulations are discussed in some detail.

Information remedies

It was mentioned above that the regulation of information can play an important role in product safety. Although limited in the extent to which it can avoid externalities, information can help to provide protection for consumers from dangerous products in two main ways. First, by

---

[26] See the Committee on Safety and Health at Work (the Robens Committee) (1972 Cmnd 5034 at para. 29).

[27] See Howells, *Consumer Product Safety*, pp. 7–8.

[28] It could be argued that this should be referred to as a target standard. See Ogus, *Regulation*, p. 166.

supplying information such as warnings and instructions for use with a product, a producer may ensure that that product is reasonably safe. As will be seen later, the information supplied with a product will be taken into account when judging if the product is a safe product for the purposes of the General Product Safety Regulations 1994. Secondly, information may help consumers to avoid the dangers inherent in a product, for example, by warning of the dangers of tobacco or the existence of nuts in food. Information remedies have the advantage that they allow consumers to make choices about the risks to which they are willing to be subjected. They may therefore be viewed as more consistent with the market system than the more interventionist forms of regulation. One seminal article on the role of information put it as follows:

> if consumers are not really interested in increasing the quality or safety of certain product attributes, an information remedy will not force the market to make an inefficient change (where a mandatory product standard would). Similarly, information remedies allow different consumers to strike different balances between price and product quality, while direct quality regulation almost necessarily imposes a single choice on all consumers.[29]

The most obvious way of implementing an information remedy is through a disclosure regime, which requires traders to disclose standardised information to consumers. However, measures such as prohibiting false and misleading information and improving consumer education could also be seen as information remedies. It is important that failure to disclose information should be backed up with an appropriate sanction where consumer safety is concerned. The approach of the General Product Safety Regulations to this issue is considered below.

The background to UK consumer safety legislation

The UK has had general product safety law for some time.[30] The Consumer Protection Act 1961 enabled the Secretary of State to make regulations which imposed the safety standards, backed up by the criminal law, which he thought expedient to prevent or reduce the risk of death or injury from particular goods. The 1976 consultative document *Consumer Safety* was, however, critical of the law, particularly in relation to

---

[29] H. Beales, R. Craswell, and S. Salop, 'The Efficient Regulation of Consumer Information' (1981) 24 *Journal of Law and Economics* 491.
[30] See P. Cartwright, 'The Regulation of Product Safety' in G. G. Howells (ed.), *Product Liability* (London, Butterworths, 2000).

enforcement.[31] The Consumer Safety Act 1978 addressed some concerns by introducing new techniques to deal with enforcement, but fell short of introducing a general duty to supply only safe products. By 1984, the Government's White Paper *The Safety of Goods*[32] recognised the case for imposing a general safety duty on suppliers. The White Paper argued that this would impose a greater sense of responsibility on suppliers, and facilitate speedy enforcement action against products as soon as they are found to be dangerous.[33]

The Consumer Protection Act 1987 resulted from the White Paper. The Act introduced a general safety duty by making it an offence to supply consumer goods which failed to comply with the general safety requirement. Consumer goods were obliged to be reasonably safe having regard to all the circumstances, with 'safe' meaning that there is either no risk, or only one reduced to a minimum. When deciding whether or not a product is safe a variety of factors could be considered, such as 'the existence of any means by which it would have been reasonable (taking into account the cost, likelihood and extent of any improvement) for the goods to have been made safer'.[34] It is apparent that the Government was mindful of the risk that higher standards would impose burdens upon business, and so introduced what was, in effect, a duty to supply reasonably safe products. In the 1984 White Paper the Conservative Administration announced that it had 'excluded options which could be implemented only by directing large additional resources to enforcement'.[35] This was not only a matter of concern for a Conservative Government, eager to be seen as a friend of business. Even in the 1976 Consultation Document the then Labour administration pointed out that higher product safety standards 'generally involve higher production costs which ultimately have to be paid for by the consumer'. They emphasised that the benefits in each case had to be weighed carefully against the costs.[36]

As well as introducing the general safety duty the Act also empowered the Secretary of State to make safety regulations, and contained a variety of enforcement measures, including prohibition notices, notices to warn, and suspension notices.[37] Although the general safety duty is of little practical significance following the introduction of the General Product Safety Regulations, the 1987 Act's enforcement provisions and law-making powers remain of great significance, as will be seen later.

---

[31] Cmnd 6398 (1976).   [32] Cmnd 9302.   [33] Ibid. para 34.
[34] Section 10(2)c.   [35] *Safety of Goods*, at para. 3.   [36] Ibid.
[37] See below and ch. 7.

Product safety and European integration

Product safety had been an area of concern at a European level for many years, as product safety laws had enormous potential for creating barriers to trade, under the guise of consumer protection. Integration has been both negative, in the form of striking down offending measures, and positive, in the form of harmonising product safety rules. Before 1985, harmonisation took the form of uniform, mandatory rules. While these arguably had advantages for competition and economies of scale, they led to difficulties.[38] First, they presupposed 'a homogeneity of preferences across the Community',[39] thus ignoring differences in consumers' willingness to pay for increased protection. Secondly, they risked creating 'Europroducts', and ignoring national traditions.[40] Thirdly, they risked creating significant delays in the establishment of a comprehensive system of standards.[41] In 1985, Council Resolution of 7 May saw a new approach to technical harmonisation and standards.[42] This provided that products should conform to essential safety requirements set out in the appropriate directives, and if they did, they could be sold freely throughout the Community. Although technical specifications would still be made they would not be mandatory. The producer could either follow harmonised standards, or merely show that her products conformed to the directive's essential requirements. This approach has the benefits of performance standards discussed above. In the words of McGee and Weatherill, it reconciles 'the diversity of cultural and commercial tradition in the Community with the need for a common Community approach in the pursuit of free trade and economic integration'.[43]

Despite the effect of the measures mentioned above, member states still had different approaches to the issue of general product safety. Directive 92/59 sought to overcome these differences, and tackle the difficulty of adopting Community legislation for all existing and future products, by formulating a broad horizontal legislative framework. The Directive was directed at the free movement of goods, but also sought to ensure a high level of protection of health and safety under Article 100a(3) EC. The

---

[38] The advantages and disadvantages of standards as a regulatory techniques are examined in ch. 1.

[39] Ogus, *Regulation*, p. 176.

[40] See A. McGee and S. Weatherill, 'The Evolution of the Single Market – Harmonisation or Liberalisation' (1990) 53 MLR 578 at 582.

[41] See J. Pelkmans, 'The New Approach to Technical Harmonization and Standardization' (1986–7) 25 JCMS 249 at 251–3.

[42] (1985) OJ C136/1.

[43] McGee and Weatherill, 'The Evolution of the Single Market', p. 584.

Directive was implemented in the UK by the General Product Safety Regulations 1994, and it is to these Regulations that we now turn.

The General Product Safety Regulations: a case study in safety regulation

Introduction

The background to the General Product Safety Regulations (hereafter 'the Regulations') is considered above. As the UK was used to the scheme imposed by Part II of the Consumer Protection Act 1987, the Regulations did not bring any cultural change. Indeed, by backing up the Regulations with the force of the criminal law, the UK government ensured that its tradition in consumer protection was maintained. We will examine the Regulations in some detail for two reasons. First, they are now the main source of product safety law in the UK. Secondly, they provide a useful illustration of many of the difficulties facing policy-makers in the area of product safety. The enforcement of product safety law is vital to its effectiveness and there is a detailed discussion of enforcement in chapter 7. Our examination of product safety should therefore be read in conjunction with that discussion.

Who is a producer?

Regulation 7 states that 'no producer shall place a product on the market unless the product is a safe product'. This is, to a large extent, the cornerstone of the Legislation. Regulation 2(1) provides that the term 'Producer' is to be construed widely. Producers include manufacturers established in the Community, and the term manufacturer includes those holding themselves out as manufacturers by affixing names, trade marks, or other distinctive marks to the product[44] and those who recondition products. This contrasts with s.10(4)(c) of the 1987 Act which provided that suppliers of second-hand goods were not guilty for supplying products that contravened general safety requirements.

It appears to be an aim of the Regulations that where the manufacturer is outside the Community there is always someone within the Community who is classed as a producer and against whom action can be taken. The Regulations state, for example, that where the manufacturer is not established in the Community, but has a representative there, that representative will be classed as the producer, while if there is no representative,

---

[44] Such as an own-brander.

the importer will be the producer. Other professionals in the supply chain are classed as producers 'insofar as their activities may affect the safety properties of a product placed on the market'. This ensures that those who have control over a product's safety are responsible as producers. As a result, a food distributor could be a producer if her storage of food potentially affected its safety. It has been argued that this extended meaning of producer will encompass, for example, gas installers and retailers who assemble the final product, who would more usually be described as suppliers or distributors.[45] The term 'professional' has been said by the DTI merely to mean 'a person carrying on a commercial activity'.[46] Professionals in the supply chain whose activities do not affect the safety properties of a product are classed as distributors rather than producers. As explained below, they are placed under a different set of obligations.

What is a product?

The Directive does not contain a comprehensive definition of the term 'product', something which had been included in the first draft of the Directive, but was not included in the final version. Article 2(a) of the Directive states, with some circularity, that 'product' shall mean 'any product intended for consumers or likely to be used by consumers, supplied whether for consideration or not in the course of a commercial activity and whether new, used or reconditioned'. The decision was taken that only 'consumer products' in the broad sense should be subject to the Directive. As a result, products intended for consumers will fall under the Regulations, as one might expect, as will products which are likely to be used by consumers. The first test is subjective and depends upon the intent of the producer, but the latter is objective, and therefore wider. It is also clear that products which were originally intended and expected only to be used in the course of a commercial activity, but which have 'migrated' from the professional sector to the general consumer market, are covered by the Regulations.[47] Unfortunately, neither the Regulations nor the Directive provides a comprehensive definition of 'consumer'. Instead, regulation 2(1) states, again with some circularity, that 'consumer' means any consumer acting otherwise than in the course of a commercial activity. Although regulation 2(1) repeats the definition from the Directive, it

---

[45] See G. G. Howells, 'The General Duty to Market Safe Products in United Kingdom Law' [1994] LMCLQ 479 at p. 481.
[46] The General Product Safety Regulations: Guidance for Business, Consumers and Enforcement Authorities (DTI Guidance Notes), p. 13.
[47] Review and Revision of Directive 92/59/EEC Discussion Paper (available at http://europa.eu.int/comm/dg 24), p. 7. The example given is that of laser pens.

also adds that: 'a product which is used exclusively in the context of a commercial activity even if it is used for or by a consumer shall not be regarded as a product for the purposes of these Regulations provided always and for the avoidance of doubt this exception shall not extend to the supply of such a product to a consumer'. This indicates that certain types of product which clearly could affect the safety of consumers are excluded. The Directive referred to the exclusion of 'production equipment, capital goods and other products used exclusively in the context of a trade or business'. The intention of that provision appears to have been the exclusion of products that form part of the infrastructure of business and which consumers do not encounter. However, it is probably wider than this. Howells suggests, for example, that escalators, ski-lifts, and railway carriages were the types of product intended to be excluded.[48] However, the approach taken by the UK may be wider than that envisaged by the Directive. Examples of products excluded from the Regulations might include a drier in a launderette or an escalator in a shop, even though they are clearly both 'used' by consumers. The concept of a 'product' would benefit from further elaboration. There are some products which appear to be consumer products in the loose sense, but which are likely to be excluded because they are only used in the context of a commercial activity, such as shampoo which is only supplied to hair salons. It has been argued that where smaller consumer products such as the shampoo are used 'in a very individualised manner', they should be included in the Regulations. This may be what was contemplated by the Directive.[49]

Product compliance

The Regulations do not apply to products where there are 'specific provisions in rules of Community law governing all aspects of the safety of a product'. This avoids overlap between the Regulations and any Directives which comprehensively cover safety. They also do not apply to antiques, nor to 'products supplied for repair or reconditioning before use, provided the supplier clearly informs the person to whom he supplies the product to that effect'. Antiques are said by the DTI to be products which are at least 100 years old, or which are of a type that have long gone out of circulation and are therefore unlikely to be used for their original purpose by consumers.[50] Regulation 10(1) provides that where products are only

---

[48] Howells, *Consumer Product Safety*, p. 284.
[49] Howells, 'The General Duty to Market Safe Products in United Kingdom Law' [1994] LMCLQ 479, at 482.
[50] DTI, The General Product Safety Regulations: Guidance for Business, Consumers and Enforcement Authorities, p. 11.

partly covered by a specific directive, or there is no directive, compliance with domestic consumer safety law will lead to a presumption that the product is safe. This contrasts with s.10(3)(b)(i) of the 1987 Act under which there was an automatic defence of compliance with specific UK regulations. Where no domestic laws exist, regulation 10(2) provides that certain matters will be taken into account when assessing the conformity of a product to the general safety requirement. These are: '(i) voluntary national standards of the United Kingdom giving effect to a European standard; or (ii) Community technical specifications; or (iii) if there are no such voluntary standards of the United Kingdom or Community technical specifications – (aa) standards drawn up in the United Kingdom; or (bb) the codes of good practice in respect of health and safety in the product sector concerned; or (cc) the state of the art and technology and the safety which consumers may reasonably expect'. It appears that the list is intended to represent a hierarchy.

When is a product safe?

The Regulations take a similar approach to s.10(2) of the 1987 Act by embracing the concept of optimal safety.[51] It is recognised that increased safety will frequently mean increased costs for industry which, ultimately, will be passed on to consumers in the form of higher prices. In *The Safety of Goods*, the UK Government argued that safety policy must reflect a judgement 'on the degree to which the community as a whole is prepared to pay for additional safety'. It therefore rejected measures which would 'involve major interference with the normal processes of manufacture and trade and so put up unduly the prices consumers have to pay for their products'.[52] Regulation 2(1) states that 'safe product' means 'any product which, under normal or reasonably foreseeable conditions of use, including duration, does not present any risk, or only the minimum risks compatible with the product's use, considered as acceptable and consistent with a high level of protection for the health and safety of persons'.

A product must present the minimum risk compatible with its use if it is to be deemed safe for the purposes of the Regulations. This is similar to a test of reasonable safety in all the circumstances and is an example of a broad mandatory standard. Products are expected to be free

---

[51] Section 10(2) of the 1987 Act provides that consumer goods fail to comply with the general safety requirement if they are not reasonably safe having regard to all the circumstances.

[52] Department of Trade and Industry, *The Safety of Goods*, London, DTI (1984) Cmnd 9302, para. 10.

from unnecessary or unreasonable risk rather than free from any risk. The Regulations seek to achieve the optimal balance between protecting consumers from physical harm, allowing them some choice about levels of safety, and encouraging innovation in the creation of new products. Determining optimal levels of safety is difficult, and it is important to take into account the distributive effects of standards. High safety standards may sometimes have damaging effects for consumers, particularly the least affluent. The welfare losses from not having potentially effective new drugs available has already been noted in the context of prior approval, and strict safety standards may mean that some beneficial products do not enter the market. High safety standards may also raise the price of products, taking them out of the reach of the least affluent consumers. As well as denying the consumer the benefit of the product, this may also have safety implications. For example, consumers may sometimes be put at risk by choosing dangerous substitute products where their first-choice products are prohibitively expensive. To use a simple example, a consumer may stand on a chair or table if stepladders are prohibitively expensive. Nevertheless, the positive distributive effects of safety standards should also be noted. As dangerous products will frequently be associated with low-income markets, mandatory standards may be desirable as a means of eliminating those products.[53] As we have seen, standards also get round the difficulties involved in communicating to consumers the attributes of particular products, and help to tackle the problems posed by externalities.

Regulation 2(1) lists specific factors which are to be taken into account when judging if a product provides reasonable levels of safety. They appear to be sufficiently wide to cover most factors that could affect the risk posed by the product. First, 'characteristics' is expressly stated to cover the composition and packaging of the product, and its instructions for assembly. It has already been noted that information, in the form of warnings and instructions, is an important method by which a product can be made safe. It is important to read this part of regulation 2(1) alongside the information duties in regulation 8(1). Secondly, 'effect on other products' must be considered. As a result, where it is foreseeable that the product in question will be used in conjunction with another product, it must be safe so to use it.[54] This would be so even if the product were misused. Thirdly, regard will be had to the presentation of the

---

[53] See T. Wilhelmsson, 'Consumer Law and Social Justice' in I. Ramsay (ed.), *Consumer Law in the Global Economy: National and International Dimensions* (Aldershot, Dartmouth and Ashgale, 1997), p. 217 at p. 225.

[54] See, for example, *Whirlpool (UK) Ltd* v. *Gloucestershire County Council* (1995) 159 JP 123.

product. This will be closely related to the information that is supplied with the product. Fourthly, consideration will be given to the categories of consumer at serious risk. This demonstrates that distributive matters will have to be considered. There may be groups who are particularly likely to be put at risk by a product, and this must be taken into account when judging if the product is safe. The particular example mentioned by the Regulations is children, but it is clear that other groups such as the blind, elderly, or those with a limited command of English could also be covered. It is clear that the existence of externalities will be an important factor in judging the safety of a product. Where the only person likely to be affected is the buyer, information on the packaging may be sufficient to make the product safe. Where third parties are at risk information is likely to be insufficient, particularly if they fall into one of the classes of consumers at particular risk considered above. Account must be taken of the fact that products may be misused. Many products present a risk if used carelessly, and the Regulations state that products must be safe for 'reasonably foreseeable conditions of use'. A product must therefore present the minimum acceptable risk both when used normally and when used abnormally, but foreseeably.[55]

Information requirements and conduct duties

It has already been emphasised that a product can be made reasonably safe by the provision of adequate information, such as warnings and instructions for use. The Regulations place duties on a producer both to provide information to consumers, and to inform himself of risks in his products. Regulation 8(1) states:

Within the limits of his activity, a producer shall –
(a) provide consumers with the relevant information to enable them to assess the risks inherent in a product throughout the normal or reasonably foreseeable period of its use, where such risks are not immediately obvious without adequate warnings, and to take precautions against those risks; and
(b) adopt measures commensurate with the characteristics of the products which he supplies, to enable him to be informed of the risks which these products might present and to take appropriate action, including, if necessary, withdrawing the product in question from the market to avoid those risks.

---

[55] Note the Scented Erasers (Safety) Order, SI 1984/83.

Regulation 8(2) then indicates the kind of measures envisaged in 8(1), such as marking the products or product batches, sampling, investigating complaints, and keeping distributors informed of monitoring. The rationale behind regulation 8(1)(a) is that consumers should be able to assess risks inherent but not obvious in a product and so take care to avoid being harmed. As inadequate information may mean that a product is unsafe there is a close connection between this provision and regulation 7 which provides that only safe products should be placed on the market. However, unlike regulation 7, there is no specific sanction for failing to comply with regulation 8(1)(a). It appears merely to be evidence that another provision has been breached. It is unclear for how long the duty lasts. If the duty continues after products are in the hands of consumers, then there is an obligation to inform consumers of risks which are discovered post sale. Although this interpretation would be beneficial from the point of view of consumer protection, it can be countered by the argument that Article 100A does not extend to validate any provision which relates to a product after it has left the market.[56]

Sub-paragraph (b) places additional obligations on the supplier to enable him to be informed of his product's risks and to take appropriate action, which may include withdrawal of the product. Regulation 2(2) then identifies what the measures referred to may include, wherever appropriate: marking the products or product batches so that they can be identified; sample testing; investigating complaints and keeping distributors informed of monitoring. There will be a degree of overlap here with the due diligence defence. The measures which the producer has to take to satisfy regulation 8(b) are likely to overlap with those that he must take to satisfy the defence in regulation 14(1). The duties to be informed of risks and to take appropriate action are kept deliberately vague. In relation to the taking of appropriate action, the only example given is that of withdrawing the product from the market. It is a moot point whether this duty extends to the withdrawal of products from consumers. The Consumers' Association argued that this would include products sold to and in the possession of consumers, but this is by no means clear.[57]

Duties on distributors

Regulation 2(1) states that a distributor is 'any professional in the supply chain whose activity does not affect the safety properties of a product', and

---

[56] See C. Hodges, M. Tyler, and H. Abbott, *Product Safety* (London, Sweet and Maxwell, 1996), p. 133.
[57] See Consumers' Association, *Improving Recalls of Unsafe Products* (CA 1993), p. 12.

regulation 9 provides that a distributor is required to 'act with due care' to help ensure compliance with the general safety requirement in regulation 7. Regulation 9(a) states that, in particular, a distributor 'shall not supply products to any person which he knows, or should have presumed, on the basis of the information in his possession and as a professional, are dangerous products', and regulation 9(b) adds that 'within the limits of his activities, a distributor shall participate in monitoring the safety of products placed on the market'.

The definition of distributor is quite narrow, with the result that some people who might be thought of as distributors, such as food stores and retailers who assemble products, will be classed as producers, as their activities affect the safety properties of their products under regulation 2(1). Breach of regulation 9(a) is a criminal offence, the test for liability containing both objective and subjective elements. A distributor will be guilty if he knows that the product is dangerous, or should have so known 'on the basis of the information in his possession and as a professional'. According to the DTI, the word 'professional' in this context refers to: 'the knowledge and expertise which the distributor could reasonably be expected to have available to him, either alone or with others, having regard to the nature of business activity and to other relevant factors (e.g. whether he is required to have specialist education, knowledge or training in order to enter that business)'.[58]

Sub-paragraph (b) requires a distributor to monitor the safety of products, 'within the limit of his activities'. This will be a question of fact for each case, and what is reasonable to expect of a large retailer may be unreasonable for a smaller distributor. It has long been the approach of courts in the UK to expect different standards of different businesses, depending upon the size of the business. This has particularly been so in relation to statutory defences.[59] According to the DTI's Guidance, the phrase 'within the limits of his activities' refers to 'the scale of the distributor's business and the facilities and knowledge available to him'. It is not clear precisely what is expected of different types of distributors, but matters referred to in regulation 8(2) could probably be used as guidelines where appropriate. A major retailer might be expected to sample products and a smaller retailer to investigate complaints. It is a moot point whether distributors are under a duty to monitor products which have already been supplied to consumers. The answer turns on what is meant by the term 'placed on the market'. It could be argued that products in the hands of consumers are no longer on the market,

---

[58] DTI Guidance for Business, p. 13.
[59] See for example, *Garrett* v. *Boots Chemists Ltd*, 16 July 1980 (unreported).

and that therefore there is no duty to monitor these products. Also, it is not clear to whom information must be passed. It is assumed that information should be passed to producers and consumers, but it is unclear whether this should extend to having to inform enforcement officers. The Discussion Paper argues that the duty should be extended to cover this. Perhaps surprisingly, breach of regulation 9(b) is not a criminal offence. The only sanction for failing to comply with this obligation appears to be the inability to use the due diligence defence.

Preparatory acts and offences

Regulation 13 makes it an offence for any producer or distributor to '(a) offer or agree to place on the market any dangerous product or expose or possess any such product for placing on the market; or (b) offer or agree to supply any dangerous product or expose or possess any such product for supply'. This provision appears stricter than regulation 9(a), because there is no need to prove fault. This means that although a distributor can only be convicted of supplying dangerous products where he knows or should have presumed that they were dangerous, there is no such requirement where a producer is charged with the preparatory acts in regulation 13. The reason for this distinction is unclear, but it could make enforcement agencies more likely to prosecute for the latter offences. For example, the small number of prosecutions brought under section 14 of the Trade Descriptions Act 1968 suggests a reluctance on the part of many trading standards officers to prosecute under sections where fault has to be proved. Regulation 12 makes it clear contravention of regulation 7 or 9(a) is an offence.

Defences and bypass procedures

The due diligence defence in regulation 14 is not included in the Directive, and its inclusion follows the UK's tradition in consumer protection statutes. Whether such a provision is compatible with the requirement that Directives are effectively implemented at national level is a moot point, and one on which litigation would be valuable.[60] These defences alleviate the potential harshness of strict criminal liability, and are considered in chapter 4. However, it is helpful to say a few words about the defence here. It applies both to producers who contravene regulations 7 or 13, and distributors who contravene regulations 9(a) or 13. Distributors cannot, however, rely on the defence if they have contravened

---

[60] See Howells and Weatherill, *Consumer Protection Law*, pp. 430–1.

regulation 9(b). This is consistent with the interpretation of due diligence defences in other consumer protection statutes. Reasonable precautions involves setting up a system to ensure that offences are not committed, while due diligence requires the defendant to ensure that the system works properly.[61] A distributor is specifically required to monitor products, pass on information about them, and co-operate to avoid risks, but the requirement only to act within the limits of his activities means that the duties are still relatively flexible, and that it is therefore difficult to take much guidance from decided cases.[62] It has been suggested by Parry that the courts are particularly reluctant to find that a due diligence defence is made out where product safety is concerned.[63] This may contrast with the approach taken in relation to the economic interests of defendants. In *McGuire* v. *Sittingbourne Co-operative Society Ltd*, Lord Widgery CJ warned that unless care is taken 'we may find the administration of... [the Trade Descriptions] Act falling down to the sort of slipshod level at which all a defendant has to do is say in some general terms that the default must have been due to something in the shop, one of the girls or some expression like that, and thereby satisfy the onus cast upon him'.[64]

It is uncertain whether there was any need to apply the due diligence defence to distributors, as the distributor's duty in regulation 9(a) requires proof that he knew or should have presumed that the products were dangerous. A distributor will find it difficult to claim to have taken all reasonable steps and acted with all due diligence when it has been proved that he had the requisite *mens rea* or carelessness. Where action is taken against producers, guidance can be taken from similarly worded defences in other statutes. As with distributors, an effective system must be set up and monitored, and the definition of 'safe product' considered above implies that the system ought to take account of matters which may make a product unsafe, such as packaging, instructions, and effect on other products. Furthermore, the requirements imposed upon producers by regulation 8(b) will provide some guidance as to the steps required to satisfy the defence. Marking of batches and sampling of products are likely to be required in the majority of cases.[65]

Regulation 15(1) provides that where the commission of an offence is due to the act or default of some other person 'in the course of a commercial activity of his', the other person is guilty of an offence. This provision

---

[61] See *Tesco Supermarkets Ltd* v. *Nattrass* [1972] AC 153 at 197.
[62] For what guidance can be gleaned see Cartwright, 'The Regulation of Product Safety', pp. 500–8.
[63] D. Parry, 'Judicial Approaches to Due Diligence' [1995] Crim LR 695.
[64] (1976) 147 JP 306 at p. 310.
[65] See e.g. *Rotherham MBC* v. *Raysun (UK) Ltd* (1988) 153 JP 37.

is similar to that found in s.40(1) of the Consumer Protection Act 1987. In *Warwickshire County Council* v. *Johnson*, Lord Roskill stated that 'the words "in the course of any business of his" must mean any business of which the defendant is either the owner or in which he has a controlling interest'.[66] He thereby concluded that employees such as store managers could not be prosecuted under the bypass provision, and it is assumed that the same approach will be taken in the Regulations. It appears, therefore, that while a corporation can escape liability by identifying an employee who caused the commission of the offence, that employee cannot be prosecuted under the bypass procedure. This has been criticised in relation to the 1987 Act,[67] but there are strong arguments for excluding relatively junior employees as potential defendants. Employees are 'locked in a system where they have to carry out a company's marketing scheme, in the case of junior employees, for low wages in what may be an uncreative environment'. Although it is recognised that employees are seldom prosecuted in practice, it is doubtful that companies should be able to avoid liability by shifting blame onto them.[68]

Sanctions

Enforcement of product safety is dealt with in chapter 4. However, it is worth mentioning a few points here. Regulation 17 provides that a person convicted under regulation 12 (which makes criminal offences of breach of regulations 7 and 9(a)) or 13 (above) shall be liable to up to three months' imprisonment, a fine not exceeding level 5 on the standard scale (currently £5,000 in Great Britain) or both. These sanctions appear sorely inadequate. Where a defendant knows that his products are dangerous, a stiff sentence is essential. The UK courts have said that defendants who dishonestly breach consumer protection statutes can expect custodial sentences,[69] and the need for effective sanctions is particularly great where physical integrity is involved. Research suggests that the public regards breach of product safety law as serious crime.[70] Indeed, it is the lack of an effective sanction that is one of the major weaknesses of the Regulations.

---

[66] [1993] 1 All ER 299, 304. See C. Wells, 'Corporate Liability and Consumer Protection: *Tesco* v *Nattrass* Revisited' (1994) 57 MLR 817.
[67] See e.g. R. J. Bragg, *Trade Descriptions* (Oxford, Clarendon Press, 1991), p. 146.
[68] C. Scott and J. Black, *Cranston's Consumers and the Law* (3rd edn, London, Butterworths, 2000), p. 330. See also P. Cartwright, 'Defendants in Consumer Protection Statutes: A Search for Consistency' (1996) 59 MLR 225.
[69] *Hewitt, The Times*, 21 June 1991
[70] J. Braithwaite, 'Challenging Just Deserts: Punishing White Collar Criminals' (1982) 73 JCLC 723.

The Secretary of State and safety regulations

Section 11(1) of the Consumer Protection Act 1987 provides that the Secretary of State may make the safety regulations that he considers appropriate for a number of purposes, such as to secure that goods are safe and to secure that inappropriate information is not provided in relation to goods. The Act also provides an illustrative list of the types of provisions that regulations might contain, such as the composition of goods, matters relating to their approval and their testing or inspection. Section 12 lists the ways in which an offence is committed by breaching a safety regulation, which include contravening a prohibition on supplying, offering to supply, exposing or possessing for supply goods, and contravening a requirement to provide or not to provide information. The offences in this section are subject to the due diligence defence in s.39(1) of the 1987 Act, and the bypass procedure in s.40(1). Before 1994 goods which complied with specific product safety regulations would automatically be deemed not to breach the general safety requirement in s.10 of the 1987 Act. However, following the 1994 General Product Safety Regulations, if goods comply with safety regulations, there is a rebuttable presumption that they also comply with the 1994 Regulations.

The Secretary of State's duty to make such provision as he considers appropriate is clearly subjective, and so difficult to challenge on the basis of *ultra vires*. Indeed, Lord Mottistone stated that this wording was introduced so that Regulations could not be challenged 'on the basis that they did not secure that the goods were safe'.[71] However, these difficulties are to some extent counterbalanced by the duty under s.11(5) to consult before Regulations are made. The Secretary of State must consult such organisations as appear to him to be representative of interests substantially affected by the proposal, and such other persons as he considers appropriate. Consultation enables interested parties to become involved in the law-making process where they have particular expertise to offer, and it has been argued that there has not been a problem in practice of groups being excluded.[72] Consultation requires 'the communication of a genuine invitation extended with a receptive mind, to give advice'.[73] It is important that this consultation process is taken seriously, as the use of the negative resolution procedure for delegated legislation will mean that there is relatively little scope for parliamentary scrutiny of safety regulations. There is some evidence that

---

[71] HL Debs, vol. 394, col. 474 *per* Lord Mottistone.
[72] See Howells, *Consumer Product Safety*, p. 263.
[73] *Agricultural Horticultural and Forestry Training Board* v. *Aylesbury Mushrooms Ltd* [1972] 1 All ER 280 *per* Donaldson J at 284.

the courts will be willing to challenge the Secretary of State on grounds of inadequate consultation. In *Secretary of State for Health ex p United States Tobacco International Inc*,[74] the applicants sought judicial review of the Secretary of State's power to make the Oral Snuff (Safety) Regulations 1989. The Government's Committee on Carcinogenicity had advised that oral snuff should be banned, and the Secretary of State reacted by making the 1989 Regulations. United States Tobacco successfully challenged the Regulations, arguing that the Secretary of State had failed to consult adequately. The court held that the Secretary of State was required to show a particularly 'high degree of fairness and candour' in his consultation in this case for a number of reasons. First, Taylor LJ said that the applicants had been 'led up the garden path' by the Secretary of State, as he knew that if he accepted the committee's recommendation he would be 'executing a volte-face' which would seriously affect the applicants. Secondly, he emphasised that although the Regulations were of general application, in practice they only affected the applicants as they were the UK's sole manufacturers and packagers of oral snuff. Thirdly, Taylor LJ pointed to the catastrophic effect the Regulations would have on the applicant's business, a business in which the government had encouraged them to invest substantial resources. The Regulations were accordingly quashed. Although the case does not suggest that it is always necessary to reveal the evidence upon which a decision to make regulations is based, this case indicates that the Secretary of State has to go some way to satisfy the duty to consult.

The advantages of consultation are considerable and were mentioned above; however, it will sometimes be necessary to abandon consultation in order to act quickly to protect the public from dangerous products. Section 11(5) of the 1987 Act provides for a power to make emergency safety regulations. The section states that if a safety regulation is to last no more than twelve months, and the Secretary of State believes 'the need to protect the public requires that the regulations should be made without delay', the consultation procedure can be bypassed. The Consumer Safety Act 1978 had contained a similar provision called the prohibition order which allowed the Secretary of State to prohibit the supply of goods without consultation if he believed that the risk of danger was such that the order should come into force without delay. Emergency safety regulations replaced this procedure. Where an emergency safety regulation is made it is envisaged that it will eventually be replaced by a permanent safety regulation. There is no duty to consult once the emergency

[74] [1992] 1 QB 353.

regulation is made, which seems surprising and is difficult to justify. In practice, however, this form of safety regulation is rare. Only one set of regulations was made under this procedure in the period 1993 to 1998.[75]

A useful illustration of the difficulties raised by this type of procedure is provided by the Scented Erasers Safety Order 1984, which was made under the Consumer Safety Act 1978. Following media pressure the Government introduced a prohibition order which banned the supply of scented erasers upon which it was feared that children would choke. The Order was challenged by judicial review in *R* v. *Secretary of State ex parte Ford*, where an importer argued that the Order had been made unlawfully.[76] It was shown that there was only a tiny risk of children being injured as a result of swallowing erasers, that the importer stood to lose £270,000 through inability to sell existing stock, and that the wording of the provision was highly vague. Although Woolf J expressed concern, particularly at the lack of clarity of the order, the court was not willing to interfere with the Secretary of State's decision. There was evidence which entitled the Secretary of State to conclude that he should exercise his powers, there was no evidence that he misunderstood the material on which he relied, he did not take into account irrelevant matters in deciding that the consultative process should be bypassed, and the resulting offence was not too uncertain to be upheld by the courts. Although it was pointed out that some items were more likely to lead to choking than erasers, such as nails, screws, and even fruit, there were still good reasons for taking action against the erasers, which are not only rarer than the other items, but of far less social utility. The decision is therefore to be welcomed. Although the emergency safety regulations will not necessarily be approached in the same way as the *Ford* case indicates, it looks as though it will be relatively difficult to challenge an emergency regulation by way of judicial review.

Product safety under other legislation

A number of pieces of legislation now deal with matters relating to consumer product safety. Law has regulated the production and sale of food since the Assize of Bread and Ale Act 1266. The Food Safety Act 1990, which followed the White Paper *Food Safety – Protecting the Consumer*, introduced a number of offences relating to food safety, as well as some which focused upon protecting the economic interests of consumers of food. Section 7(1) created an offence of rendering food injurious to health

---

[75] The Fireworks (Safety) Regulations 1996.
[76] (1984) unreported. Cited and discussed in Ramsay, *Consumer Protection*, p. 482.

by means of specific operations, and with the intent that the food be sold for human consumption. Section 8(1) of the Act creates offences of selling, offering, etc. for sale for human consumption food which fails to comply with food safety requirements. Food fails to comply with food safety requirements if, for example, it is unfit for human consumption or is so contaminated that it would be unreasonable to expect it to be used for human consumption in that state. When the Act was introduced, food had been excluded from the general safety duty of the Consumer Protection Act 1987, largely because of the 'considerable body of existing legislation',[77] and there remain a large number of detailed regulations governing food. However, food is a product for the purposes of the General Product Safety Regulations 1994, and it will be interesting to see the extent to which prosecutions in relation to food are brought under that legislation. The creation of the Food Standards Agency also has important implications for consumer product safety, as the agency now has considerable powers pertaining to the protection of public health. It is not proposed to go into these powers here, and recourse to a specialist text is necessary for the reader wanting an in-depth examination of these provisions. However, it should be noted that the agency was designed to ensure that the interests of food safety were examined separately from those of the food industry, and that it has among its objectives the protection of public health in relation to food and the protection of the wider food standards interests of consumers, such as food labelling.

Other areas where specialist safety legislation exists include medicines and health and safety at work. Medicines are controlled mainly by the Medicines Act 1968 which requires a manufacturer to obtain a licence before a drug can be marketed. The Medicines Control Agency undertakes the procedure of licensing, acting closely with the Committee on the Safety of Medicines and the Medicines Commission. Section 19(1) of the Medicines Act 1968 provides that before a drug is awarded a licence, the authorities must take into account its safety, efficacy, and quality. The Medicines Control Agency also has responsibility for post-licensing supervision of medicines, in recognition that not all characteristics of medicines can be identified prior to authorisation. The efficacy of prior approval as a regulatory technique is examined above and in chapter 2. Health and safety at work are largely governed by the Health and Safety at Work Act 1974. Section 6 of the Act imposes a number of duties on manufacturers, importers, and suppliers of articles and substances for use at work. It is not proposed to examine this here.

---

[77] HL Debs, vol. 485 col. 914 (9 March 1987) *per* Lord Lucas.

Conclusions

The protection of health and safety is one of the most basic and fundamental aims of consumer protection law. The UN Guidelines for Consumer Protection require governments to adopt appropriate measures
to ensure that products are safe, and consumer safety remains a central
feature of many consumer laws. The justifications for intervening in the
market place to ensure that consumers are not injured are considerable.
In terms of economic justifications, information deficits and externalities provide ample justification for intervention. Social justifications, in
particular paternalism, may also justify regulation. The variety of techniques available is also numerous. Prior approval will tend to be reserved
where the consequences of unsafe products reaching the market are particularly great, for example, in the case of pharmaceuticals. Information
remedies will be sufficient in some cases, but the main technique will
be the standard. Specification standards can be justified in limited cases,
but performance and target standards appear to provide the best means
of balancing the interests of consumer safety with the interests of the
producer.

The UK has had general criminal legislation on product safety since
1987. The main difficulties which legislators face is in producing laws
which allow for the free movement of goods, thus complying with international obligations, while ensuring that consumers are adequately protected from dangerous products. These difficulties are clearly illustrated
by the General Product Safety Regulations. This balance has not been
easy to achieve. What can be said about the regime is that it appears to take
an objective, flexible, and rational approach to the question of whether
a product is safe, although there has been a suggestion that deregulation
may have gone too far.[78] The General Product Safety Regulations 1994
provide a framework for removing dangerous products from the market,
while ensuring that safe products can be sold throughout the European
Community. The Regulations provide a broad definition of producer,
and ensure that it is reasonably easy to identify someone within the EU
against whom action can be taken. The definition of product is of more
concern, partly because of its lack of clarity, but also because it appears to
exclude some products which can put consumers at risk. However, until
the scope of the term is clarified it is difficult to say much more here.

The test for whether a product is safe is sufficiently broad to allow
a court to consider all the characteristics of the product when forming
a decision. It is important that the needs of vulnerable consumers are

---

[78] See H. Micklitz, 'Perspectives on a European Directive on the Safety of Technical Consumer Goods' (1986) 23 CMLR 617, and Ogus, *Regulation*, at pp. 203–4.

addressed and the explicit reference to consumers at particular risk is to be welcomed. The inadequate levels of sanctions are, however, a major matter for concern. We have already noted the difficulties faced by consumers in seeking justice through the civil law. Consumers rely upon public regulation to ensure that dangerous products do not reach the market, and this can only be done if a sufficient deterrent is available. No regime is likely to receive the unmitigated praise of consumer groups and producers, but, for all its weaknesses, the present system appears to provide a reasonable balance between the competing interests.

6   The protection of economic interests

Introduction

It was argued in the previous chapter that the criminal law has an important role to play in the protection of a consumer's safety. Indeed, research by Braithwaite suggests that regulatory offences which protect safety are viewed by the public as being as serious as violent crimes.[1] There may be debate about the extent to which producers should be strictly liable, either under the law of tort or the criminal law, but the need to ensure that unsafe products are controlled is generally seen to justify a tough stance from the state. It is more difficult to establish the role that the criminal law should play in the protection of consumers' economic interests, although it should be noted that there will be overlap between safety and economic interests in a number of ways. A victim of a dangerous product may be primarily concerned with the economic loss suffered as a result of missing work or undergoing treatment. Adulterated food will be tackled by the criminal law regardless of whether the adulteration makes it dangerous, or merely different from what the consumer intended. It is also possible to bring an action under a statute aimed at protecting economic interests such as the Trade Descriptions Act 1968 where the product is dangerous.[2]

The importance of economic interests has been recognised at both national and international level. Statutes such as the Trade Descriptions Act 1968 are aimed primarily at removing false or misleading information. Article 129A of the EC Treaty gives the EU a mandate to contribute to a high level of consumer protection through actions which 'support and supplement the policy pursued by the Member States to protect the ... economic interests of consumers and provide adequate information to consumers'. Furthermore, the UN Guidelines for Consumer

---

[1] See J. Braithwaite, 'Challenging Just Deserts: Punishing White Collar Criminals' (1982) 73 JCLC 723.

[2] See for example *Hicks* v. *Sullam* (1983) 147 JP 493.

Protection state that '[g]overnment policies should seek to enable consumers to obtain optimum benefit from their economic resources' and
note that 'the promotion and protection of the economic interests of
consumers' are legitimate needs which the Guidelines are intended to
meet. However, deciding on which economic interests are deserving of
protection, and how they should be protected, is far from easy. It is an
area where the respective boundaries of criminal and civil law are particularly difficult to draw, and one that raises questions about the role
of information and disclosure. Therefore, this topic should be viewed
in close conjunction with the discussion in chapters 1 and 2 of this
book.

The purpose of this chapter is to examine the extent to which the
criminal law is, and should be, used to protect the economic interests
of consumers. It begins by looking at the rationales for protecting the
economic interests of consumers, and then looks briefly at the legal techniques that can be used to achieve their objectives. The chapter then
examines in outline the main statutes which use the criminal law to protect consumers' economic interests: the Trade Descriptions Act 1968,
the Consumer Protection Act 1987, the Food Safety Act 1990 and the
Property Misdescriptions Act 1991. It will be argued that there are three
main ways in which the criminal law could be used to protect consumers' economic interests. The first way is by correcting information
failure. In the UK, the main way in which the criminal law has been
used is by prohibiting the supply of false and misleading information.
Criminal sanctions are less common as a means of ensuring that accurate information is disclosed, but there are examples of it being used
in this way. The second way is by ensuring that consumers' expectations are fulfilled. The law of contract requires that goods sold to consumers be of satisfactory quality and it would be possible to extend the
ambit of criminal sanctions like this, as has been done in the case of
food. The third way in which economic interests could be protected is
through provisions which outlaw unfairness. This could apply both to
unfair procedure, such as high-pressure selling, and unfair substance,
which would involve examining the content of the agreement. It will be
argued that the criminal law should continue to play a major role in
addressing information deficits, and could play a role in ensuring that
expectations are fulfilled. In relation to unfairness, although it would be
possible to utilise the criminal law further, it will be suggested that administrative action, through a reformed version of Part III of the Fair
Trading Act 1973 would be the most appropriate way of tackling unfair
conduct.

Rationales for intervention to protect consumers' economic interests

In chapter 1, the rationales for consumer protection were examined. Under the market-based approach, it was argued that consumer law should be used to correct market failure. In the previous chapter, we saw that the main ways in which markets fail in relation to dangerous products were by information deficits and externalities. To some extent, these rationales also apply where consumers' economic interests are concerned.

Information deficits

Consumers who purchase products frequently do so under conditions of imperfect information. Chapter 1 explains why markets may not provide perfect information. In some cases this will be because of the nature of the product. For example, credence goods such as pensions will tend to be purchased under conditions of uncertainty. However, even for search and experience goods, we may find the market providing inadequate information. First, fly-by-night traders who do not depend on repeat purchasers will be under little incentive to provide consumer satisfaction. Secondly, producers will be unlikely to disclose the poor quality of their wares, and competitors may be reluctant to correct the information deficits caused. Thirdly, information about quality is likely to be treated with scepticism by consumers and so may not be economical to provide. Furthermore, where products and the information supplied with them are complex, bounded rationality means that consumers are likely to find it difficult to act upon that information. This will be so even if the information is accurate and comprehensive. As a result, there may be a role for the law to step in and correct these information deficits.

Externalities

Where product safety is concerned, the risk of externalities is a major justification for intervention. This is not so apparent when dealing with economic interests. The financial loss of one person may cause distress and hardship to those close to the victim, but its impact on third parties will be limited. However, it is possible to justify some measures designed to protect economic interests under this heading. For example, depositor-protection schemes protect a proportion (generally 90 per cent) of a customer's deposit up to a set limit (currently £20,000), in the event of a bank's insolvency. These are frequently seen as consumer protection measures, explicable on the grounds that consumers are unlikely to have adequate information on the risk posed by a financial institution at the time of making a deposit.[3] However, it is also suggested that insolvency may lead to a run on other, perfectly healthy banks with financial contagion (an externality) resulting.[4] Therefore, deposit protection schemes are aimed largely at overcoming externalities, in the form of loss to consumers unconnected with the failure of the original institution.

Paternalism

Another justification for intervening to protect economic interests is paternalism. A number of provisions appear concerned to protect consumers from themselves. In chapter 1 we saw that standards can be described as paternalistic to the extent that they prevent the consumer from dictating the level of safety or quality to which she wishes to be subject. If the law requires goods to be of satisfactory quality then traders will be forced to respond to this with a resulting reduction in consumer choice. The justification can be seen as paternalistic – ensuring that consumers are not put at risk by poor quality products – although it is also possible to explain such provisions on information grounds. For example, we might emphasise how difficult it is for consumers to identify quality.[5] The law in the UK tends not to make it an offence to supply goods of less than satisfactory quality unless there is a false or misleading description. However, the criminal law requires food to be of the quality demanded by the purchaser, and so there is a precedent for the use of the criminal law to ensure product quality. This could perhaps be explained on grounds of paternalism, although it is submitted that it is better to justify such intervention on grounds of information deficits.

It is possible to view some provisions that control the supply of information as paternalistic. For example, where we control advertising which is deemed unfair (rather than misleading or deceptive) we might justify this on the grounds of the risk that consumers will make choices which are not in their best interests. The criminal law has tended to limit itself to false and misleading claims rather than unfair claims, leaving the latter to be controlled by self-regulation. However, this is an area where the criminal law could become increasingly involved. Controls over taste and

---

[3] R. MacDonald, *Deposit Insurance* (London, Bank of England, 1996), p. 6.

[4] J. R. Macey and G. P. Miller, *Banking Law and Regulation* (2nd edn, New York, Aspen, 1997), pp. 22–3.

[5] See G. Akerlof, 'The Market for Lemons: Qualitative Uncertainty and the Market Mechanism' (1970) 84 QJEcon 488.

decency in advertising can also be interpreted as paternalistic, although they are not concerned with economic interests.[6]

Distributive justice

The extent to which the criminal law is concerned with distributive justice is unclear. Provisions which require information to be explained in a certain manner, or which prohibit information which might be misleading to one section of the population, may have a distributive effect. The cost of providing information which benefits only a small section of the community will be likely to be passed on to all purchasers equally. The standard by which we judge information such as advertisements and descriptions is relevant here. It is clear that information will sometimes be unlikely to mislead the average consumer, but more likely to mislead a credulous consumer. If the standard adopted is that of the credulous, rather than the average or reasonable consumer, this could be seen as based on distributive justice. Traders will have to tailor their marketing practices to take account of the risk of misleading the credulous, naïve or poorly educated. Anti-discrimination laws can also be interpreted as consumer laws which protect consumers' economic interests on the grounds of distributive justice.[7] More generally, any provision based upon the concept of inequality of bargaining power could be viewed as distributive as between trader and consumer.

Techniques for protecting economic interests

Prior approval

In the previous chapter we saw how prior approval can be used to protect consumers from dangerous products. It was noted that this tends to be used where the consequences to the consumer of making a wrong choice are particularly severe, and where there is a risk of externalities. Prior approval is also used to protect consumers' economic interests. Under s.21 of the Consumer Credit Act 1974, all proprietors of consumer credit or hire businesses have to be licensed by the Director General of Fair Trading. The Director General will only grant a licence if he is satisfied that the applicant is a fit and proper person to hold the licence. When determining whether to award a licence, the Director General will consider a wide

---

[6] See C. Scott and J. Black, *Cranston's Consumers and the Law* (London, Butterworths, 2000), ch. 2.
[7] See T. Wilhelmsson, 'Consumer Law and Social Justice', in I. Ramsay (ed.), *Consumer Law in the Global Economy* (Aldershot, Dartmouth and Ashgale, 1997), p. 217.

variety of matters, including whether the applicant has engaged in 'practices appearing to the Director to be deceitful or oppressive or otherwise unfair or improper (whether unlawful or not)'. In addition to refusing to grant a licence, the Director General can renew, vary, suspend, or revoke a licence already awarded. The main justification for using prior approval in this context seems be to the extent of harm that a consumer may suffer from entering a contract with an unfit supplier. However, it can also be explained on other grounds, such as the difficulty of obtaining reliable information, and the influence of vested interests in trying to discourage competition.[8]

Standards

Standards are used to protect consumers' economic interests in both civil and criminal law. Where criminal law is concerned, standards generally take the form of broad target standards which require traders not to provide false and misleading information in the course of business. As mentioned above, they may also be used to ensure that consumers receive goods of reasonable quality, although this only appears to be used in the case of food. Where standards are used to ensure fairness, they are generally backed up by administrative controls, rather than by the criminal law. However, as will be argued below, it would be possible to give the criminal law a wider role to play in controlling unfair behaviour.

Information remedies

It is where the economic interests of consumers are concerned that the relationship between information remedies and standards is particularly apparent. Statutes such as the Trade Descriptions Act 1968 are concerned to prohibit false and misleading information. The criminal law has been less prominent in requiring the disclosure of information, although there are examples of disclosure regimes being backed up with criminal sanctions. For example, regulation 5 of the Food Labelling Regulations 1996 provides that food labels must set out, *inter alia*, the food's name, ingredients, minimum durability, storage requirements, instructions for use.[9] Furthermore, non-disclosure may make a statement false or misleading, and where this occurs an offence may be committed.[10] The discussion below of the leading statutes will reveal the difficulties

---

[8] See W. Gelhorn, 'The Abuse of Occupational Licensing' (1976) 44 U Chicago LR 6.
[9] SI 1996/1499.
[10] See for example the Property Misdescriptions Act 1991 s.1(5).

and limitations presented by basing a legislative regime on the prohibition of false and misleading information.

The statutory framework

The Trade Descriptions Act 1968

The first major statute to deal with the protection of the economic interests of consumers was the Trade Descriptions Act 1968, although a degree of protection had been provided by the Merchandise Marks Acts 1887–1953.[11] Sir George Darling, the President of the Board of Trade at the time of the Act's inception, said that its aim was 'to protect consumers, the buyers of goods and services, from swindles, unfair practices, misdescriptions and false claims which are perpetrated by a relatively small minority of traders'.[12] The wording chosen by the Minister might suggest that the Act was targeting those who had been dishonest, but its scope is wider than that.

Section 1 of the 1968 Act deals with traders who make false trade descriptions about goods, or supply or offer to supply goods bearing a false trade description. Section 1(1) states '[a]ny person who, in the course of a trade or business – (a) applies a false trade description to any goods; or (b) supplies or offers to supply any goods to which a false trade description is applied; shall, subject to the provisions of this Act, be guilty of an offence'. Two main classes of defendant are targeted by s.1. First, s.1(1)(a) deals with those who actually apply false trade descriptions to goods. The word 'applies' is to be interpreted broadly. Section 4(1) provides that applying includes, for example, affixing or annexing the description to the goods or anything with which they are supplied, as well as using the trade description 'in any manner likely to be taken as referring to the goods'. Section 4(2) makes it clear that an oral statement can be an application, something which had not been recommended by the Molony Committee.[13] Section 4(3) provides that 'where goods are supplied in pursuance to a request in which a false trade description is used and the circumstances are such as to make it reasonable to infer that the goods are supplied as goods corresponding to that trade description, the person supplying the goods shall be deemed to have applied that trade description to the goods'. This means that where a buyer orders goods and specifies certain requirements when he does so, an offence may be

---

[11] For a detailed discussion of those Acts see the Report of the Committee on Consumer Protection (hereafter the Molony Committee) (1962), Cmnd 1781, paras. 573–720.
[12] HL Debs, 22 February 1968, col. 675.
[13] 1962 Cmnd 1781, para. 155.

committed if the goods do not meet these requirements when they are subsequently supplied. This applies provided that it is reasonable to infer that the goods corresponded to that description.[14]

In s.1(1)(b) 'supplying' is given a broad meaning. In most cases, the supply will be a sale, but the term will also include hiring and, presumably, free samples, as there appears to be no requirement that the supply is for consideration. 'Offering to supply' extends beyond the contractual meaning of offer. For example, it includes displaying goods in shop windows, advertising them in newspapers, and having them in possession for supply.[15] This is important as enforcement authorities need to be able to take action at an early stage, preferably before a consumer is misled.[16] Here, there was once a suggestion that carelessness might have been a requirement of the sub-section, but this was later shown not to be the case.[17]

The term 'goods' is said under s.39(1) to include 'ships and aircraft, things attached to land and growing crops', but this list is not exhaustive. Despite attempts to argue that real property is included, the majority view appears to be that buildings are not goods.[18] Misdescriptions of property are now covered by the Property Misdescriptions Act 1991. This is examined below.

A trade description is defined in s.2(1) as 'an indication, direct or indirect, and by whatever means given, of any of the following matters with respect to any goods or part of goods . . .' The matters then listed include: quantity size or gauge; method of manufacture, production, process, or reconditioning; fitness for purpose, strength, performance, behaviour, or accuracy; and any physical characteristics not included in the preceding paragraphs, to name but a few. The list includes most matters which could induce a sale. The trade description must be 'false', but as we will see later, this has been interpreted broadly, and includes descriptions that are misleading.

Section 14(1) of the Act deals with false statements about services. It states that '[i]t shall be an offence for any person in the course of any trade or business: (a) to make a statement which he knows to be false; or (b) recklessly to make a statement which is false; as to any of the following matters . . .' In contrast to s.1, s.14 includes a requirement of

[14] *Shropshire CC* v. *Simon Dudley Ltd* (1997) 16 *Trading Law Reports* 69.
[15] *Stainthorpe* v. *Bailey* [1980] RTR 7.
[16] It is clear that there is no need for a consumer to have been misled. See *Chidwick* v. *Beer* [1974] RTR 415.
[17] *Southwood* [1987] 1 WLR 1361.
[18] See G. Stephenson, 'Estate Agents and Trade Descriptions' [1980] *Conveyancer* 249.

mens rea. The main reason for this was the novelty of the provisions. As the then President of the Board of Trade stated: '[i]n one way or another, misdescription of goods has been in the statute books for a long time, but to apply the same laws to services is a legal innovation. Because of this, an offence in regard to services will be committed only where a false statement is made knowingly or recklessly.'[19]

The requirement of proving *mens rea* in s.14(1) has caused some difficulty for the courts. The Act provides a partial definition of recklessness in s.14(2)(b). This states that 'a statement made regardless of whether it is true or false shall be deemed to be made recklessly, whether or not the person making it had reasons for believing that it might be false'. Case law demonstrates that there is a duty upon the defendant to consider whether her statement is true or false. *MFI Warehouses Ltd* v. *Nattrass* stated that the Act imposes on defendants 'a duty to give active consideration to whether their statements were true or false'.[20] If this was not done, the prosecution could contend that the statement was made recklessly.[21] There is no need to show that the defendant closed his eyes to the truth or was dishonest. There is very little case law on the meaning of knowledge, and it is unclear how far the meaning of the term extends.[22]

The subject matter of s.14 has produced some difficult cases. In *Newell and Taylor* v. *Hicks,* Goff LJ held that 'services in this context should be regarded as doing something for somebody' whereas 'a facility is providing someone with the wherewithal to do something for himself'.[23] For example, a tennis lesson would be a service, and a tennis court a facility. One difficult case is *Ashley* v. *London Borough of Sutton*[24] where the appellant advertised a book which was a guide to profiting on betting. The advertisement guaranteed to refund the purchase price to customers, a guarantee which was not honoured. The Divisional Court was asked whether a guarantee to refund the purchase price of a book was a statement as the provision of services. The Court, rather surprisingly, asked itself whether the book itself was a service, and concluded, even more surprisingly, that it was. Scott-Baker J justified this decision by saying that the customer wanted the information in the book rather than the book itself. Other cases have found that a promise to refund the difference if goods are purchased cheaper elsewhere was not a statement about services, but that to state wrongly that goods are available 'carriage free' is an offence under s.14. It is suggested that some of these cases are not easy to

---

[19] 759 HC Debs, col. 683.   [20] [1973] 1 WLR 307 at p. 312.
[21] Ibid.   [22] See *Yugotours* v. *Wadsley* [1988] BTLC 300.
[23] [1984] RTR 135 at 148.   [24] (1995) 15 *Trading Law* 350.

reconcile. Indeed, it is difficult to see how the *Ashley* case, in particular, can be defended.[25]

The other main difficulty caused by s.14 is the relationship between the *mens rea* and *actus reus* elements. Two issues have troubled the courts. The first is whether a person is said to make a statement which he knows to be false when the statement relates to something to be done in the future.[26] This is discussed below in the context of whether a statement about the future can be false or misleading. The second issue is whether a defendant is guilty where a statement is made on a person's behalf in the course of business, and its content is false to the knowledge of that person, but the person believes he has corrected the information. This was the issue in *Wings Ltd* v. *Ellis*, where a tour operator tried, but failed, to correct false information in a brochure, and a consumer read an uncorrected brochure.[27] The House of Lords held that the offence was established. The statement was made when the complainant read the brochure, and at that time Wings knew it to be false. This decision has not escaped criticism.[28] Although the decision appears to follow the literal meaning of the words in s.14(1)(a), it means that the offence is to be understood as imposing semi-strict liability, something which may not have been intended by Parliament.

Enforcement authorities have sometimes gone to considerable lengths to avoid the requirement of establishing *mens rea*. In *Formula One Autocentres* v. *Birmingham City Council*[29] the Divisional Court decided that a trader who carries out a service on a car where that service does not comply with a prior description can be convicted of supplying goods to which a false trade description is applied under s.1(1)(b) of the 1968 Act when he returns that car to its owner. The natural provision under which to bring a prosecution was s.14, but the enforcement authority tried to bring the case under s.1 in order to avoid the *mens rea* requirement. The Divisional Court's decision is questionable, and blurs the distinction between ss.1 and 14.[30]

The case law under the Act reveals some odd discrepancies between s.1 and s.14. *Wings* v. *Ellis* holds that a defendant can be guilty of an offence under s.14 even if he does not know a statement is being made, provided that he knows that the information in it is false. By contrast, *Cottee* v.

---

[25] See P. Cartwright, 'A Service Fault in the Divisional Court' [1996] JBL 58.

[26] Compare *Beckett* v. *Cohen* [1972] 1 WLR 1593 with *British Airways Board Ltd* v. *Taylor* [1976] 1 WLR 13.

[27] [1985] AC 272.

[28] G. Stephenson, 'Unknowingly Making a Knowingly False Statement' (1985) 125 NLJ 160.

[29] (1999) 163 JP 234.

[30] P. Cartwright, 'Servicing and Supplying: A Judicial Muddle' [2000] Crim LR 356.

Douglas Seaton (Used Cars) Ltd holds that it is a prerequisite for an offence under s.1 that the defendant knows that a description is applied to goods, even if he does not know the description to be false.[31] Similar discrepancies are found in relation to post-contractual statements. In *Breed* v. *Cluett* it was said to be an offence under s.14 for a builder to describe a bungalow as having a guarantee when it did not, even though the statement was made after exchange of contracts.[32] By contrast, in *Wickens Motors (Gloucester) Ltd* v. *Hall* it was not an offence under s.1(1)(a) wrongly to describe a car as having nothing wrong with its steering as the description was applied after the car had been sold.[33] These discrepancies are difficult to justify in principle.

The 1968 Act endeavours to ensure that only those who are at fault are liable to be convicted by including a due diligence defence in section 24. This enables defendants to escape liability where they have taken all reasonable precautions and exercised all due diligence to avoid the commission of the offence. Section 23 is also important in that it contains a bypass procedure which enables action to be taken against anyone who has caused an offence to be committed by their act or default. These types of provisions were considered in some detail in chapter 3.

The Consumer Protection Act 1987

Part III of the Consumer Protection Act 1987 replaced s.11 of the Trade Descriptions Act 1968, and the Price Marking (Bargain Offers) Order 1979, and now contains the law on misleading price indications. The main offence is contained in s.20(1) which states that 'a person shall be guilty of an offence if, in the course of any business of his, he gives (by any means whatever) to any consumers an indication which is misleading as to the price at which any goods, services, accommodation or facilities are available'. There is also an offence in s.20(2) where a price indication 'has become misleading'. The latter offence concerns where a price indication is given which is accurate initially, but something happens subsequently which makes the original indication false. It will only be an offence where '(b) some or all of those consumers might reasonably be expected to rely on the indication at a time after it has become misleading; and (c) [the defendant] fails to take all such steps as are reasonable to prevent those consumers from relying on the indication'. It has been suggested that this offence is most likely to occur where brochures are

---

[31] [1972] 1 WLR 1408.   [32] [1970] 2 QB 459.   [33] [1972] 1 WLR 1418.

printed with a long life expectancy, but prices are likely to increase.[34] The 1987 Act is wider than the previous legislation on pricing in dealing with services, facilities, and accommodation as well as goods. The Act therefore includes the pricing of credit, banking services, and holidays. It also includes new housing offered in the course of business, but not second-hand housing. The latter is now covered by the Property Misdescriptions Act 1991.

The essence of the s.20(1) offence is giving a misleading price indication. In relation to the meaning of price indication it is helpful to look at *Toys R Us* v. *Gloucestershire CC*.[35] Here, the Divisional Court held that where one price is indicated on a label, but another is displayed at a till, the commission of an offence will depend upon which price the defendant intended the consumer to be charged. In that case the company policy was to charge the lower price, and staff were instructed to check that this happened. Section 21(1) sets out when an indication can be described as misleading and s.21(2) explains when a method of determining price is misleading. It is not proposed to examine these in detail here. Problems raised by false and misleading indications are considered below.

When re-formulating the laws on pricing, the Government decided to follow the recommendation of the Inter-Departmental Working Party and introduce a statutory code of practice. Section 25(1) of the 1987 Act empowers the Secretary of State to approve a code of practice for the purpose of:

(a) giving practical guidance with respect to any of the requirements of section 20 . . . and (b) promoting what appear to the Secretary of State to be desirable practices as to the circumstances and manner in which any person gives an indication as to the price at which any goods, services, accommodation or facilities are available or indicates any other matter in respect of which any such indication may be misleading.

In pursuance to s.25 the Secretary of State approved the Code of Practice for Traders on Price Indications.[36] Contravention of the code is not automatically an offence. Rather, evidence of contravention of or compliance with the code may be relied on as evidence that an offence has, or has not, been committed.

Two matters pertaining to the ambit of the Act are worthy of comment at this stage. First, for the price indication to constitute an offence it must

---

[34] C. J. Miller, B. W. Harvey, and D. L. Parry, *Consumer and Trading Law: Text, Cases and Materials* (Oxford, Oxford University Press, 1998), p. 694.

[35] (1994) 13 *Trading Law* 276.

[36] It was made by the Consumer Protection (Code of Practice for Traders on Price Indications) Approval Order 1988 (SI 1988/2078).

be made by the defendant 'in the course of any business of his'. The case of *Warwickshire County Council* v. *Johnson*[37] held that this means 'any business of which the defendant is either the owner or in which he has a controlling interest'. This means that in cases under s.20, the defendant will either have to be the corporation itself, or someone very senior in it, presumably someone who constitutes its directing mind and will. It was argued in chapter 4 that it is important to ensure that junior employees are not convicted of consumer protection offences for a variety of reasons. However, the existence of a due diligence defence in s.39 means that a corporation will be able to escape liability under the Act by blaming an employee, safe in the knowledge that the employee will not be prosecuted. This is likely to make the prosecution's task difficult.

The second issue which should be noted is that the price indication is only misleading if it is given 'to consumers'. There is no need for a consumer to have been misled, and indications given to trading standards officers, for example, will be covered.[38] However, it is clear that business-to-business transactions which involve a misleading price indication will be outside the Act. The meaning of 'consumer' was considered at some length in chapter 1, and it is not proposed to revisit that here. What is interesting to note is the contrast between the 1987 Act and the Trade Descriptions Act 1968 which does cover false trade descriptions given by one business to another. On balance, it is submitted that statutes aimed at protecting consumers should be limited to consumers. Where the only indication is given to another business, and there is no prospect of consumers being misled, the matter should be dealt with through the civil law or, if sufficiently serious, the criminal law. Allowing businesses to take advantage of consumer protection law leads to litigation of the type criticised in *Simon Dudley* v. *Shropshire CC*, considered below.[39]

The Food Safety Act 1990

The Food Safety Act 1990, like the Property Misdescriptions Act 1991, was a speedy response to public concern. It was passed in a climate of fear, and even panic, following scares about salmonella, listeria, and BSE, to name but three. Despite its slightly misleading title, it is concerned with more than just food safety. The Act was also designed to protect the economic interests of consumers.

---

[37] [1993] AC 583.   [38] *Toys R Us* v. *Gloucestershire CC*.   [39] (1997) 16 Tr LR 69.

The two main offences which deal with economic interests are contained in s.14 and s.15 of the Act. Section 14(1) states that '[a]ny person who sells to the purchaser's prejudice any food which is not of the nature or substance or quality demanded by the purchaser shall be guilty of an offence'. Section 15 makes it an offence to falsely describe, advertise, or present food. There is clearly overlap between the 1990 Act and the Trade Descriptions Act 1968, and many offences under the former will also be offences under the latter. The 1990 Act, although much narrower in terms of subject matter, is wider in terms of the kinds of misdescriptions which will give rise to criminal liability. In relation to subject matter, s.1 of the Act states that food includes drink, articles of no nutritional value, chewing gum, and articles and substances used as ingredients in the preparation of food, but generally excludes live animals and birds, animal fodder, and medicines. In relation to the kinds of misdescriptions which will give rise to liability, the Act provides that it is an offence to sell to the purchaser's prejudice food that is not of the nature, substance, or quality demanded by the purchaser. The term 'nature' is wide. Food will not be of the nature demanded if it is different from that which was ordered, the test being based on what the ordinary consumer would expect. For example, it was held to be an offence to supply toffee containing coconut fat when butter toffee was ordered, as the ordinary consumer would expect butter toffee to contain no fat except butter.[40] Food will not be of the substance demanded if it fails to comply with minimum regulatory standards,[41] contains a foreign body to which the consumer may reasonably object,[42] or fails to comply with a generic definition given to a particular type of food.[43] It is in relation to quality that the most stark contrast between the 1990 Act and the other statutes is revealed. Under s.4(3) of the 1968 Act an offence will be committed where a trader supplies goods which fail to comply with a prior description applied by the consumer. The 1990 Act seems to go further. The courts will consider the quality that an ordinary consumer would expect to receive, even if there cannot be said to be any false description. The test appears to be very similar to that of satisfactory quality under the Sale of Goods Act 1979.[44] This is considered further below.

The sale must be to the customer's prejudice. This does not mean that the consumer needs to have suffered any form of injury, and the

---

[40] *Riley Brothers (Halifax) Ltd* v. *Hallimond* (1927) 44 Tr LR 238.
[41] *Tonkin* v. *Victor Value Ltd* [1962] 1 All ER 821. But see *Few* v. *Robinson* [1921] 3 KB 504.
[42] *Hall* v. *Owen Jones* [1967] 3 All ER 209.
[43] *Anderson* v. *Britcher* (1914) 110 LT 335.
[44] G. Howells, R. Bradgate, and M. Griffiths, *Blackstones Guide to the Food Safety Act 1990* (London, Blackstone Press, 1990), p. 38.

requirement seems to be interpreted broadly. It will be enough if the customer merely receives something different from that which she was expecting. For example, in *McDonald's Hamburgers* v. *Windle*, an offence was committed when a customer ordered diet cola, but received regular cola.[45]

Section 15 contains a number of offences of falsely describing, advertising, or presenting food. Section 15(1) contains the offences of selling, offering, or exposing for sale, or possessing for sale, food with a label which is either false or likely to mislead as to the food's nature, substance, or quality. Section 15(2) contains the offences of publishing or being party to the publication of an advertisement which falsely describes food or is likely to mislead as to its nature, substance, or quality. Section 15(3) contains the offence of selling, etc. food, the presentation of which is likely to mislead as to its nature, substance, or quality. It is not proposed to examine these offences in any detail, but a few points should be noted. First, whether the description is false or likely to mislead is judged on the basis of how the ordinary consumer would understand the description. Therefore, descriptions commonly used in the food industry may still be false or likely to mislead if the ordinary consumer would be misled.[46] Secondly, the offence in s.15(3) allows the court to convict those who present food in such a way that it is likely to mislead. This might allow a conviction in a case where there has been no false description as such, but the food has a misleading appearance. This approach obviates some difficulties found in statutes such as the 1968 Act where it is difficult to find a false description.[47]

The Property Misdescriptions Act 1991

The Property Misdescriptions Act 1991, described at the time of its inception as 'draconian',[48] was seen from the outset as a powerful weapon against the malpractices of two much-reviled business groups, estate agents and property developers. The Act prohibits the making of a false or misleading statement about prescribed matters in the course of an estate agency business or a property development business. It arose partly as a result of political expediency, and partly as a result of the uncertainty surrounding the scope of other consumer protection statutes. In particular, it was unclear whether or not the Trade Descriptions Act's provisions were wide enough to deal with misdescriptions of real property. Although

---

[45] [1987] Crim LR 200.   [46] *Amos* v. *Britvic* (1985) 149 JP 13.
[47] See *R* v. *AF Pears Ltd* (1982) 90 ITSA MR 142.
[48] *The Independent*, 3 April 1993.

s.14 of the Act refers to 'accommodation', the general view was that this did not include real property.[49] It was also generally accepted that although the definition of goods in the 1968 Act included 'things attached to land', this was not sufficiently wide to cover property misdescriptions. The Methven Committee[50] saw this as a matter for concern, and suggested that the Act be reformed to include property. Instead of amending the Act, the Government decided to create a new statute to deal with the perceived problem, and the Property Misdescriptions Act 1991 was the result.

Section 1(1) of the Act states that '[w]here a false or misleading statement about a prescribed matter is made in the course of an estate agency business or a property development business, otherwise than in providing conveyancing services, the person by whom the business is carried on shall be guilty of an offence under this section'. The Act is not of general application, and only applies where a false or misleading statement about a prescribed matter is made 'in the course of an estate agency business or a property development business, otherwise than in providing conveyancing services'.[51] This means that private sales are excluded, and also offers some protection to solicitors and licensed conveyancers. However, builders of new houses are covered by the Act, as are those who renovate houses that they intend to sell.

The Act takes an unusual approach to the prosecution of employees. It provides that where the offending statement is made, 'the person by whom the business is carried on' shall be guilty of an offence. This is a rare example of explicit vicarious liability, and as such is to be welcomed. However, the bypass procedure in s.1(2) states that 'where the making of the statement is due to the act or default of an employee the employee shall be guilty of an offence under this section'. This means that where the employee is at fault he can be prosecuted for causing his employer to commit an offence. It contrasts particularly sharply with s.40(1) of the 1987 Act, under which employees specifically cannot be prosecuted. The Act contains a due diligence defence in s.2(1), which makes it a defence for the defendant to show that he took all reasonable steps and exercised all due diligence to avoid the commission of the offence. Where the defendant relies on the act or default of another person in trying to establish the defence, regard will be had: '(a) to the steps he took, and those which might reasonably have been taken, for the purpose of verifying the information; and (b) to whether he had any reason to disbelieve

[49] See Stephenson, 'Estate Agents and Trade Descriptions' for an argument that the Act could be interpreted broadly.
[50] (1976) Cmnd 6628.
[51] For the meaning of 'estate agency business' see s.1 of the Estate Agents Act 1979.

the information'. In the context of estate agency, this aspect of the defence is interesting, because statements made by vendors are extremely likely to be over-enthusiastic. It is noticeable that many estate agents now make it clear whether or not they have checked matters such as whether appliances work, and are more explicit in their presentation of room dimensions.

The conceptual framework

When examining the extent to which the criminal law should be used to protect consumers' economic interests, it is important to consider how the law is used, and how it could be used. It is suggested that there are four main ways in which the criminal law can protect economic interests: first, by prohibiting the supply of false and misleading information; secondly, by requiring the disclosure of accurate and helpful information; thirdly, by protecting consumers' expectations; and fourthly, by providing a duty to trade fairly. Although these are conceptually distinct, there will be a degree of overlap. For example, the failure to disclose vital information might make a transaction unfair. At present, the law in this area is a mixture of statutory controls, common law, and self-regulation. It will be argued that it would be possible for criminal sanctions to play a greater role in the protection of economic interests and that this would be of benefit to consumer and honest trader alike.

Prohibiting the supply of false and misleading information

Perhaps the main way in which consumer law protects consumers' economic interests is by prohibiting the supply of false and misleading information. Where a claim is false, there is no benefit to anyone except the errant trader who makes it. False claims distort the market, and where a market is filled with such claims, consumers may lose confidence in all traders within that market.[52] In addition, false claims are widely viewed as immoral and so prohibition can be justified on such grounds. False information can also be damaging from a social perspective, as false information is likely to be more damaging to the most vulnerable classes of consumer. Misleading claims raise more difficulties, as they may sometimes be only misleading to certain groups of consumers. We have to consider the extent to which the law should protect the credulous and the ignorant as well as the sophisticated and the informed. It may be

---

[52] See I. Ramsay, 'Framework for Regulation of the Consumer Marketplace' (1985) 8 JCP 353 at p. 361.

unfeasible, and undesirable, to insist on 'truth at all costs' as the flow of market information will be restricted unnecessarily.[53] However, if the law is to address issues of distributive justice, and is to ensure that the most vulnerable consumers are informed in the marketplace, it needs to look closely at how misleading statements are judged.

All the statutes mentioned above have the control of false and misleading information as one of their prime aims. The *actus reus* of these offences is very similar, and it is submitted that there is no material difference between applying descriptions, giving indications, and making statements, all of which have wide meanings. In *Doble* v. *David Greig* Melford Stevenson J said 'the choice of the word "indication" as distinct from such word as representation plainly shows that... [the Trade Descriptions Act] with which we are here concerned is extended over conduct or signs of many different kinds and its width and significance... cannot be too widely and clearly recognised'.[54] It is submitted that 'descriptions' and 'statements' are to be similarly widely interpreted. There also seems little difference between applying, making, and giving. It is central to these offences that the information which gives rise to the offences is either false or misleading. This has caused some difficulty for the courts, revealing problems of statutory interpretation and policy.

False to a material degree. Section 3(1) of the Trade Descriptions Act 1968 provides that a description must be false 'to a material degree' if it is to give rise to an offence under s.1 of the Act. Similar wording is used in other statutes, such as s.1(5) of the Property Misdescriptions Act 1991. It has long been recognised that the law's emphasis upon prohibiting falsity has its limitations. Goffman commented that 'communication techniques such as innuendo, strategic ambiguity and crucial omissions allow the misinformer to profit from lies without, technically, telling any'.[55] This demonstrates the difficulty in separating true descriptions from false descriptions, something that is addressed to some extent by the provision for misleading descriptions.

The word 'material' has been said to relate to the degree of deception involved.[56] Under the Merchandise Marks Acts, it appears that this meant that the false description had to be capable of inducing a purchase,[57] and the Molony Committee stated that the description which could not 'fairly

---

[53] Ibid.   [54] [1970] 1 WLR 703.
[55] E. Goffman, *The Presentation of Self in Everyday Life* (Harmondsworth, Penguin, 1969), p. 69. Cited in I. Ramsay, *Consumer Protection: Text, Cases and Materials* (London, Weidenfeld and Nicolson, 1990) at p. 374.
[56] See Richard J. Bragg, *Trade Descriptions* (Oxford, Clarendon Press, 1991), p. 44.
[57] Ibid.

be regarded as capable of inducing a purchase' would be 'mere puff' and so not caught by the Act.[58] However, it is clear that the statement need not in fact induce a purchase, as post-contractual statements will in some cases be covered.[59] Furthermore, there is no requirement that the purchaser is in fact deceived.[60] It has been argued that the phrase is a way of disregarding trivial inaccuracies, and the court clearly has some flexibility when using the concept.[61] Under the Property Misdescriptions Act 1991, the requirement that false statements must be false to a material degree was included 'to ensure that trivial errors or discrepancies in descriptions will not constitute an offence'.[62] It is, nevertheless, difficult to know when offences are committed. A number of particularly difficult issues are examined below.

Material falsity, opinions, and subjectivity. One major difficulty is in deciding whether something which appears to be a statement of opinion can be false. In *Robertson* v. *Dicicco*[63] a Ford Anglia was described in an advertisement as being a 'beautiful car'. Indeed, the purchaser found the car to be 'pleasing to the eye', and so bought it. The car turned out to be so seriously corroded internally that it was unroadworthy. The Divisional Court found that the justices had erred in law when they decided that it was not a false trade description to describe the car as being beautiful. Lord Widgery said: 'in the ordinary use of such an adjective as "beautiful", when applied to a motor car, it is at least likely that the person hearing that description of the car will think that it is intended to refer not only to the outside appearance, but also to the quality of its running and matters of that kind'.[64] As a result of this approach, the Divisional Court decided that a description such as 'beautiful' would be 'likely to be taken as an indication' that the car runs beautifully, and so would be a false trade description as to performance. Melford Stevenson J said that

---

[58] (1962) Cmnd 1781.
[59] Also, of course, there may be an offence where a product is merely advertised for sale and no sale takes place. This is clear by the inclusion of the offence of offering for sale in s.1(1)(b).
[60] See *Heywood* v. *Whitehead* (1897) 76 LT 781. Otherwise, a purchase by a trading standards officer would not be covered. Note also *Chidwick* v. *Beer* [1974] RTR 415 *per* McKenna J.
[61] Contrast *Harrison* v. *Freemaster* (1972) 80 MR 75 with *Goldup* v. *John Manson Ltd* [1982] QB 161. The cases are discussed in Bragg, *Trade Descriptions*, pp. 42–3.
[62] 'The Property Misdescriptions Act 1991' (DTI Guidance Note). It has, however, been noted that consumers can be put to great expense by visiting houses, sometimes on the strength of what appears to be a minor misdescription. See D. Oughton, 'The Property Misdescriptions Act 1991' [1992] *Professional Negligence* 59 at p. 62.
[63] [1972] RTR 431.
[64] Ibid.

he based his decision on the meaning of 'misleading' in s.3(2), which is considered below. There appear to be two ways of viewing the decision. The first is to say that the use of the word beautiful is false because it is likely to be taken as an indication of the performance of the vehicle, a matter which is covered by s.2(1)(d). The second is to say that the word is false because it is misleading under s.3(2). Whichever is so, it constitutes an offence under the Act. A further authority which indicates that statements of opinion can constitute offences under s.1 is *Holloway v. Cross*.[65] Here, a car dealer was asked what he estimated the mileage of a car he was selling to be. He suggested 45,000 miles. It later turned out that the correct mileage was 73,000 miles. The Divisional Court decided that the dealer had applied a false trade description to the car. Donaldson LJ suggested that it was probably a false trade description within s.2(1), but even if it was not, it was 'likely to be taken by the purchaser as an indication of the history of the car'.[66] There were reasons to suggest that the estimation of mileage was to be taken seriously. For one thing, D gave P a warranty which only applied to cars which had done less than 60,000 miles. But this may indicate no more than that D honestly believed the mileage to be less than 60,000.

As well as indicating that statements of opinion are covered by the Act, *Robertson v. Dicicco* suggests that vague and apparently subjective concepts like beauty can be false to a material degree and fall foul of the criminal law. By contrast, there is the case of *Cadbury Ltd v. Halliday*.[67] Here some chocolate bars were advertised for sale as being 'extra value'. They were offered for sale at the same time as some virtually identical bars which offered more chocolate for less money. The Divisional Court quashed the convictions. Ashworth J said that the words 'extra value' could not be an indication of any of the matters in s.2, which, he thought, 'were all matters in respect of which truth or falsity can be established as a matter of fact'.[68] Lord Widgery CJ stated that the words 'extra value' could not be an indication of quantity 'when the wrapper also contained a specific and correct statement of what the quantity was'.[69]

It appears difficult to reconcile the cases of *Robertson v. Dicicco* and *Cadbury v. Halliday*. The solution may be to say that beauty can be objectively determined in a way that value cannot. The latter may be 'mere puff', whereas the former conveys a clear message. Other terms which the courts have found to be false for the purposes of the Act include

---

[65] [1981] RTR 146.   [66] Ibid. at p. 151.   [67] [1975] 1 WLR 649.
[68] Except, he conceded, perhaps fitness for purpose.
[69] Page 654 of the case *Cadbury v. Holliday*. This must be treated with some caution at the very least following the decision in *R v. AF Pears* and *Dixons v. Barnett* (below).

'immaculate condition',[70] 'mechanically superb – very good bodywork',[71] 'good little engine',[72] and 'excellent condition throughout'.[73] From this it can be seen that the courts have interpreted the requirement of falsity quite broadly.

Misleading descriptions. It was stated above that misleading descriptions are deemed to be false by s.3(2) of the 1968 Act. This states: '[a] trade description which, though not false, is misleading, that is to say, likely to be taken for such an indication of any of the matters specified in section 2 of this Act as would be false to a material degree, shall be deemed to be false trade description'. This ensures that descriptions which are literally true are deemed false if they are misleading. The Property Misdescriptions Act 1991 also provides that misleading statements will be subject to the Act.[74] In *Dixons Ltd* v. *Barnett*[75], Dixons described a telescope which they were selling as having 455 times magnification. Although this was literally true, its maximum useful magnification was 120 times. The court decided that the description was misleading, as ordinary members of the public would understand the description to mean that the telescope had a useful magnification of 455 times. Similarly, in *R* v. *Inner London Justices ex p Wandsworth LBC*,[76] a car was described as having had one owner, when it had been hired out to several different individuals. This was an offence under the Act, as although strictly true it was misleading. The inclusion of misleading descriptions raises particular difficulties where the statement may be misleading to naïve or credulous consumers. This is considered below.

Things likely to be taken as an indication. A further complication is added by Section 3(3) of the Act. This says: '[a]nything which, though not a trade description, is likely to be taken for an indication of any of those matters and, as such an indication would be false to a material degree, shall be deemed to be a false trade description'. The meaning of Section 3(3) of the Act is not entirely clear, and Bragg argues that there are two main interpretations of the section's aim. The first is that it may be a general section 'adding to s.2 where that section is deficient'. However, where this has occurred, for example in *Holloway* v. *Cross* and *Robertson*

---

[70] *Kensington and Chelsea (Royal) LBC* v *Riley* [1973] RTR 122.
[71] *Furniss* v. *Scott* [1973] RTR 314.
[72] *Fletcher* v. *Sledmore* [1973] Crim LR 195.
[73] *Chidwick* v. *Beer* [1974] RTR 415. These cases are examined in *Butterworths Trading and Consumer Law*, paras. 47.1–47.5.
[74] Section 1(5).   [75] (1989) 8 Tr LR 37.   [76] [1983] RTR 425.

v. *Dicicco*, offences could be established by s.2 alone. Bragg's second interpretation of the section is that it might be aimed at catching goods which are 'self descriptive'. An example is *Cottee* v. *Douglas Seaton*.[77] Here, the seller of a car disguised a defect with filler paste. The work was painted over by a later owner, and then sold on twice. After an accident, the defect came to light. The Divisional Court had to consider the liability of the seller who knew nothing of the defect, nor its covering up. Lord Widgery CJ said that 'an alteration of goods that causes them to tell a lie about themselves may be a false trade description', although on the facts the defendant was not guilty as he was unaware that any description had been applied to the car.

It is difficult to know when repairing goods causes them to tell a lie in the way envisaged by Lord Widgery, and the implications of this approach have not been as significant as might originally have been thought. The case illustrates that a trade description may arise from the way that a product is presented, even if no specific statement has been made about the matter in question.[78] Bragg illustrates the idea that goods may be 'self-descriptive' by saying that 'if, for example, a motor car is displayed, it is self descriptive to the extent that it must be roadworthy'.[79] This is an interesting and potentially far-reaching analysis, the consequences of which could be considerable. There is some support for this approach in the case of *R* v. *AF Pears Ltd*[80] where a jar of face cream appeared to contain more cream than it did. This was held to amount to a false trade description, despite the fact that the weight stated on the jar was correct. There is the difficulty of deciding whether a trade description is applied here,[81] but Bragg obviates this by arguing that there could be said to be an application merely by manufacturing goods or packaging in such a way as to convey a false impression.

It is difficult to know how far this approach can be taken, but it is clear that the courts will treat misleading descriptions seriously. Where a product is presented in such a way as to create a particular expectation on the part of a consumer, they may be able, under s.3, to regard this as a false trade description. The related issue of the extent to which the criminal law should criminalise the sale of unsatisfactory goods is considered below.

Statements false and misleading by omission. A further area of difficulty concerns descriptions which are misleading by what they fail to say.

---

[77] [1972] 1 WLR 1408.
[78] See also s.15(3) of the Food Safety Act 1990.
[79] Bragg, *Trade Descriptions*, p. 48.
[80] (1982) 90 ITSA MR 142.
[81] See G. Woodroffe, 'False Bottoms, Thick Skins' (1982) 79 LSG 62.

This causes problems for the courts, because statutes such as the 1968 Act do not generally require information to be disclosed; they merely require that false and misleading information is not disclosed. However, it is well accepted that a half-truth can be misleading, or even false, by what it fails to say. In *R* v. *Bishirgian*, it was stated that a statement may be false where 'the withholding of that which is not stated makes that which is stated false... such as a non-disclosure as to render the document misleading'.[82] A more recent attempt to tackle this difficult area is found in the Property Misdescriptions Act 1991. Section 1(5) of the Act states that a statement will be misleading if it is not false, but 'what a reasonable person may be expected to infer from it, or from any omission from it, is false'. Similar wording is used in s.21(1) of the Consumer Protection Act 1987. There was concern at the time that the 1991 Act was being debated that there would be liability for failing to supply information, but it is clear that the Act does not impose a duty of positive disclosure.[83] It does recognise, however, that statements can be misleading by what they omit, and many cases where this could arise can be envisaged, although the provision has not yet been tested in the courts. For example, given that a statement may be contained in a photograph, it could be argued that a photograph taken from a particularly flattering angle might fall foul of the Act in appropriate circumstances.

An alternative approach to one of providing a general duty not to give misleading information is to list in detail the circumstances in which a statement will be misleading. Section 21 of the Consumer Protection Act 1987 explains the circumstances in which a price indication will be classified as misleading, and recognises that an indication may be misleading by omission. Interestingly, the Act does not state that it prohibits false price indications, but it is clear that false indications are deemed to be misleading indications. This contrasts with the 1968 Act where misleading indications are deemed to be false.

False statements about the future. Section 14(1) of the 1968 Act makes it an offence for any person in the course of any trade or business: '(a) to make a statement which he knows to be false; or (b) recklessly to make a statement which is false; as to any of the following matters...' It is under this section that the courts have had to consider whether a statement can be said to be false when it relates to matters in the future. The courts have often found difficulty in distinguishing between statements which are false when made, and statements which are merely of future

---

[82] [1936] 1 All ER 586.
[83] See Oughton, 'The Property Misdescriptions Act 1991', p. 62.

intention. In *Beckett* v. *Cohen*, Lord Widgery CJ said that Section 14(1) 'has no application to statements which amount to a promise with regard to the future, and which therefore at the time when they are made cannot have the character of being either true or false'.[84] He continued by saying that 'Parliament never intended nor contemplated for a moment that the Act of 1968 should be used in this way, to make a criminal offence out of what is really a breach of warranty.' On the facts of the case, the decision was probably correct. The respondent promised to build a garage for the complainant which the former said would be completed within ten days and be just like his neighbour's. He achieved neither. However, there was no evidence at the time he made the promise that he was being dishonest, in the sense of realising that this would not be done. Unfortunately, this case gave rise to the impression that statements about services to be provided in the future were not actionable under the Act.[85] The matter was clarified, to some extent, by the case of *British Airways Board* v. *Taylor*.[86] Here, the complainant booked a flight with an airline. He was told orally that he had a definite booking, and this was later confirmed by letter. The complainant was refused a place on the flight as it had been overbooked. The House of Lords decided that an offence was committed under s.14(1)(a) of the 1968 Act as a false statement had been made. Viscount Dilhorne said that the letter was clearly false because 'it clearly implied that they had reserved a seat for him and would keep one reserved for him when it was always their intention, should more passengers arrive for the flight than there was room for, not to carry one or more of those for whom reservations had been made'. He continued, 'it was false because it did not state the qualification to which it was subject, and it was false, in my view, to their knowledge'.[87]

Looked at this way, there is a distinction between a promise as to the future, as in *Beckett* v. *Cohen*, and a false statement of existing fact, as in *BAB* v. *Taylor*. The airline was purporting to guarantee something which it knew it could not guarantee, and it was that which amounted to an offence under the Act. Both would be a breach of contract, but only one a criminal offence. However, the line between them is not as clear as it might at first appear. It would be quite possible, were the facts of *Cohen* to be repeated, for the court to convict. It would not be unreasonable for the court to view the defendant's words as a promise or guarantee that the garage would be completed on time. If he knew at the time he made the statement that

---

[84] [1972] 1 WLR 1593

[85] This was the view of many enforcement officers. See R. Cranston, *Regulating Business* (London, Macmillan, 1979) at p. 118.

[86] [1976] 1 WLR 13.

[87] Ibid.

he could not make that guarantee, if for example he realised that it might well not be completed on time, he could be convicted. Often, a person will make a promise intending to keep the promise, but realising that he might not be able to. The essentially honest but over-optimistic builder may find himself falling foul of the contract/criminal law line more easily than might originally have been thought. What the cases certainly show is that many matters which might be thought to be purely contractual will fall into the realms of the criminal law. This approach also bears similarity to the approach taken in relation to the law of misrepresentation.[88]

Misleading descriptions and credulous consumers. The statutes in question say little of the standard against which consumers' understanding is to be judged. When the court is deciding if a statement or description is misleading, it may find that some people would be misled by it, but that others would not be. It is important to know whether consumers are expected to reach certain standards of credulity. Statements which are only found to be misleading by a tiny minority of consumers will be unlikely to distort the market for the product in question, but there may be equitable or distributive reasons for protecting that minority.[89] Case law provides us with some guidance as to how the issue might be addressed, but is far from definitive.

It has been argued that the appropriate test for the standard to be expected of a consumer is that found in *Burleigh* v. *Van den Berghs and Jurgens Ltd.*[90] Here, it was stated that the description must be likely to mislead 'the average reasonable member of the [shopping] public', and that 'it is not enough that we should be sure that an unusually careless person might be misled ... [or] a person who is dyslexic, short-sighted, or of less than average intelligence'.[91] Under this approach, an objective test is used, with the reasonable consumer providing the standard. The Molony Committee Report stated that one of the aims of the 1968 Act should be to encourage consumers to go 'shopping with their eyes open and their wits reasonably alert'.[92] Similarly, the Consumer Protection Act 1987 implies that an objective test should be used as to whether a price indication is misleading. Section 21(1) states that 'an indication given to any consumers is misleading if what is conveyed by the indication, or what those consumers might reasonably be expected to infer from the

---

[88] '[T]he state of a man's mind is as much a fact as the state of his digestion ... A misrepresentation as to the state of a man's mind is, therefore, a misstatement of fact' (*Edgington* v. *Fitzmaurice* (1885) 29 ChD 459 at p. 483 *per* Bowen LJ).
[89] See Ramsay, 'Framework for Regulation', p. 361.
[90] See Bragg, *Trade Descriptions* at p. 43.
[91] [1987] BTLC 337 p. 339.
[92] Cmnd 1781, para. 813.

indication or any omission from it, includes any of the following . . . ' It then lists a variety of matters. The inclusion of the reasonableness test shows that the courts will consider whether the particular interpretation a consumer might put on an indication is reasonable. However, the use of the expression 'those consumers' suggests that the courts can consider that a particular group of consumers might be more likely to interpret an indication in a particular way than consumers more generally. For example, if a statement was contained in an advertisement for credit targeted particularly at low-income groups, the question could be whether members of that group might be misled. If the advertisement was aimed at the public generally, but certain groups might be misled, it is unclear to what extent this can be considered.

Where a statement is so outrageous, or so obviously 'mere puff', that it is clear to all groups of consumers that it is not to be taken literally, then this is unlikely to fall foul of the law, even though it is not strictly true. A television advertisement which proclaimed that a video recorder was so simple that 'even the cat can use it' would presumably be an example of this. If humour and irony are to be allowed in advertising then traders need to be able to make statements that are not true. Of course, claims which are merely trade puff need not be outrageous: they may merely be vague. Where the statement is so vague as to be lacking in an identifiable meaning then the statement would presumably not amount to an offence.[93] However, the courts have held some apparently vague claims to fall foul of the 1968 Act. This seems reasonable. A claim that a car is 'in good condition' is vague, but some cars are undoubtedly in poor condition. Where such a statement applies to one of those cars an offence should be committed. Where a statement is capable of more than one meaning, only one of which is true, it is submitted that the statement would be capable of being false, provided a reasonable person might attribute that false meaning to it.[94]

Focusing on the reasonable, or ordinary consumer as a point of reference has been subjected to criticism. Ramsay, for example, argues that assumptions are frequently made about how consumers act which are not reflected in a pluralist society.[95] An illustration of some of the difficulties is found in *Charles of the Ritz* v. *FTC*. In that case, the defendant had marketed a cream which it claimed gave skin a 'wonderfully rejuvenating bloom'. The Federal Trade Commission (FTC) argued that no cosmetic

---

[93] See e.g. *Cadbury Ltd* v. *Halliday* [1975] 1 WLR 649.

[94] See *MFI Warehouses Ltd* v. *Nattrass* [1973] 1 WLR 307.

[95] See Ramsay, *Consumer Protection*, I. Ramsay, 'Consumer Law and Structures of Thought: A Comment' (1993) 16 JCP 79 and I. Ramsay, *Advertising, Culture and the Law: Beyond Lies, Ignorance and Manipulation* (London, Sweet and Maxwell, 1996).

product could overcome the ageing of skin, and that the company had therefore made false representations. The company argued in its defence that no reasonable person would believe that the cream could actually rejuvenate the skin. The Federal Circuit Court of Appeal rejected this argument, saying: 'while the wise and worldly may well realise the falsity of any representations that the present product can roll back the years, there remains that vast multitude of others who . . . still seek a perpetual fountain of youth'.[96]

The case is often taken to illustrate how the FTC saw itself as having a role in protecting 'the ignorant, the unthinking, and the credulous',[97] although it could be criticised for demonstrating a sexist and patronising attitude, which sees women consumers as incapable of making rational judgements to protect themselves and 'indict[s] the intelligence of the general public'.[98] Indeed, later cases showed a move away from the approach in *Charles of the Ritz*, with the FTC providing protection where a statement would be likely to mislead a customer who is 'acting reasonably in the circumstances'.[99] This seems closer to the position adopted in the UK. But is there value in the approach taken in *Charles of the Ritz*? Despite possibly sexist overtones, it can be seen as reflecting the truth that consumers are not always, if ever, part of a homogeneous entity with the same capacity to understand. Kennedy argues that the FTC's decision recognises that the paternalism shown by the FTC is necessary because 'we are all "idiots", subject to the false consciousness of consumer capitalism'.[100] The idea of the 'reasonable consumer' results from the free market concept of the rational consumer, and is subject to all weaknesses embodied by that which were discussed in chapter 1. Bourgoignie also doubts the utility of focusing on the reasonable, rational consumer, suggesting that the concept 'constitutes a dangerous abstraction which hardly recognises the heterogeneity of consumers as a group and the concomitant blend of interests'.[101]

It is one thing to recognise that statements can be interpreted in different ways, and that 'consumers' are not a homogeneous entity. We have to decide how the law should approach statements which might mislead consumers. Sunstein suggests that 'almost all substantive advertisements

---

[96] 143 F.2d 676 2d Circuit, 1944.
[97] Ibid.
[98] J. Spanogle and R. Rohner, *Consumer Law* (1979). Cited in Ramsay, *Advertising, Culture and the Law*, p. 78.
[99] *Clifford Associates* (1984) 103 FTC 110.
[100] D. Kennedy, 'Distributive and Paternalist Motives in Contract and Tort Law with Special Reference to Compulsory Terms and Unequal Bargaining Power' (1981–2) 41 *Maryland Law Review* 563.
[101] T. Bourgoignie, 'Characteristics of Consumer Law' (1991) 14 JCP 293 at p. 301.

will deceive at least some people in the light of the exceptional heterogenity of listeners and viewers'.[102] One approach would be to say that only statements which can be substantiated should be permissible.[103] Taken to an extreme, this would remove the possibility of the most extreme sales puff. It is submitted that this would go too far. Consumers benefit from humour, for example. However, where extreme claims are made about a product which might be interpreted as true by a consumer, the trader should bear the consequences of this. The celebrated case of *Carlill* v. *Carbolic Smoke Ball Company* is often derided, but in that case the consumer believed that she would be protected from influenza by using a smoke ball. Bowen LJ accepted that the defendants' claims were extravagant, but concluded that this was no reason for him not to be held to them.[104] If this had been a trade descriptions case, would there have been a conviction? It is submitted that there would. The claim in *Carlill* was not misleading; it was false. Moreover, there were factors to suggest that the information in the advertisement was to be taken seriously as a guarantee. It is submitted that where a trader makes an exaggerated claim, which is untrue, an offence should be committed, unless it would be clear even to a naïve consumer that the claim was not intended to be taken seriously.

The second issue is how to deal with misleading claims. It is submitted that what is necessary is a recognition that consumers interpret statements in different ways, and that consumers who might not have the same understanding as the 'average', or 'normal' consumer are entitled to protection. Indeed, it may be those consumers who are particularly in need of protection. Where a statement might be interpreted by a consumer in a way which is false, it should be open to the court to find that statement to be misleading, even if the average, informed consumer might not interpret it in this way. This can be justified on a number of different grounds. First, we might argue that by encouraging traders to address their minds to ambiguous statements we improve the clarity, and therefore the quality, of information, and thus have economic benefits. Secondly, we might justify this approach on social grounds of distributive justice. The cost of greater scrutiny of advertising might be borne by all consumers, while only benefiting the naïve, credulous, or poorly educated, but if it is the more vulnerable whom we protect this can be

---

[102] C. Sunstein, *Free Markets and Social Justice* (New York, Oxford University Press, 1997), p. 284.

[103] Article 6 of the 1978 proposal for a Directive on misleading advertising provided that where an advertiser makes a factual claim, the burden of proof that it is true should be placed on him. This was eventually changed. See G. Howells and T. Wilhelmsson, *EC Consumer Law* (Aldershot, Dartmouth and Ashgale, 1997), p. 140.

[104] [1893] 1 QB 256 at p. 268.

justified on distributive grounds. Thirdly, we might emphasise the issue of community values. Ramsay suggests that the rationale for a credulous consumer test might not be protection for the weak, but the reinforcement of trust.[105] The private law increasingly recognises concepts such as good faith, and has long recognised the value of fiduciary obligations, and perhaps the criminal law should do more to take this on board.

There would be difficulties with a test which requires traders to consider how statements might be interpreted by vulnerable, credulous, and ignorant consumers. First, there is the risk of uncertainty. Traders may find it more difficult to know whether their sales pitch will cause them to fall foul of the law. But the burden should not be an unnecessarily heavy one. The law already requires traders not to mislead consumers, and if the effect of a different approach is to require them to think harder about how their advertisements might be viewed, this would be a positive step. Secondly, there is the objection that there might be an increased cost for traders, but this is likely to be marginal, and the social benefits could be argued to compensate for this. Thirdly, there is the risk that sales literature might become bland, but this need not be the case. The law should take a balanced approach and recognise the value of marketing language insofar as it does not mislead the most vulnerable of consumers. It should also be remembered that enforcement authorities have a discretion to decide whether or not to prosecute, and some reliance can be placed upon their using this discretion wisely. We have already noted the advantages of over-inclusive provisions in deterring undesirable conduct and ensuring compliance. Any change in the law has to be interpreted in the light of the reality of enforcement practice. This is considered in more detail in the next chapter. A final point to note is that some jurisdictions have adopted an approach which takes account of the needs of the vulnerable. Nordic law, for example, adopts the 'passive glancer', rather than the average consumer, as the dominant consumer image, and German law is also willing to find statements misleading when only a small proportion of consumers might be misled.[106]

The criminal law and mandatory information disclosure

It has been argued above that prohibiting the supply of false information can be justified on economic as well as social grounds. False information distorts the market and leads to an inefficient allocation of resources. However, the importance of consumers receiving accurate information,

[105] Ramsay, *Advertising Culture and the Law*, p. 85.
[106] Howells and Wilhelmsson, *EC Consumer Law*, p. 138.

as well as not receiving false and misleading information should not be underestimated. Market transparency is emphasised by free market economists as fundamental to the effective working of the market, and ensuring that consumers receive optimal information is an important part of this. Ippolito and Mathios, authors of an influential study on the role of advertising in providing consumers with information, argued that an effective consumer protection policy requires 'that we focus as much on increasing the flow of truthful information as we do on stopping deceptive or misleading claims'.[107] Our discussion of the role of information in consumer protection in chapter 1 suggested that consumers typically want to know the price of the product in question and of other products, the quality of the product relative to substitutes, and the terms of trade.[108] To what extent does, and should, the criminal law play a role in requiring the supply of such information in order to protect consumers' economic interests?

In some cases, the criminal law requires information to be disclosed. For example, under s.77(1) of the Consumer Credit Act there is an obligation to supply certain information to a debtor under a fixed-sum credit agreement. Under the Business Advertisements (Disclosure) Order 1977 it is an offence for a person in the course of business to publish or cause to be published an advertisement offering goods for sale to consumers unless it is clear that it is a business sale. The Price Marking Order 1991 requires that the selling price of goods is indicated in writing. The other way in which disclosure is relevant is where non-disclosure makes a statement false or misleading. Here, the law is not punishing non-disclosure, but punishing the making of a statement which is false or misleading because of what it fails to say. This is considered above.

If market transparency and the supply of optimal information are so important, should the law go further in requiring disclosure? Some argue so. Stauder has argued that banning misleading advertising is important, but that specific disclosure requirements should also be set.[109] He gives examples of information that should be disclosed. These would include 'all consumer relevant characteristics of a good or service'. In the goods sector, this would include matters such as composition, volume, quality, and after-sales service. In the service sector it might include the allocation

---

[107] P. M. Ippolito and A. D. Mathios, 'The Regulation of Science Based Claims in Advertising' (1990) 13 JCP 413 at p. 441.
[108] See *Consumer Detriment under Conditions of Imperfect Information* (OFT Research Paper 11, August 1997), pp. 5–20.
[109] B. Stauder, 'The Protection of the Economic Interests of the Consumer' in F. Maniet and B. Dunaj (eds.), *The Scope and Objectives of Consumer Law* (Louvain, Centre de Droit de la Consommation, 1994) at pp. 47–9.

of risks and the nature and features of the services. Price should always be disclosed, Stauder argues, and this should include factors determining price, conditions of payment, etc. Disclosure regulation has advantages if we see consumer law as having a role in correcting market failure. In the words of Beales, Craswell, and Salop, '[r]emedies which simply adjust the information available to consumers still leave consumers free to make their own choices, thus introducing less rigidity into the market'.[110] This was an important part of the philosophy followed by the FTC under Robert Pitofsky in the 1970s. He suggested that an effective consumer-oriented programme of action should 'emphasise required disclosure of accurate and important product information that consumers could then use to protect their interests in advance of injury'.[111] The main way in which this was effected was by arguing that conduct could be unfair because of insufficient disclosure. As Ramsay notes, a similar approach is taken by s.17(2) of the Fair Trading Act 1973, which states that withholding adequate information from consumers may amount to an unfair trade practice.[112] This provided part of the justification for legislating to make it an offence for traders to advertise without revealing that they were acting in the course of business, mentioned above. By arguing that non-disclosure can be unfair as well as deceptive, we might see the law as moving beyond economic justifications for disclosure. One approach is to say that there is a constitutional right to information, and that this justifies requiring traders to disclose information about their products.[113] As we have already seen, it is also possible to justify disclosure on grounds of distributive justice. If vulnerable consumers are relatively ill-informed then disclosure will help their position relative to other consumers.[114]

Stauder does not suggest that the obligations to disclose should be backed by the force of the criminal law, favouring the use of administrative, competition, and contract law. However, it should be pointed out that he is viewing these matters from the perspective of a legal tradition that does not frequently use the criminal law to protect consumers. If the UK were to follow this lead, should they include these provisions in the

---

[110] Beales, R. Craswell, and S. Salop, 'The Efficient Regulation of Consumer Information' (1981) 24 *Journal of Law and Economics*.

[111] R. Pitofsky, 'Beyond Nader: Consumer Protection and the Regulation of Advertising' (1977) 90 Harvard LR 661 at 675.

[112] Ramsay, *Consumer Protection*, p. 404.

[113] See T. Emerson, 'Legal Foundations of the Right to Know' [1976] Wash ULQ 1 and R. Vaughan, 'Common Access to Product Safety Information and the Future of the Freedom of Information Act' (1991) 5 Adm LJ 673.

[114] See A. Schwartz and L. Wilde, 'Intervening in Markets on the Basis of Imperfect Information: A Legal and Economic Analysis' (1979) U Penn LR 630. But see also G. Schuker, 'The Impact of the Saccharin Warning Label' (1983) 2 *Journal of Public Policy and Marketing*, p. 46.

criminal law? It is suggested that the extent of disclosure championed by Stauder would be inappropriate for criminal sanctions. For example, it would not be appropriate to require traders to disclose information about the durability of goods with a criminal penalty if they fail. However, this does not mean that the criminal law should play no part in requiring disclosure of information. The solutions mooted by Ramsay are to impose a duty to disclose information where consumers have difficulty in checking the relevant attribute, or where there are serious losses from consumer mistakes and the costs of disclosure are not high, or to identify those product markets where disclosures are justified and write detailed disclosure requirements.[115] Under these solutions, a different approach might be taken in relation to a chocolate bar, where the consumer may be a 'repeat player' and there is a large incentive on the part of the producer to ensure consumer goodwill, and a motor car, where the consumer is likely to suffer from a significant information deficit.[116] Certainly, there are sectors of the economy where the consequences of a bad decision are so huge, and information is so difficult for many consumers to process, that disclosure should be required by legislation. It is submitted that the best approach is to merge Ramsay's suggestions, rather than present them as alternatives. The areas where information deficits and consequences of error are great, and the costs of disclosure low, should be identified, and disclosure requirements produced. Where this occurs it is important that the manner in which information has to be disclosed is addressed. It is not just what is disclosed that matters, but how it is disclosed. An obvious example is that the price of credit in an advertisement should be set in a uniform manner in accordance with a uniform method of calculation. There are other sectors, for example, motor cars, where standard criteria could be devised as a means of increasing the information available to consumers. Disclosure regimes can be backed up by other methods of increasing consumer information such as standardised scoring and consumer education.[117] Together they can bring important benefits to consumers but, as is discussed in chapter 1, they are subject to limitations which adversely affect the benefits they bring.

Protecting economic interests by fulfilling expectations

So far we have examined the role of the criminal law in protecting consumers' economic interests by prohibiting the supply of false and

---

[115] Ramsay, *Consumer Protection*, p. 229.
[116] Ibid. p. 223.
[117] Beales, Craswell, and Salop, 'The Efficient Regulation of Consumer Information'.

misleading information, and encouraging the supply of accurate information. It is now time to look at the role of the criminal law in protecting
expectations. Where expectations are generated by specific statements on
the part of the trader, but are not fulfilled, the law will step in, provided
the statement can be said to be false or misleading when made. This section begins by examining the situation where the buyer describes goods
she wants, but receives goods which do not correspond to that description. Under s.4(3) of the 1968 Act the buyer's description is deemed to
be applied by the trader, provided it is reasonable to infer that the goods
correspond to the description. This obviates any difficulty in holding the
description to be made by the seller that might otherwise have arisen. The
chapter then goes on to consider whether we should take this a step further and make it an offence to supply goods which are of unsatisfactory
quality where the consumer is entitled to expect that the goods would
meet that standard. It will be argued that while this may appear to be a
major extension to the law, it would not be as great a change as might
at first appear, and could bring significant benefits. Indeed if the need
for consumer policy is based on 'the gap between what the consumer
intended and expected and what the consumer in fact got', this topic is
of central importance.[118]

Compliance with descriptions. Section 4(3) of the Trade Descriptions Act 1968 states that where goods are supplied in pursuance of a
request in which a trade description is used 'and the circumstances are
such as to make it reasonable to infer that the goods are supplied as goods
corresponding to that trade description, the person supplying the goods
shall be deemed to have applied a trade description to the goods'. In
Shropshire CC v. *Simon Dudley Ltd*,[119] Shropshire put out a tender for
supply of a fire engine, and accepted the bid by Simon Dudley. The bid
contract was later varied with the consent of both parties. When the fire
engine was delivered, it did not meet the specifications, either in the initial, or the amended, contract. The respondents were prosecuted under
s.1(1)(b) of the Trade Descriptions Act with supplying goods to which
a false trade description is applied. They were acquitted at first instance
but convicted, albeit with some reluctance on the part of the judges, on
appeal. Hooper J held that s.4(3) made it clear that on supplying the
fire engine the respondent 'shall be deemed to have applied' the trade
description which was used in the 'request' made by Shropshire for the

---

[118] G. K. Hadfield, R. Howse, and M. J. Trebilcock, 'Information-Based Principles for
Rethinking Consumer Protection Policy' (1998) 21 JCP 131 at 163.
[119] (1997) 16 Tr LR 69.

fire engine. He further stated that even without s.4(3) the representations made by the respondents 'continued in force and were applicable at the time moment [*sic*] of delivery'. As a question of statutory interpretation, this decision has to be correct. Whether it is appropriate for defendants to be convicted in such situations is more doubtful. Certainly, Phillips LJ seemed reluctant to see the respondents convicted. He said:

> If the 1968 Act takes effect in the way that I have postulated, it follows that the offences under the Act will be committed on many occasions where a breach occurs of a contract for the sale of goods . . . I do not think that this is a satisfactory state of affairs, but it may be justified by the need to attempt to ensure fair trading in a very wide variety of circumstances. The consequence is, however, that technical offences will be committed in circumstances where a civil law claim is the only remedy that the facts of the case require. Trading standards officers must exercise discretion when deciding whether or not a particular case warrants the intervention of the criminal law.[120]

There must be doubts about the utility of prosecuting this case. Before the decision to prosecute was made, civil proceedings for breach of contract had begun. The case did not involve 'consumer protection' in the sense of protecting individuals against errant traders. The parties in this case were in a roughly equal bargaining position. It is submitted that enforcement officers should use their discretion wisely to ensure that only appropriate cases are brought before the court. But this is no reason to criticise the decision in *Simon Dudley*. The law is clear, and the interpretation of the Divisional Court surely correct. It is the buyer's reasonable expectation that is being protected. The case may look more like a mere breach of contract than a criminal offence, but the relationship between the 1968 Act and the law of contract is closer than is often realised.

Supplying goods of satisfactory quality and implied descriptions. Section 14(2) of the Sale of Goods Act 1979 states that where the seller sells goods in the course of a trade or business, there is an implied term that the goods supplied under the contract are of satisfactory quality and reasonably fit for their purpose. There has been debate about whether traders who sell goods which fail to meet statutory implied terms should be guilty of criminal offences, in particular under the 1968 Act. In *R* v. *Ford Motor Co. Ltd* Bridge LJ argued that: 'it would be very startling if . . . the effect of the 1968 Act were to make a criminal of every seller of goods by description who delivers goods in breach of the condition of merchantable quality which is implied by s.14(2) of the Sale of Goods Act 1893'.[121]

---

[120] Ibid. p. 82.   [121] [1974] 1 WLR 1220.

Debate about the role of the criminal law in this area took place before the Methven Committee, which had been set up to review the working of the Trade Descriptions Act, and reported in 1976.[122] A number of bodies, including the Consumers' Association, argued before the Committee that the Act should be amended to cover 'implied' trade descriptions, where the appearance of goods is taken as an indication of satisfactory quality and fitness for purpose. There were several arguments advanced in favour of this. First, consumers are often forced to make assessments on the basis of appearance because of the proliferation of goods being sold pre-wrapped, and the effect of the Act in discouraging the provision of adequate information. Secondly, there was increasing concern about quality of goods, and the limitations on consumers' ability to exercise their legal rights in this area. Thirdly, there was thought to be a need for additional powers which would be given to enforcement officers to help consumers who have been the victim of defective goods, and enable such officers to target manufacturers by use of the bypass procedure. Finally, it was pointed out that if the consumer had asked the right questions about the goods, and the seller had been forced to describe them, the Act would have applied.

These arguments did not convince the Committee. They believed that there would be several difficulties with such an extension of the law. First of all, they argued that it would be impossible, in many cases, to decide what is to be implied. Secondly, they were concerned that the concept of *caveat emptor* would be removed. It has already been noted that there was concern at the time that the need for the 1968 Act was being debated that consumers should be encouraged to 'go shopping with their eyes open'.[123] A third criticism was that the distinction between criminal and civil liability would become blurred. Manufacturers could become liable for 'normal' defects inherent in a percentage of some mass-production goods. Fourthly, it was felt that the enforcement authorities would be put under an additional burden to pursue individual claims. Finally, they argued that the aim of the Trade Descriptions Act is to ensure accurate descriptions, including some which involve an assessment of quality, but that it is not concerned with the promotion of quality. They concluded that '[t]here would be a real risk that trading standards officers dealing with more serious offences... would be overwhelmed by a plethora of complaints, many of which would... amount to little more than disputes about value for money'. They also saw a risk that 'to legislate in this way would in the end be counter-productive because it would

---

[122] Cmnd 6628 paras. 140–4.   [123] Cmnd 1781, para. 813.

discourage shoppers from taking even minimal care to protect their own interests'.[124]

While there are some strengths to these arguments, it is possible to overstate them. It may well be difficult to ascertain precisely what is to be implied, but in the case of breach of a statutory implied term of satisfactory quality and fitness for purpose this is a problem with which the civil courts frequently are forced to deal. There is a wealth of case law for the purposes of the Sale of Goods Act 1979, and while this would not be binding on the criminal courts, it could provide some useful guidance. As for the removal of *caveat emptor*, this again can be overplayed. It is important to encourage consumers to look after their own interests, but this is frequently more easily said than done. It is often difficult to ascertain the quality of goods prior to purchase, and the transaction costs of civil law actions are liable to put off all but the most persistent of litigants. The third point, regarding the blurring of the distinction between civil and criminal law, appears fair, but ignores a number of important points. First, there is already a substantial overlap between the civil and the criminal law in the area of consumer protection. As has already been pointed out, if the consumer asks for information and the trader supplies false or misleading information, even innocently, this will amount to both breach of contract and an offence under the Trade Descriptions Act. Imposing criminal liability for breach of an implied term is merely taking the law one step further. Secondly, it should be remembered that the Trade Descriptions Act has been described as a statute which is 'not criminal in any real sense'.[125] These offences are not 'sins with legal definitions'.[126] Although there is no formal or agreed distinction in English law between offences *mala prohibita* and those *mala in se*, it is generally accepted that trade descriptions offences are part of the former, and that the general principles of the criminal law do not apply to them.[127] With this in mind, it may be easier to accept criminal liability for breach of an implied term. Next, manufacturers may become liable for 'normal defects' in mass-production goods, but if the role of the criminal law is seen to be an improvement in trading standards rather than the enforcement of the criminal law, this may not be too objectionable. It should be noted, for example, that in one leading trade descriptions case, Lord Scarman commented that the 1968 Act 'is not a truly criminal statute. Its purpose is

---

[124] Cmnd 6628, para. 144.
[125] *Sherras* v. *De Rutzen* [1895] 1 QB 918 at 919.
[126] G. Borrie, *The Development of Consumer Law and Policy: Bold Spirits and Timorous Souls* (Hamlyn Lectures, London, Steven and Sons, 1984), p. 46 (quoting Lord Devlin).
[127] See ch. 3.

not the enforcement of the criminal law but the maintenance of trading standards.'[128] In practice, the effect of such a change would largely be to transfer the risk from the consumer to the trader. If any new offence were to be subject to due diligence defences, as it is submitted it should be, the faultless defendant would be able to escape liability. In many cases, the retailer will be able to use the due diligence defence and the manufacturer may be pursued under the bypass procedure. This point is developed later. The next criticism, that enforcement officers may be put under an additional burden, is a reasonable one, but this is always the case when new consumer protection legislation is introduced. If trading standards officers are given insufficient resources to meet their statutory obligations then the legislator should address that alongside addressing the change in the law.

The final criticism is particularly interesting. It is argued that the aim of the Trade Descriptions Act is to ensure accurate descriptions and not to promote quality. As already mentioned, one of the difficulties with the Act as it stands is that it may have the effect of discouraging the flow of useful information as a result of the requirement to tell 'nothing but the truth'. Disclosure duties can overcome this to some extent. But it could also be argued that an important aim of consumer law is to help consumers to get goods of the quality they are entitled to expect.[129] A product which is not reasonably fit for what is obviously its purpose should not be sold. Provided that the courts adopt a flexible view of what is satisfactory and what the purpose of the goods was in all the circumstances, the duty should not cause injustice.

A further point to note is that if it is seen as a major step to make sellers responsible under the criminal law for goods which are not of satisfactory quality or fit for their purpose, it is important to remember that a similar obligation is placed upon the sellers of food. Section 14(1) of the Food Safety Act states that: '[a]ny person who sells to the purchaser's prejudice any food which is not of the nature or substance or quality demanded by the purchaser shall be guilty of an offence'. The standard is to be judged in the light of what the purchaser expected to receive.[130] The reference to 'quality' in this section makes it clear that food which is not of satisfactory quality, but which the consumer was entitled to expect would be, would give rise to an offence. Although there is a reference to the consumer having 'demanded' food of a particular quality, it does

---

[128] *Wings* v. *Ellis* [1985] AC 272 at 282.
[129] Hadfield, Howse, and Trebilcock, 'Information-Based Principles for Rethinking Consumer Protection Policy', p. 163.
[130] *McDonalds Hamburgers Ltd* v. *Windle* (21 October 1986, unreported).

not appear necessary for the consumer to have said anything specific to the seller about the standards he expected. In the case of *Goldup* v. *John Manson Ltd*, Ormrod LJ said that, in the absence of evidence of specific circumstances, 'it will be inferred that the purchaser demanded an article which corresponds in substance or quality with that normally sold in the trade... Where the article is sold by description... the purchaser impliedly demands a product which is of merchantable quality.'[131]

This demonstrates that criminal law has a role where food does not meet the requirement of satisfactory quality. Should this be applied to goods generally? There is no doubt that food holds particular concern for consumers. This is one reason why Parliament reacts so quickly to food scares, and why they generate such interest.[132] However, s.14 goes beyond matters of safety by making criminal the selling of food which is perfectly safe, but not of the quality expected. There are arguments against extending this approach to other goods. These are considered in the discussion of implied trade descriptions above. One point not examined there is that such a duty would remove from the market cheap, low-quality products for which there is demand, particularly from less affluent consumers. However, traders are already under a civil law duty not to supply goods which are unsatisfactory and not reasonably fit for their purpose. As a result, the only reasons why the trader's conduct should change are first, because he might be more likely to be held to account for failing in his legal duty, and secondly, because fear of criminal liability carries greater stigma than civil liability. An increasing likelihood of being forced to comply with existing obligations is an unconvincing argument against change. If the law were to be extended along the lines suggested it would be important to introduce safeguards. The due diligence defence would play a role here, and it is suggested that exceptions similar to those contained in s.14(2C) of the 1979 Act should be included. For example, no offence would take place where a defect is drawn to the consumer's attention. This would be consistent with the rationale of protecting consumers' legitimate expectations. In addition, the provision should apply only to consumers. The *Simon Dudley* case considered above reveals the unfortunate effects of using a statute primarily designed to protect consumers in business transactions.[133] Any extension of the law should be limited to where the trader deals with a consumer. With these safeguards, an extension to the law would be easier to justify.

---

[131] [1982] QB 161.
[132] See C. Scott, 'Continuity and Change in British Food Law' (1990) MLR 785.
[133] (1997) 16 *Trading Law* 69.

Economic interests and fairness

The statutes examined so far could all be interpreted as prohibiting unfair conduct. However, the offences contained in those pieces of legislation are all quite specific. If one aim of protecting consumers' economic interests is to ensure that consumers are treated fairly in the marketplace a more general provision would be necessary. Unfairness is about more than being misled, or failing to have legitimate expectations fulfilled. A provision which forbade unfair conduct would have to address a number of other matters.

First, unfairness may involve unfair competition. Although competition legislation benefits consumers it is generally viewed separately from consumer protection law, and is beyond the scope of this book.[134] Secondly, unfairness may concern conduct which puts unreasonable pressure on the consumer. An obvious example would be where physical force was used. Any transaction concluded under such conditions would be liable to be vitiated, and the mainstream criminal law could be invoked. However, there is no general consumer protection offence designed to combat such behaviour. Furthermore, pressure need not be physical to be unfair. The civil law recognises notions such as undue influence as grounds for avoiding a contract, although using undue influence is not generally an offence, either under consumer protection or general criminal law.[135] A third aspect of unfairness is exploitation. Ramsay notes, for example, that one of the complaints made by the FTC about the advertisements for 'Wonder Bread' was that they 'exploit the emotional concerns of parents for the healthy development of their children'.[136] Conduct which targets vulnerable groups such as children, the elderly, or the ill could also easily fall foul of a requirement of fairness. However, exploitation as an example of unfairness can cause difficulties for consumer law. For example, advertising, by its very nature, tries to change consumer consciousness by persuading the consumer to purchase particular goods or services. When does this, apparently legitimate, commercial conduct become unfair or exploitative, and so deserving of legal redress? Ramsay classifies one area of unfairness as 'psychological exploitation'.[137] Advertisements might be unfair, for example, if they

---

[134] See G. G. Howells and S. Weatherill, *Consumer Protection Law and Theory* (Sydney, The Law Book Company, 1980), ch. 15.
[135] See D. Capper, 'Undue Influence and Unconscionability: A Rationalisation' (1998) 114 LQR 479.
[136] Ramsay, *Consumer Protection*, p. 405.
[137] Ibid. pp. 404–6.

claim to induce a euphoric state or satisfy emotional anxieties or fears when they are unlikely to do so.[138] In such cases, the law is still protecting the economic interests of the consumer; it is recognising that the consumer may be persuaded to part with his resources under unfair conditions. Where the law becomes involved in this way it can be justified, and criticised, on grounds of paternalism. The consumer is seen as unable to make an informed decision for himself because he has been exploited. If we argue that the state's intervention is designed to ensure that the consumer gets what he would have wanted, then we might argue that our intervention is consistent with market rhetoric. To this extent, we are merely correcting information deficiencies, and ensuring that the consumer's true wishes are fulfilled. In reality we may be deciding what the consumer should have wanted, or even what the state believes it would have wanted had it been in the consumer's position – a form of paternalism.

Another way in which conduct may be unfair is through a failure to provide relevant information. We have already examined where nondisclosure makes information misleading, but it has been argued that non-disclosure could also be described as unfair where: '(1) consumers currently lack the information in question (2) consumers would choose differently if they had the information . . . and (3) the benefits of better consumer decisions and improved seller performance are not outweighed by the costs of supplying the information'.[139] The role of the criminal law in disclosure regulation is discussed above and so it is not proposed to go into further detail here. Suffice it to say that one justification for disclosure might be the unfairness of non-disclosure and, similarly, one method of tackling unfairness might be to insist upon disclosure.

The discussion so far has focused upon the fairness of traders' conduct, and therefore on procedural fairness. It would also be possible for the law to insist on substantive fairness.[140] Although historically the law of contract has been primarily concerned with fairness in relation to procedure, it has shown an increasing willingness to intervene in the substance of contracts.[141] The rationale for this may be largely based on procedural matters, such as unequal bargaining power, but the focus has been on substance. The Unfair Terms in Consumer Contracts Regulations are

---

[138] See O. L. Reed and J. Coalson, 'Eighteenth Century Legal Doctrine and Twentieth Century Marketing Techniques'. Cited in Ramsay, *Consumer Protection*, p. 405.

[139] R. Craswell, 'Identification of Unfair Acts and Practices by the FTC' [1981] Wisc LR 107 at p. 123. Cited in Ramsay, *Consumer Protection*, at p. 404.

[140] Although it should be recognised that the distinction between procedural and substantive unfairness is not always easy to draw. See ch. 1.

[141] See ch. 1.

a clear example of the willingness of the civil law to strike down unfair terms, albeit only in certain types of contract.[142] The question for us to consider concerns the extent to which the criminal law should be used to address issues of fairness.

The bold solution to the inadequacies of the present law would be to create a general offence prohibiting unfair conduct. Writing in 1990, the Director General of Fair Trading noted the support for such a provision from organisations representing trading standards officers, but concluded that criminal sanctions are not appropriate for the enforcement of general prohibitions on misleading and unconscionable conduct.[143] There is no doubt that there would be difficulties in creating such a general criminal offence if it were couched in terms of unfairness. Unfairness would be a relatively low threshold for the prosecution to overcome, and there is comparatively little tradition of challenging transactions on grounds of unfairness in the UK, particularly through the use of criminal sanctions. However, if a higher standard were envisaged, the creation of a criminal offence would be possible. It would be feasible, for example, to create an offence which prohibited deceptive and unconscionable conduct rather than merely unfair conduct. Deceptive conduct will already constitute an offence where the deceiver is dishonest and receives an advantage from the victim.[144] It would be possible to make proof of dishonesty a prerequisite of any new provision based on deception. Unconscionability also reflects a high degree of culpability. The OFT argued that conduct could be described as unconscionable where 'a stronger party to a transaction knowingly takes *wholly unfair advantage* [my italics] of that position to the detriment of the less powerful party'.[145] It would be conduct that 'grossly contravenes ordinary principles of fair dealing'. It is therefore submitted that it would be possible to create a new offence along the lines of dishonestly engaging in deceptive or unconscionable behaviour towards a consumer in the course of business. This could be defined, at least in part, by the statute, and fleshed out with non-exhaustive examples. Although there would be opposition to such a provision, it should be remembered that enforcement authorities are frequently 'firing at a moving target'.[146] A general offence along the lines suggested might provide them with a more accurate weapon.

---

[142] Ibid.   [143] *Trading Malpractices* (OFT July 1990).
[144] See for example the Theft Act 1968.   [145] *Trading Malpractices*, para. 1.8.
[146] Borrie, *The Development of Consumer Law and Policy*, p. 64.

Fair Trading Act 1973 Part III and the obtaining of assurances

Although the criminal law could be extended to provide better protection for consumers' economic interests, it should be recognised that this has drawbacks, and is politically unlikely to take place. Another way forward, which would be more likely to receive political support and would also address some of the difficulties we have identified, is to reform Part III of the Fair Trading Act 1973. Part III enables the Director General of Fair Trading to seek assurances from individual traders who carry on a course of conduct which is detrimental to the economic, health, safety, or other interests of consumers in the UK, and is unfair to consumers according to the criteria set out in the Act. It has been argued that the powers in Part III are intended to 'reinforce' criminal enforcement of trading standards at the local level.[147] Sir Geoffrey Howe, the Minister for Trade and Consumer Affairs at the time of the Fair Trading Act's inception, stated that the purpose of Part III is 'to create a climate in which the overwhelming majority of traders, who deal fairly with the public, can continue to flourish without interference and in which the minority of traders, who maintain an unhelpful attitude to justified complaints by consumers, will see sense and, in the end, the necessity of mending their ways and improving their standards'.[148] The specific wording of the provision is as follows:

34(1) Where it appears to the Director that the person carrying on a business has in the course of that business persisted in a course of conduct which –

(i) is detrimental to the interests of consumers in the United Kingdom, whether those interests are economic interests or interests in respect of health, safety or other matters, and
(ii) in accordance with the following provisions of this section is to be regarded as unfair to consumers,

the Director shall use his best endeavours, by communication with that person or otherwise, to obtain from him a satisfactory written assurance that he will refrain from continuing that course of conduct and from carrying on any similar course of conduct in the course of that business.

The matters which are regarded as unfair to consumers are then listed. These involve contraventions of duties, prohibitions or restrictions

---

[147] I. Ramsay, 'The Office of Fair Trading: Policing the Consumer Market Place' in J. Baldwin and C. McCrudden (eds.), *Regulation and Public Law* (London, Weidenfeld and Nicolson, 1987) 177 at p. 195.
[148] 848 HC Official Report, col. 454, 13 December 1972.

imposed by the criminal law whether or not the person has been convicted, and breaches of contract or other civil duties whether or not proceedings have been brought. The Director General must be satisfied that the trader has 'persisted' in the course of conduct, and in order to decide this, the Director General can take into account complaints received by him and any other information collected by or furnished to him. Once persistence is established, the Director General must try to obtain a written assurance from the trader that he will refrain from the conduct in question. It seems clear, therefore, that once the evidence has come to the Director General's attention he is under an obligation to try to obtain the assurance. This will usually involve a written request and a reminder sent four weeks later. If the process fails, the Director General may bring proceedings before the Restrictive Practices Court or the County Court. The court can accept an undertaking, or can make an order against the trader. Where this is breached, an action lies for contempt of court.

Part III and its weaknesses

Persistence and procedure. A former Director General of Fair Trading stated that Part III 'is not an alternative means of enforcement, nor does it give new rights or avenues of redress for consumers, but is designed to correct unlawful business practices of particular traders, and provide a sanction where those business practices continue unabated'.[149] The OFT has recognised that one of the most difficult problems it faced was that of judging whether the trader has persisted in a course of conduct. Initially, the only indication of persistence in a course of conduct that the OFT has is the number of complaints about a trader. The OFT has said that 'there cannot be said to be a course of conduct unless there are several breaches having a common thread or of a similar type'.[150] The OFT has recognised that a number of other issues also need to be considered: the seriousness of individual complaints within the total; the period which the complaints cover; and the overall picture shown by the total complaints when compared with the size of the trader's business. The Office added that persistence could also be shown if the trader had been warned by a trading standards officer, but continued with the offending course of conduct. However, it appears that there are still difficulties in showing that the criteria are met. Writing in 1990, the Director General stated that the OFT had been advised that the statutory wording meant that for small traders, a minimum of ten to fifteen well-documented complaints about a

---

[149] *Trading Malpractices*, pp. 29-30.   [150] Ibid. p. 30.

similar kind of misconduct over a year would be necessary. Proportionally more complaints would be needed where the firm was large. Recently, the DTI has stated that courts considering applications under Part III 'require a very large number of instances of unlawful conduct' before they are willing to find persistence in a course of conduct.[151] However, in its 1997 document *Part III Assurances* the OFT stated that between six and ten complaints would be sufficient for a trader to be approached, provided that they clearly illustrate breach of the law and the trader's intention to disregard the law.[152] No precise figure can be laid down because each case is examined on its own facts. An additional difficulty with persistence is that the OFT regards it as involving an element of deliberation by the trader. Careless conduct may therefore fall outside the scope of the provision.

There are strong arguments for removing the requirement that the trader has persisted in the course of conduct. The National Consumer Council suggested that all the Director General should need to show is that the kind of unfair conduct is 'more than an isolated example'. This would give him the power to act before the conduct becomes persistent.[153] The DTI now proposes that it should be possible to apply for an injunction where 'it appears that a person carrying on a business has engaged in a course of conduct consisting of breaches of legal obligations which are unfair and detrimental to the interests of consumers'.[154] Engaging in a course of conduct seems to make it easier to take action at an earlier stage and so nip unlawful conduct in the bud. This is to be welcomed.

The difficulties with the procedure under Part III are well established. The OFT has recognised that it is time consuming, convoluted, and susceptible to delay,[155] and the Better Regulation Task Force described it as 'cumbersome and ineffective'.[156] The procedure works as follows. First, as has already been noted, the Director General must be satisfied that a trader has persisted in a course of conduct which is detrimental to the interests of consumers in the UK and is unfair to consumers on the stated criteria. If the Director General decides to act, he must first use his best endeavours to obtain a written assurance from the trader agreeing that he will refrain from that or a similar course of conduct. In practice, the OFT approaches the trader in writing asking for a signed assurance about his future conduct. This will be done by recorded delivery and will

---

[151] *Reform of Part III of the Fair Trading Act 1973* (DTI, 2000), p. 1.
[152] *Part III Assurances* (OFT, 1997), p. 8.
[153] *Unfair Trading: Recommendations for Reform of Part III of the Fair Trading Act* (National Consumer Council, 1997), p. 7.
[154] *Reform of Part III*, p. 2.
[155] *Consumer Affairs: The Way Forward* (OFT, 1998), p. 12.
[156] *Better Regulation Task Force Report on Consumer Affairs* (1998), p. 10.

include a covering letter which sets out the Director General's powers, the implications of not signing the assurance, and how the assurance may be publicised. If the Director General does not get such an assurance, or if he does but the assurance is subsequently broken, the Director General may bring proceedings before the Restrictive Practices Court or the County Court. The Court can either obtain an undertaking from the trader to refrain from the offending course of conduct or make an order against the trader.

There can be little doubt that the procedure under Part III has contributed to its lack of success. Even where the conduct is grossly improper and there is ample evidence of numerous breaches, the Director General must 'use his best endeavours' to obtain an assurance. By that time, the trader may have sold all the goods which formed the basis of the malpractice. The trader might conclude that there is little or no incentive to co-operate with the Director General. By prolonging the proceedings, the longer it will be before the matter comes to court, and in the meantime the trader may well continue with the offending conduct. The Director General has given examples of simple tactics that the trader might use, such as refusing to accept recorded-delivery letters, or avoiding personal approaches asking him for an assurance.[157] If the trader breaks the assurance, all the court will do, in effect, is tell him not to do it again. It can be time consuming and wasteful of resources to pursue unscrupulous traders in order to get assurances. Even when the court becomes involved there are difficulties, as the court needs to be satisfied, not just that the trader persisted in the course of conduct, but that it is likely to be continued. There is an incentive for the trader to improve his conduct temporarily to persuade the court that he has changed his ways. Even if a court order is breached or an undertaking unfulfilled, proceedings must be brought for contempt of court. This involves the criminal standard of proof.

One step forward has been the increased use of warnings by the OFT and by local trading standards officers.[158] Warnings can be given at a number of different stages, including when problems with the trader begin. Ignoring a warning may be used as evidence of persistence in a course of conduct. The increasing use of warnings by trading standards officers has been welcomed by the OFT. In particular, the officers will inform the trader that if an unlawful course of conduct persists, it will be referred to the OFT. However, the use of warnings brings its own difficulties, including putting the trader on guard that he is being investigated.

---

[157] *Trading Malpractices*, p. 31.   [158] *Part III Assurances*, pp. 13–14.

The DTI's latest proposals overcome many of the procedural weaknesses with Part III. It is proposed to dispense with the requirement to seek assurances, allowing enforcement authorities to apply to the court directly for an injunction. However, authorities will be encouraged, as a matter of good enforcement practice, to obtain an informal assurance first. When deciding whether to award an injunction, the court will be able to consider whether the trader has complied with any previous assurance given.

The role of publicity. When the OFT has obtained an assurance against a trader it is important that the trader's conduct is monitored to ensure that he does not continue with that, or any similar, course of conduct. As a result, it is necessary to bring the assurance to the attention of those who are likely to discover whether such conduct is continued. The most effective way of doing this is to publicise the assurance.[159] The Divisional Court has recognised that the Director General 'has to ensure that others who are likely to learn of conduct which would constitute a breach of the assurance must be made aware that the assurance has been given and encouraged to report breaches to his office'.[160] This can sometimes only be done through publicity.

To whom action will be publicised will depend on all the circumstances. All assurances appear in the Director General's reports and details are always sent to trading standards officers where they have an interest in the matter. However, in other cases the OFT will go considerably further than this, and publicise far more widely. Indeed, if it is seen as important that consumers are aware of an assurance so that they will be encouraged to inform the OFT of subsequent lapses, it will be necessary to publicise in media to which the public are likely to pay attention. In *R v. Director General of Fair Trading ex p FH Taylor & Co. Ltd*[161] the Divisional Court noted that there are different reasons for publicising assurances, ranging from informing a trading standards department so that they can inform the office of future breaches, to informing the general public as a way of punishing the trader by adverse publicity. The court made it clear that widespread publicity would only be appropriate where its main purpose was to warn the public rather than to punish the trader. Publicity designed purely as a punishment was inappropriate. The court set out a number of questions which it said the Director General should ask

---

[159] See E. Gellhorn, 'Adverse Publicity by Administrative Agencies' (1973) 86 Harvard LR 1380.
[160] *R v. Director General of Fair Trading ex p FH Taylor and Co.* [1981] ICR 292.
[161] Ibid.

when deciding whether to publicise the assurance.[162] First, who should be informed that assurances have been given? It gave examples of the sorts of people who would be likely to be appropriate, such as the trade press, trading standards officers, and consumer protection bodies. Caution should be exercised before informing the wider public, and the Office should carefully consider whether wider publicity would improve the flow of information, or would 'merely tend to put the person concerned out of business'. The second question concerns the form in which the information should be disseminated. The court noted that it is easier to ensure that information is publicised widely and cheaply if the information is presented in a colourful way, but that this will in some cases be unfair to the trader. The third and fourth questions relate particularly to the facts of the specific publicity used in relation to the assurance in *Taylor*. The third question was 'is it really relevant to say, however accurately, that the assurances were only given after a threat of legal proceedings?' In the publicity in that case, attention had been drawn to the fact that the company and its managing director had only given assurances after they had been warned that, if they did not do so, proceedings would be started. The court pointed out that such a threat is implicit in a request for written assurances in any case. It could be argued that by drawing attention to this the Office was being unfair to the trader as it implied that there was something particularly improper in this case. However, the court did concede that it may have been necessary to emphasise the threat in this particular case. The fourth question concerned the decision by the OFT to publish an expression of gratitude to trading standards officers of the three authorities involved, and was simply whether this was appropriate. There was a suggestion that this might have been done to increase the likelihood of obtaining a reference in the local press to the fact that an assurance had been given. If this was done for the purpose of improving the supply of information then this might be acceptable but, again, it would presumably not be so if it merely had the effect of driving the trader out of business through adverse publicity.

The approach of the court in the *Taylor* case has caused difficulties for the OFT. The basic principle, that the OFT must have regard to whether or not it is being fair to the trader in publicising the assurance, is relatively straightforward. The difficulty comes when the OFT is aware that publicity is likely to have an adverse effect upon the trader. It is clear from the case that this will be permissible in some cases, particularly where it is necessary to improve the flow of information. However, the balance that has to be drawn is a difficult one, and there was some evidence of the

---

[162] Ibid. pp. 297–8.

OFT being reluctant to publicise assurances soon after the decision.[163] This is in sharp contrast to the FTC which issues a press release immediately upon filing a complaint.[164] However, in 1989 the Office signalled a new approach to publicity.[165] Details of assurances may now be found not just in OFT press releases, but in local and national newspapers and magazines relevant to the business of the trader. The Office ensures that all letters seeking assurances contain a standard paragraph which states that the Director General may publicise assurances if he thinks fit. The OFT has stated that where a court order has been made against a trader, the Office is especially keen to see that the order is publicised, in order to see whether it is being observed. However, as Miller, Harvey, and Parry note, since the introduction of the new arrangements for publicity there has been a reduction in the number of assurances given.[166]

It is not just the OFT that has power to publicise assurances. Local authorities will, in some cases, see fit to publicise assurances relating to their areas. *Part III Assurances*, a document which is aimed at trading standards officers, states that in every case where the authority has an interest, the OFT will pass the details of the assurances to the authority, with guidance concerning publicity. It continues '[w]here there is no restriction, you will be able to publicise them in whatever way you think would best serve the purpose of publicity – namely, to monitor the observance of the assurances by the trader'.

The proposed new procedure will have an enhanced role for publicity. The OFT will establish and maintain a register of injunctions and proceedings brought alleging contempt for breach of an injunction. This register will be open to public inspection on terms similar to those relating to s.35(3)–(5) of the Consumer Credit Act 1974 and s.8 of the Estate Agents Act 1979. Unfortunately, it is proposed to charge a fee to the public to inspect the register, which may make it more difficult to obtain vital information about rogue traders.

Types of offending conduct. It is a limitation of Part III that the trader's conduct must be detrimental to the interests of consumers in the UK and 'unfair' to consumers in accordance with the terms in the Act. It is clear that the conduct need not only be detrimental to such consumers: a trader whose activities adversely affect UK and overseas consumers will, of course be covered, as will a trader whose activities affect businesses as well as consumers. Unlike Part II of the Act, which

---

[163] See Ramsay, *Consumer Protection*, p. 305.
[164] See Gellhorn, 'Adverse Publicity' and Ramsay, *Consumer Protection*, p. 305.
[165] *Part III Assurances: A New Approach* (OFT booklet, 1989).
[166] *Consumer and Trading Law*, p. 552.

is only concerned with the protection of economic interests, Part III also protects health and safety. As a result, breaches of the General Product Safety Regulations 1994 or the safety provisions of the Food Safety Act 1990 could give rise to action under Part III. Unfairness for the purposes of Part III is interpreted narrowly, and only involves breach of either the civil or criminal law. Typical examples of conduct that will give rise to an action under Part III are failing to deliver goods in breach of contract, failing to return money to which consumers are entitled, and making false statements about goods or services.

There are many examples of conduct that is improper and unfair in the loose sense but will not found an action under Part III because they do not involve breaches of the law. In his 1990 report, *Trading Malpractices*, the Director General suggested widening the provisions which define an unfair course of conduct. The Director General suggested adding two general provisions, each of which would be supported by a 'shopping list' of illustrative acts or practices. The first general provision 'would be cast in terms of business practices which are deceptive or misleading'. The general provision would then be supported by a list of acts or practices which would be treated as falling within it. This list would be illustrative rather than exhaustive. The second general provision concerns acts, practices, or conduct that are unconscionable. These are practices which are not deceptive, but are unacceptable or objectionable for different reasons. Again the OFT recommended a non-exhaustive list of factors or circumstances that could be taken into account when deciding if the conduct was unconscionable. Examples included that the consumer was subjected to undue pressure to enter into the consumer transaction, and that the terms and conditions on, or subject to which the consumer's transaction was entered by the consumer are so harsh or adverse to the consumer as to be inequitable. More recently, the OFT has suggested that new legislation could create a statutory test of unfairness, 'which goes beyond breaches of civil or criminal law and tackles new and fast-moving practices which give rise to consumer detriment, exploiting the imbalance favouring traders at the expense of consumers, or show a lack of good faith'.[167] An alternative would be for the OFT to develop codes of practice for problem industries, breach of which could count as evidence of unfair conduct. This was suggested by the National Consumer Council. The Council was particularly eager to ensure that conduct which did not breach a legal duty could nevertheless be challenged.[168]

---

[167] *Consumer Affairs: The Way Forward*, para. 4.11.
[168] *Unfair Trading*, pp. 33–6.

It is unfortunate that the DTI seems to lack ambition in respect to the types of conduct that can be challenged. The proposal is that 'unfair' should continue to mean breach of the civil or criminal law. There are strong arguments for extending the law to cover deceptive or unfair conduct that is not currently against the letter of the law. There have to be safeguards, of course, and a test of unfairness might be too wide. But if the law were to be limited to tackling unconscionable or deceptive conduct, this would seem to find an appropriate balance. Indeed, there may even be an argument in favour of a lack of clarity and consistency. In the words of Ramsay 'a certain degree of unpredictability may have a "chilling" effect on the Holmesian "bad men" operating on the fringes of the market-place',[169] although it would be of concern if this unpredictability were taken too far.

Persons by whom action can be taken. An additional weakness of Part III is that the power to take action rests with the Director General of Fair Trading. A number of the reports that have called for reform have suggested broadening this so that action can be taken by trading standards officers. In his 1982 Annual Report, the Director General argued forcibly against local enforcement, claiming that the need for a consistent application of principle and the potential severity of sanctions under Part III meant that it would be neither feasible nor efficient for trading standards officers to take on powers under Part III. By 1990, the Director General had come out in favour of shared enforcement with local authorities, and the DTI now proposes that this should be followed. Trading standards departments will be able to take action, as will the Secretary of State, although it is suggested that the latter will use his power sparingly. In order to avoid duplication of effort and unnecessary burdens on business the DTI proposes that the OFT should provide a co-ordination mechanism similar to that which operates in relation to unfair terms in consumer contracts.[170] So that the OFT can carry this out effectively, it is proposed that authorities be required to give the Office twenty-eight days' notice before taking action.

The proposal to share power between the OFT and trading standards officers is a major step forward. It has been a grave cause of concern that most traders who fall foul of Part III operate at a local level, but that trading standards officers have to refer matters to the OFT to take action. Concerns have been expressed at non-uniform enforcement, but it is submitted that these can be overcome by the measures that the DTI

[169] Ramsay, 'The Office of Fair Trading', p. 197.
[170] *Reform of Part III*, p. 2.

suggests. Furthermore, as will be examined in the next chapter, there
are already safeguards in place, operated by LACOTS, to ensure that
businesses are not subjected to uneven enforcement.

Part III and banning orders

One major improvement that the DTI has proposed in relation to Part III
is the creation of a power to prohibit a person from carrying on a course
of business with consumers. The proposal is that enforcement authorities
(including trading standards officers) should be able to apply to the court
for a banning order:

if it believes that the trader has breached an injunction awarded against him; or
has committed an offence involving fraud, or other dishonesty or violence; or has
engaged in conduct which is unfair and detrimental to consumers (these expressions having the same meaning as they have for the purposes of the injunctions
power) of such frequency or over such a period of time or over such a wide geo-
graphical area as to demonstrate that the respondent is not a fit person to engage
in business with consumers.

This is a significant weapon and, not surprisingly, it is proposed that it
be subject to safeguards. First, at least a month before making an application, the authority will have to inform the trader of its intention, giving
him the opportunity to make representations. Where the case goes to
court, the court will consider whether it is necessary to make an order to
protect the interests of consumers. If the court decides that it is, it will be
able to impose a ban for up to fifteen years, although if the ban was made
on the grounds of a criminal offence, it will expire when the conviction
becomes spent. The recipient of a banning order will be able to apply to
the court to release or vary the ban on the grounds that it is no longer
necessary to protect the interests of consumers, or that it could be varied without a significant risk of causing further detriment to consumers.
Breach of a banning order will be a criminal offence. The Public Register
will apply to banning orders as it does to injunctions.

Bearing in mind the likely opposition to any attempt to extend the
criminal law in the area of unfair activity, it may be that reform of Part III
is the best approach. As it stands, Part III is undoubtedly inadequate as a
mechanism for consumer protection. However, with some amendments it
could become a powerful weapon. The proposals set out by the DTI are to
be welcomed. In particular, the removal of the persistence requirement,
the allocation of powers to local authorities and the creation of the power
to make banning orders would greatly improve the potential for consumer
protection. If these powers were increased along the lines proposed, there

would be less need to reform the criminal law in relation to protecting economic interests.

Part II of the Fair Trading Act

When the Fair Trading Act 1973 was passed, the Government thought it necessary to have some 'reasonably swift and sensitive piece of machinery'[171] which could lead to the making of secondary legislation to protect the economic interests of consumers. Under Part II of the Act, the Director General of Fair Trading was empowered to propose criminal law regulations to tackle consumer trade practices which appear adversely to affect consumers' economic interests. These proposals were scrutinised by a body called the Consumer Protection Advisory Committee (CPAC), which was supposed to act as a kind of 'jury' to assess proposed new offences. The Committee could modify or reject the Director General's proposals. Assuming that the CPAC did not reject the Director General's proposal, the Secretary of State then decided whether to follow the Director General or the Committee, or to do nothing. Just four references have been made, with only three orders resulting. No references have been made since 1976.[172] As a result of this, it seems that the procedure has been something of a failure. Nevertheless, it is worth looking at Part II, first because it teaches us something about the use of criminal sanctions to protect consumers' economic interests, and secondly because the DTI have produced proposals for the reform of Part II, which would be an important step forward if enacted.

It is clear that there were several problems with the use of Part II. First, the procedure under which it operates is time consuming. Under s.17, a reference can be made to the CPAC who investigate the reference. They then report to the Secretary of State, stating first whether the trade practice affects the economic interests of consumers and, if it does, whether it is likely to have one of the effects required by s.17(2). If these criteria are met then the CPAC may agree with the Director General's proposals, suggest modifications to them, or disagree with them. If the Committee either agrees with the proposals, or agrees subject to modifications, the Secretary of State can make an order and lay it before Parliament. The average length of time between making a reference and an order resulting

---

[171] An observation which has not found support with all commentators. Richard Lawson describes the procedure as 'nothing if not tortuous' (R. Lawson, 'Fair Trading Act 1973: A Suitable Case for Treatment' 1992 SolJ 544 at p. 544).

[172] For a detailed examination of the process and its deficiencies, see Ramsay, *Consumer Protection: Text, Cases and Materials*, pp. 270–80.

was two years.[173] It has been pointed out, however, that the CPAC should not be blamed for this delay, as the evidence is that they generally worked quickly and effectively.[174]

A second problem with the procedure was that it was necessary to show that the problem concerned a 'consumer trade practice', which must affect the 'economic interests of consumers'. This is rather prescriptive. A former Director General of Fair Trading has stated that he would have liked to have used these powers to deal with property misdescriptions but the term 'consumer trade practice' was too narrow to allow this, as it only concerned goods and services. It has also been suggested that the requirement to show that 'economic detriment' was present caused difficulties for the OFT, and that rather than using any accepted economic theory, the office had only a muted 'exploitation theory'.[175]

A further difficulty with the procedure in Part II is that the only laws to which it could lead were criminal laws. It may be that there was a reluctance to use such powers, both on the part of the Director General and the CPAC. The Director General's concern about using the criminal law has been emphasised by successive Directors General.[176]

It has been suggested that the reality of the CPAC's involvement may have been different from that which was intended. Cranston has noted that the CPAC has shown that it will 'closely and systematically scruti-nize a proposal from the Office of Fair Trading to determine whether all the necessary effects are produced and whether the proposals for control are requisite for the purpose of preventing a practice'.[177] This may be far more rigorous and interventionist than was anticipated. It has been argued that the CPAC was established with a 'fifth wheel' constitution, meaning that it would not be effective and would not have a high calibre of membership.[178] It has been suggested that there may be weaknesses in the CPAC's approach. Ramsay argues that its lack of reference to em-pirical or economic literature reveals an approach 'reminiscent of that of many English Royal Commissions ... suffused with "Judgment, wisdom

---

[173] See Ramsay, 'The Office of Fair Trading: Policing the Consumer Market Place' in Baldwin and McCrudden (eds.), *Regulation and Public Law*, p. 177 at p. 189.

[174] B. W. Harvey and D. L. Parry, *The Law of Consumer Protection and Fair Trading* (5th edn, London, Butterworths, 1996), p. 327.

[175] See Ramsay, *Consumer Protection*, p. 281.

[176] See the discussion in Harvey and Parry, *The Law of Consumer Protection and Fair Trading*, p. 327 n. 9.

[177] R. Cranston, *Consumers and the Law* (2nd edn, London, Weidenfeld and Nicolson, 1984), p. 338.

[178] Ramsay, relying on information from an informant. This is backed up by the fact that the Committee was given only three months in which to respond to a reference (Ramsay, 'The Office of Fair Trading', p. 189).

and common sense"'.[179] The CPAC itself should not be criticised for taking this approach, however. The Parliamentary debates reveal that the Committee was intended to 'use its broad experience and common sense' rather than to engage in academic analysis.[180] Ultimately, whether action is taken depends upon the Secretary of State. The decision will therefore be political, notwithstanding the removal of the early parts of the procedure from the political process. One alternative might be to give a law-making power to the Director General, although it is questionable whether this would be seen as constitutionally acceptable.

Sir Gordon Borrie described Part II as 'an example of a bold idea smothered by an excess of nervous caution so that the resulting provisions have inevitably been a disappointment'.[181] Certainly, the procedure is dormant. However, the DTI have recently proposed changes to Part II which may lead to its re-awakening. The main proposals are that the CPAC be abolished and the procedure for making an order be changed. The justification for abolition of the CPAC is that the OFT now uses rigorous appraisal techniques to determine the necessity of legislation, and so the Committee is no longer necessary. The new procedure would be that the Director General would identify an appropriate trade practice, and issue a notice explaining its adverse effects, giving opportunities for representations to be made which he would be obliged to consider. The Director General would then publish a report setting out the recommended action. If the Secretary of State agrees with the Director General, he would then be able to make secondary legislation accordingly. However, before issuing the order, the Secretary of State would be obliged to publish a notice of his intentions, and invite written representations. If the Secretary of State decides not to make an order, he will have to give his reasons to the Director General and publish them. The new power can be used both to protect consumers, and to protect individuals 'who are receiving or seeking to receive goods, services, etc., with a view to establishing a business, and who are not currently carrying on a business involving the supply of goods or services of any kind'. This is designed to protect vulnerable individuals who may fall prey to unscrupulous traders such as 'vanity publishers' and who may not currently fall under the definition of consumers.

The proposed changes to Part II should be given a cautious welcome. It is regrettable that the procedure has become moribund, as it should have provided a means of creating protective legislation without the need for

---

[179] Ramsay, *Consumer Protection*, p. 274.
[180] Standing Committee B HC 436-38 22 February 1973.
[181] Borrie, *The Development of Consumer Law and Policy*, p. 127.

precious Parliamentary time, but with adequate safeguards. The abolition will streamline the process, and recent Directors General have shown an admirable willingness to suggest how new legislation could be implemented to provide increasing consumer protection. A re-vamped Part II, coupled with the changes to Part III already discussed, may become one of the most important methods for protecting consumers' economic interests.

Conclusion

The law can protect consumers' economic interests in a number of ways. First, it can make it an offence to supply false or misleading information about goods or services. The tradition in the UK has been to focus upon this, particularly where the criminal law is concerned. Secondly, the law can insist that information be disclosed. It is relatively rare for the law to require disclosure under pain of criminal sanctions, but there are examples where this technique has been used. Thirdly, the law could ensure that traders fulfil consumers' reasonable expectations, for example by making it an offence to supply goods which are not of satisfactory quality. Although it has been suggested that this would muddy the distinction between breach of the criminal law, it is sometimes forgotten that consumer protection statutes already go a long way towards making breach of contract into a criminal offence. Under the Trade Descriptions Act 1968, for example, goods may be found to 'lie about themselves' if they are presented in a misleading way, promises as to future conduct may be criminal if the maker of the statement purports to guarantee something which he knows that he cannot, and a trader will be deemed to have applied a false trade description to goods if he delivers them when they do not comply with the recipient's request. This is a small step away from criminal liability for supplying unsatisfactory goods. Where the goods in question are foodstuffs, an offence will be committed if they are not of the quality demanded by the purchaser, even if the purchaser has not explicitly stated his requirements. Although it is unlikely that new legislation would impose criminal liability for the supply of unsatisfactory goods, provided the offence was subject to a due diligence defence and enforced with an appropriate compliance strategy, it need not be feared unduly by honest traders.

The fourth way in which the criminal law could be used to protect consumers' economic interests is by prohibiting unfair conduct. Again, although this might appear attractive from the point of view of consumer protection, it is unlikely to find support from the Post-1997 Government. Indeed, an offence of unfair conduct seems too wide. One possibility would be to introduce an offence couched in terms of unconscionability or deceptiveness, but this too seems unlikely to be introduced. But the problem of unfair conduct remains significant. A Government committed to championing the consumer and tackling the causes of 'Rip-Off Britain' needs to take action against conduct which is unacceptable, but does not fall squarely under an existing offence. It is submitted that the most appropriate solution would be to reform and revitalise Parts II and III of the Fair Trading Act 1973. Reform along the lines suggested above would give enforcement authorities a valuable weapon to tackle trading malpractices, and would, when the need arises, enable criminal offences to be created swiftly and effectively.

7 The enforcement of regulatory consumer law

Introduction

If the criminal law is to be effective in protecting consumers then it needs effective enforcement. Some of the earliest consumer protection statutes created criminal offences, but frequently relied upon private individuals to take action. For example, the Adulteration of Food and Drink Act 1860 made it an offence knowingly to sell food containing an injurious ingredient or which was adulterated. Although local authorities were empowered by the Act to appoint public analysts they were under no duty to do so, and individuals wanting samples to be analysed were required to pay for the service. It was only with the passing of the Adulteration of Food, Drink, and Drugs Act 1872 that the appointment of analysts became obligatory and that local authority inspectors were empowered to procure samples for analysis. Since that time, the enforcement of consumer law by public bodies has become a major characteristic of the system in the UK.[1]

The purpose of this chapter is to examine the ways in which regulatory consumer protection statutes are enforced. Consumer law in the UK is enforced predominantly at local level, by officers employed by local authorities, who will be responsible for a particular geographic area. However, at a national level the Director General of Fair Trading and the Secretary of State for Trade and Industry also have some enforcement powers, for example under Part III of the Fair Trading Act 1973, and under the Consumer Protection Act 1987.[2] To understand the reality of enforcement, it is important to say something about the strategies which may be invoked, and to look at the available theoretical and empirical evidence. We will see that trading standards officers, in common with other

---

[1] See P. Smith and D. Swann, *Protecting the Consumer: An Economic and Legal Analysis* (Oxford, Martin Robertson, 1979), pp. 118–19. Private prosecutions are still possible, and there have been examples of prosecutions by competitors. See *Donnelly* v. *Rowlands* [1971] 1 All ER 9.

[2] This book does not consider the enforcement of consumer law by bodies outside the UK, such as the European Commission.

212

enforcement agencies, rely extensively on compliance strategies.[3] These
are characterised by persuasion and negotiation, and may be contrasted
with deterrence strategies, which are characterised by prosecution. Nevertheless, prosecution remains an important weapon for trading standards
officers, and it is important to investigate when this will be invoked. It
will be concluded that enforcement of consumer protection law in the
UK displays many of the characteristics of the 'tit for tat' strategy championed by Ian Ayres and John Braithwaite, and that such an approach is
to be welcomed.[4]

After examining law enforcement in theory and practice, this chapter looks doctrinally at some of the statutory provisions which facilitate
enforcement. The focus of this part of the chapter is on enforcement
techniques available to deal with dangerous products. Product safety
provides a useful case study to illustrate the difficulties faced by those
seeking to ensure effective enforcement of regulatory consumer law. If a
particular product is found to be dangerous, there has to be a method
of ensuring that it does not infiltrate the market. In some cases there is
the need to target a particular supplier, in others the need to tackle a
variety of suppliers. In some cases it may be enough to ensure that the
product is accompanied by a warning, while in others we need an out-
right ban. Some powers are only exercisable by the Secretary of State,
whereas others can be utilised by trading standards officers. Attention
will also be paid to the protection of economic interests by examining
enforcement powers which apply both to matters of safety and economic
interests.

Enforcement strategies

Compliance and deterrence

Although consumer protection law imposes upon enforcement authorities a duty to enforce the legislation, this does not mean that there is a duty
to prosecute as a matter of course.[5] Authorities generally have a discretion
as to what action, if any, to take.[6] They have limited resources at their disposal, and will want to make optimal use of those resources. Authorities

---

[3] I use the term 'enforcement agency' to mean a specialist body charged with the implementation of regulatory criminal law. I use the term 'enforcement authority' when
focusing specifically on trading standards departments.

[4] I. Ayres and J. Braithwaite, *Responsive Regulation: Transcending the Deregulation Debate*
(Oxford, Oxford University Press, 1992).

[5] See *Smedleys Ltd* v. *Breed* [1974] AC 839 *per* Viscount Dilhorne.

[6] Note the comments by Lord Shawcross (Hansard HC vol. 483 col. 681, 29 January
1951).

have a choice of enforcement strategies, the main two of which have been categorised as deterrence strategies and compliance strategies.[7] The aim of a deterrence strategy is 'to secure conformity with the law by detecting violation, determining who is responsible for the violation, and penalising violations to deter violations in the future, either by those who are punished or by those who might do so were violations not penalised'. By contrast, a compliance strategy has as its aim 'to secure conformity with law by means of ensuring compliance or by taking action to prevent potential law violation without the necessity to detect, process and penalise violations'.[8] It 'seeks to prevent a harm rather than punish an evil'.[9] There is also a third enforcement strategy, the retributive strategy, which is seldom employed.[10] The empirical evidence on enforcement indicates that enforcement officers overwhelmingly adopt compliance strategies, with prosecution as a last resort.[11] Indeed, it has been said that: '[enforcement officers'] normal attitude is to see their major role as one of attempting to acquire compliance with legislation by information and persuasion... in many authorities prosecution is seen as a last resort and, sometimes, even as an admission of failure'.[12]

Seeking optimal strategies

A considerable quantity of literature has emerged on what might be called the economic theory of crime. One aim of this approach is to explain when an offence is likely to be committed, and to use that information to devise an appropriate enforcement strategy. If the aim of enforcement is optimal deterrence, i.e. 'to minimise the harm resulting from contraventions

---

[7] A. J. Reiss, 'Selecting Strategies of Social Control Over Organisational Life' in K. Hawkins and J. Thomas (eds.), *Enforcing Regulation* (Dordrecht, Kluwer Nijhoff, 1984).

[8] Ibid. pp. 23–4.

[9] C. Veljanowski, 'The Economics of Regulatory Enforcement' in Hawkins and Thomas (eds.), *Enforcing Regulation*, p. 172.

[10] This is where 'sanctions are imposed for their own sake as punishment': G. Richardson, 'Strict Liability for Regulatory Crime: The Empirical Research' [1987] Crim LR 295 at 299. For a discussion of the role of retributive theories of crime see ch. 3. There will be cases where retribution is relevant to regulatory offences. See 'Developments in the Law: Corporate Crime' (1978–9) 92 Harvard LR 1227 at 1231.

[11] Although it is possible for an enforcement agency to adopt a compliance strategy in relation to most types of wrong but a deterrence strategy in particular types of case. See J. Rowan-Robinson, P. Q. Watchman, and C. R. Barker, 'Crime and Regulation' [1988] Crim LR 211 at pp. 216–17.

[12] R. J. Bragg, *Trade Descriptions* (Oxford, Clarendon Press, 1991), p. 202. Evidence shows that this strategy is favoured in the context of trade descriptions legislation. See also R. Cranston, *Regulating Business: Law and Consumer Agencies* (London, Macmillan, 1979).

of regulation at lowest administrative cost',[13] we need some idea of how a trader is likely to behave under different circumstances. In particular, we need to be able to predict when a trader will obey or break the law. According to a simplified version of the main economic theories of crime, the trader will comply with the law where $pD > U$. Here, P is the perceived probability of apprehension and conviction, D represents the costs incurred as a result of apprehension and conviction, and U represents the benefits resulting from violation.[14] The enforcement agency should use resources up to the point where the marginal cost of those resources is equal to the marginal benefit which arises from the expenditure in terms of reduced violations.[15]

Ogus sets out the model, but recognises that there are huge difficulties in applying it in practice. First, it assumes that the trader is rational, influenced only by the costs and benefits of his actions. In reality, it is unclear to what extent rational cost-benefit decisions are made by those considering committing offences,[16] and much economic analysis of crime assumes a degree of rationality on the part of the offender which is difficult to accept.[17] Gardiner comments that the depiction of individuals as rational beings who always think before they act is questionable, and that '[a]mongst criminals, foresight and prudent calculation is even more conspicuous by its absence'.[18] Similarly, the 1990 White Paper *Crime, Justice and Protecting the Public* commented that 'it is unrealistic to construct sentencing arrangements on the assumption that most offenders will weigh up the evidence in advance and base their conduct on rational calculation'.[19] However, it has been argued that we might be able to differentiate businesses from other criminals in respect of rational decision-making:

while criminals generally do not carefully calculate the probable consequences of their actions and therefore are often not deterred by the threat of punishment, this cannot be said of the corporate criminal. Since corporate activity is normally

[13] A. I. Ogus, *Regulation: Legal Form and Economic Theory* (Oxford, Clarendon Press, 1994), p. 90.

[14] See G. Becker, 'Crime and Punishment: An Economic Approach' (1968) 76 J Pol Econ 169 and Ogus, *Regulation*, p. 91.

[15] See Ogus, *Regulation*, and R. Posner, 'The Behaviour of Administrative Agencies' (1972) 1 J Legal Stud 314.

[16] Becker, for example, assumes that 'a person commits an offence if the expected utility to him exceeds the utility he could get by using his time and other resources at other activities'. See Becker, 'Crime and Punishment', at p. 176. For a criticism of this approach see T. Gibbons, 'The Utility of Economic Analysis of Crime' (1982) *International Review of Law and Economics* 173.

[17] See Gibbons, 'The Utility of Economic Analysis of Crime'.

[18] G. Gardiner, 'The Purposes of Criminal Punishment' (1958) 21 MLR 117 at p. 122.

[19] (1990) Cm 965 para. 2.8.

undertaken in order to reap some economic benefit, corporate decision-makers choose courses of action based on a calculation of potential costs and benefits.[20]

Although traders may be better placed to weigh costs and benefits than the majority of offenders, it is unlikely that they will do it in the way that the economic approach to crime envisages. One reason for this is that many traders will have a genuine desire to obey the law, even if it is costly for them to do so. The reason for this is that people make choices for a wide variety of reasons, and not just because of the economic satisfaction they derive. 'They choose to do things out of a sense of duty, altruism, or because they have been taught to do a job in a particular way.'[21] Ayres and Braithwaite similarly note the importance of norms, arguing that whereas '[s]ome corporate actors will only comply with the law if it is economically rational for them to do so; most corporate actors will comply with the law most of the time because it is the law'.[22] Kagan looked at the motivation of a corporation by suggesting that they can be divided into three separate categories: amoral calculators, political citizens, and the organisationally inept.[23] Amoral calculators are those that carefully weigh up the benefits and costs of complying with the law. Political citizens may not be deterred by conviction, as they aim to comply with the law in the first place, while the organisationally inept may be unable to comply even if they wish to. In the context of consumer law it is clear that many offences are due to organisational failures rather than calculated decisions.[24] In the context of Health and Safety at Work legislation, Baldwin divides up employers into the following categories: well-intentioned and well-informed; well-intentioned and ill-informed; ill-intentioned and ill-informed; and problematic.[25] In the area of pollution control, Hawkins found that enforcement officers divided up polluters into the categories of socially responsible, unfortunate, careless, and malicious.[26] It is therefore

---

[20] 'Developments in the Law: Corporate Crime' (1978–9) 92 Harvard LR 1227 at p. 1231. See also J. Braithwaite and G. Geis, 'On Theory and Action for Corporate Crime Control' (1982) 28 *Crime and Delinquency* 292.

[21] B. J. McCormick, *Introducing Economics* (2nd edn, London, Penguin, 1977), p. 176. Cited in Gibbons, 'The Utility of Economic Analysis', p. 178. It may be possible to incorporate this into the economic model by saying that these factors are part of the costs for the perpetrator.

[22] Ayres and Braithwaite, *Responsive Regulation*, p. 19. See also C. Sunstein, *Free Markets and Social Justice* (New York, Oxford University Press, 1997), ch. 2.

[23] R. Kagan and J. Scholz, 'The "Criminology of the Corporation" and Regulatory Enforcement Strategies', in Hawkins and Thomas (eds.), *Enforcing Regulation*.

[24] See I. Ramsay, *Consumer Protection: Text, Cases and Materials* (London, Weidenfeld and Nicolson, 1990), p. 190.

[25] R. Baldwin, 'Why Rules Don't Work' (1990) 53 MLR 321 at p. 324.

[26] K. Hawkins, 'Compliance Strategy' in K. Hawkins, *Environment and Enforcement* (Oxford, Oxford University Press, 1994).

difficult to make generalisations about how traders will react to different legal rules and enforcement policies, and this makes the creation of an optimal enforcement model particularly problematic.

A second difficulty with the model is that it involves a high degree of imprecision in its implementation. There will be little evidence of the likelihood that a firm will be prosecuted and convicted, and of what punishment, if any, they are likely to receive. As a result, it is likely that traders will differ greatly in their perception of the probability of conviction (P) and the likely costs of conviction (D). As well as the fine imposed, D will include the cost of defending the case in court and any costs that result from negative publicity; these will be extremely difficult to quantify. This is not to say that the defendant will not be deterred. Indeed, he may greatly fear the consequences of conviction, in particular the loss of business which might result from a highly publicised case.[27] However, quantifying this is likely to be extremely difficult. It may be easier for them to identify the probable benefits of contravention (U), but this may also be hard to assess. As a result, even if the offender is rational, he may not find it possible to come to any conclusion about the values of the variables. The enforcement agency will therefore find it equally difficult to establish the optimal level of enforcement. Furthermore, the content of the variables in our equation will be largely outside the control of the agency. The agency can increase the number of prosecutions (subject to budgetary constraints), and this may increase the perception of the likelihood of conviction. The agency can press for maximum sentences to be imposed, but those sentences will be a matter for the judge, following the limits set down by the legislature. As most consumer protection offences are dealt with by the magistrates' court, even the maximum sentences may be low. The enforcement agency may have some influence over the adverse publicity suffered by the trader, but its ability to do this will be limited. The agency has little control over the benefit to the trader from contravention.

Perhaps the main difficulty for the enforcement agency in trying to ensure optimal deterrence is how to weigh up the value of different types of harm.[28] For example, it may be difficult for an agency to balance severe harm to an individual against minor harm to a larger group. Although we place monetary value on death and personal injury for the purposes of tort law, this is both contentious and imprecise.[29] Nevertheless, as will be

---

[27] C. Wells, *Corporations and Criminal Responsibility* (Oxford, Oxford University Press, 1993), p. 37, B. Fisse and J. Braithwaite, *The Impact of Publicity on Corporate Offenders* (Albany, State University of New York, 1983).

[28] Ogus, *Regulation*, p. 92.

[29] See M. W. Jones-Lee, *The Economics of Safety and Physical Risk* (Oxford, Blackwell, 1989).

seen below, there is likely to be broad agreement about the seriousness of offences, and an enforcement agency will have to form some view of the severity of a particular type of harm when weighing up the decision as to whether to prosecute.

The strengths of deterrence strategies. An agency that aims for optimal deterrence might be expected to prosecute on a regular basis, and regular prosecution is a characteristic of a deterrence strategy. However, we know that in practice very few prosecutions are brought under regulatory legislation. To use an extreme example, Lidstone, Hogg, and Sutcliffe found that the Wages Inspectorate discovered about 40,000 offences under the Wages Act 1976 to have been committed, but chose not to prosecute in any case.[30] In consumer protection, prosecutions are also infrequent. Publishing his findings in 1979, Cranston found that of over 21,000 infringements of the Trade Descriptions Act he identified over a six-month period, just 1,003 were prosecuted while 14,542 were resolved by giving advice. Recent figures from the OFT reveal only prosecutions and formal action rather than infringements discovered, but it is generally recognised that prosecutions remain the exception rather than the rule.[31] It is clear that a wide variety of factors influence the decision to bring a prosecution on any given facts, and these are considered below.[32] One explanation for the paucity of prosecutions is that enforcement agencies are liable to be 'captured'. This capture theory, which is primarily associated with Bernstein, is characterised by the idea of enforcement agencies going through a 'life-cycle'. This was summarised memorably by Galbraith as follows: 'Regulatory bodies, like the people who comprise them, have a marked life-cycle. In youth they are vigorous, aggressive, evangelistic, and even intolerant. Later, they mellow, and in old age – after a matter of ten or fifteen years, they become, with some exceptions, either an arm of the industry they are regulating or senile.'[33]

Capture theory suggests that enforcement agencies' close connections with industry lead to the public interest being subordinated to the interests of the industry. This may be because of the revolving-door theory – that enforcement agencies are made up of former members of the business

---

[30] K. Lidstone, L. Hogg, and F. Sutcliffe, *Prosecution by Private Individuals and non-Police Agencies*, Royal Commission on Criminal Procedure Research Study No. 10 (HMSO 1980).

[31] See recent annual reports of the Director General of Fair Trading.

[32] For useful accounts of the findings of the main empirical studies, see Richardson, 'Strict Liability for Regulatory Crime' and Rowan-Robinson, Watchman, and Barker, 'Crime and Regulation' [1988] Crim LR 211.

[33] J. K. Galbraith, *The Great Crash* (Boston, Houghton Mifflin, 1955), p. 171. Cited in Ramsay, *Consumer Protection*, at pp. 77–8. See also M. Bernstein, *Regulating Business by Independent Commission* (Princeton, Princeton University Press, 1955).

they are regulating, and officers who aspire to take up well-paid positions in those businesses. Research by Grabosky and Braithwaite found that prosecutions were less frequent where regulators and the regulated were close in terms of social background (the so-called relational distance hypothesis), and that prosecutions were less frequent for large firms than small firms (the company size hypothesis). This might lead us to conclude that the agencies had been captured by those they were regulating.[34]

If we are sensitive to the risk of capture, this may lead us towards favouring deterrence strategies, where prosecutions are taken as a matter of course. Such strategies might reduce the risk of certain forms of capture, for example, corruption, by reducing discretion on the part of the agency.[35] A study by Bardach and Kagan found that strict enforcement brings reduced risks and improved standards by inducing firms to change their corporate culture and introduce new management schemes.[36] To some extent due diligence defences may encourage traders to set up management schemes, as the main indicator of whether a firm has taken all reasonable precautions and exercised all due diligence is found in the system established by the trader to ensure that offences are not committed. Empirical research by Cranston found that while a minority of consumer agencies were 'prosecution minded', there were vocal adherents of deterrence strategies. In the words of one enforcement officer: 'there's nothing that brings home an infringement more than a prosecution. You can issue cautions until you're blue in the face. If you don't enforce the law you get a fall in the trading environment, and you get more complaints.' Despite this, Cranston found that even prosecution-minded authorities settle the majority of matters informally.[37]

A further advantage of deterrence strategies is that they may reduce the likelihood of inconsistent enforcement. In chapter 3 we examined the argument put forward by Ashworth that it is a fundamental principle of the criminal law that like cases should be treated alike.[38] If an enforcement agency has a fixed policy of prosecution following contravention there is less scope for the unfairness that results from unequal treatment. Indeed, Ashworth argued that '[a] system of criminal justice that allows the differential enforcement of its laws is not a system that honours the

---

[34] P. Grabosky and J. Braithwaite, *Of Manners Gentle: Enforcement Strategies of Australian Business Regulatory Agencies* (Melbourne, Oxford University Press, 1986).

[35] There are other ways in which the risk of capture can be minimised, for example through tripartism, where public interest groups are formally included in the regulatory process. See Ayres and Braithwaite, *Responsive Regulation*, ch. 3.

[36] E. Bardach and R. Kagan, *Going by the Book: The Problem of Regulatory Unreasonableness* (Philadelphia, Temple University Press, 1982).

[37] Cranston, *Regulating Business*, p. 100.

[38] A. Ashworth, 'Is the Criminal Law a Lost Cause?' (2000) 116 LQR 225 at 245.

principle of equal treatment'.[39] Inconsistent enforcement may lead to a greater breakdown in trust between regulator and regulated than strict but consistent enforcement.

The strengths of compliance strategies. A number of arguments can be made in favour of compliance strategies. First, despite the one-time popularity of capture theory, the theory has been largely discredited. Many regulators appear to be worthy adversaries of their industries, and it may be that compliance strategies, far from indicating capture, merely demonstrate the determination of enforcement agencies to place compliance with the law at the top of their agendas. Research by Makkai and Braithwaite cast doubt upon capture, the authors concluding that their data 'indicate little support for the theory that regulatory enforcement is under the hegemony of the private interests from which so many regulators come – or to which they hope to go'.[40] Similarly, the arguments in favour of deterrence-based approaches are questionable. Bargaining and negotiation, rather than being the easiest options for the regulated trader may be the most effective options for the enforcement agency. The perception that prosecution is a last resort is an important aspect of a compliance strategy. If compliance with legislation can be ensured by informal measures then the prime purpose of the legislation is fulfilled cost-effectively. 'Punishment is expensive; persuasion is cheap.'[41] Veljanowski found that prosecution was from eight to ten times more time consuming than the typical factory visit.[42] When the Trade Descriptions Act 1968 was being debated, the Government emphasised the importance of trading standards officers being able to use discretion. One Minister commented that '[w]e do not want a spate of trivial prosecutions where, when the mistake is drawn to the attention of the department store, or whatever it is, the customer is immediately appeased, the mistake admitted, and the loss to the customer, whatever it may be, corrected'.

There are other difficulties with deterrence-based schemes. First, the cost of regular prosecution may be prohibitive. As will be argued later, if cost were the major factor in the decision not to prosecute then that would be deeply concerning, but it is not clear that this is the case.

[39] Ashworth, 'Is the Criminal Law a Lost Cause?', p. 246.
[40] They did, interestingly, find some support for Bernstein's life-cycle theory in that 'tougher inspectors leave the [regulatory] programme earlier, while less tough peers stay on as regulators'. See T. Makkai and J. Braithwaite, 'In and Out of the Revolving Door: Making Sense of Regulatory Capture' (1995) 1 *Journal of Public Policy* 61 at p. 78.
[41] Ayres and Braithwaite, *Responsive Regulation*, p. 19.
[42] See C. Veljanowski, 'Regulatory Enforcement: An Economic Study of the British Factory Inspectorate' (1983) 5 Law and Pol Q 75 at p. 86.

Secondly, there is the possibility that enforcement officers will find it more difficult to obtain information from the industry, and therefore to exercise effective control, if there is a culture of hostility between regulator and regulated. If compliance strategies increase trust between regulators and regulated then this may improve the flow of information between them, which in turn leads to more effective enforcement. Painter has argued that successful enforcement 'depends upon goodwill and co-operation between manufacturers, distributors, and enforcement officers. Unless trades people can discuss problems freely, uninhibited by fear of prosecution, the quality of service must suffer.'[43] Where a strategy is based predominantly on punishment it may foster 'an organised business subculture of resistance to regulation'.[44] This view has been expressed in a number of different areas.[45] Adopting punishment as a first-choice strategy may be seen as 'unaffordable, unworkable, and counter productive in undermining the good will of those with a commitment to compliance'.[46]

Compliance and tit for tat. A recent approach to enforcement which involves many of the characteristics of compliance strategies is that set out by Ayres and Braithwaite in *Responsive Regulation*.[47] They argue in favour of seeing regulators as 'benign big guns', who have a variety of sanctions at their disposal, but rely upon moral suasion as the primary means of ensuring compliance. They argue that the most effective method of regulation is what they term tit for tat (TFT). This means that 'the regulator refrains from a deterrent response as long as the firm is co-operating; but when the firm yields to the temptation to exploit the cooperative posture of the regulator and cheats on compliance, then the regulator shifts from a cooperative to a deterrent response'.[48] Ayres and Braithwaite argue that TFT strategies are effective in controlling both the Holmesian 'good men' who look to the law as a guide for proper action, and 'bad men', who try to evade those laws.[49] Furthermore, they argue that 'all corporate actors are bundles of contradictory commitments to values about economic rationality, law abidingness, and business responsibility'.[50] This is important because the pressures on such actors, to maximise profits, to comply with

[43] A. A. Painter, 'Why Prosecute?' (1974) 76 *British Food Journal* 38 at p. 38.
[44] Ayres and Braithwaite, *Responsive Regulation*, p. 20.
[45] See Bardach and Kagan, *Going by the Book*, G. Richardson, A. Ogus, and P. Burroughs, *Policing Pollution* (Oxford, Clarendon Press, 1982), p. 126 and Cranston, *Regulating Business*.
[46] Ayres and Braithwaite, *Responsive Regulation*, p. 26.
[47] Ibid.   [48] Ibid. p. 21.   [49] Ibid. p. 20.   [50] Ibid. p. 23.

legal, business, and moral norms, and so on, will manifest themselves to different extents at different times. Strategies based purely on compliance are likely to be exploited where actors are motivated by economic rationality, while strategies based mostly on punishment will undermine the goodwill of those who are motivated by a sense of responsibility. The key is to strike some sort of 'sophisticated balance' between the two models, to 'establish a synergy between punishment and persuasion'.[51]

In practice, it seems that the approach of trading standards officers in the UK bears many similarities to the TFT strategy that Ayres and Braithwaite favour. Although prosecutions may occur without deliberation on the part of the trader in exceptional cases, the emphasis is on prosecution as a last resort. In the words of Cranston, '[c]ourt proceedings are seen as a backstop to be used where advice or persuasion have failed, or for unscrupulous businesses which are immune from other reformative action'.[52] So, for example, a more deterrence-based strategy might be used where there is a practice which suggests the existence of *mens rea* and is seen as a major problem.[53]

One inherent difficulty is that regulation inevitably produces a response in the regulated. Sunstein argues that nearly all the paradoxes of regulation, where regulation produces a result directly opposed to that intended, 'are a product of the government's failure to understand how the relevant actors – administrators and regulated entities – will adapt to regulatory programmes'.[54] Effective enforcement only works to the extent that there is either a genuine desire to comply with the law, or a real fear that continuance with a course of conduct will lead to an effective sanction. The specificity of many criminal sanctions means that new forms of conduct may arise which offend the spirit, but not the letter, of the legislation. However, the move towards more general legislation in a number of areas has already been noted, and the existence of broad rules makes it easier to threaten action if compliance is not forthcoming.[55]

The decision to prosecute. Our discussion of compliance strategies and TFT demonstrates that although prosecutions are less frequent than might be expected, they remain a significant part of enforcement agencies' work. The important point to consider now is what the factors are that will lead trading standards officers to prosecute for breach of consumer

---

[51] Ibid. p. 25.
[52] Cranston, *Regulating Business*, p. 99.
[53] Rowan-Robinson, Watchman, and Barker, 'Crime and Regulation', pp. 216–17.
[54] Sunstein, *Free Markets and Social Justice*, p. 276.
[55] Note, for example, the General Product Safety Regulations discussed in ch. 5 and the calls for a re-vamped Part III of the Fair Trading Act made in ch. 6.

protection law. TFT emphasises primarily the attitude of the trader, but there appear to be several important factors in the decision to prosecute. These may be found in official guidance or inferred from empirical studies.[56] One recent document is the Enforcement Concordat, issued by the Cabinet Office on 4 March 1998. This states:

The effectiveness of legislation in protecting consumers or sectors of society depends crucially on the compliance of those regulated. We recognise that most businesses want to comply with the law. We will therefore take care to help business and others meet their legal obligations without unnecessary expense, while taking firm action, including prosecution where appropriate, against those who flout the law or act irresponsibly.[57]

The concordat requires local authorities to improve their dealings with business, for example by identifying the performance that business and the public can expect, providing and disseminating information on the rules that enforcement officers apply, and exercising their duties fairly and consistently. However, it remains for the enforcement authority to have its own enforcement policy, and there is therefore the possibility of different policies being used by different authorities.[58] One example of detailed policy enforcement guidelines is those produced by LACOTS in relation to food safety. They provide that prosecutions may be pursued:

(i) Where there has been such a flagrant breach of the law that the health, safety or well-being of consumers has been put at risk;
(ii) Where the suspected offender has failed to correct a serious identified risk, having been given a reasonable opportunity to comply with the lawful requirements of an authorised officer;
(iii) Where the offence involves a failure to comply (fully or partly) with a statutory notice;
(iv) Where there is a history of similar offences related to a risk to public health.[59]

This detailed guidance has not been introduced in other areas, and so a wider range of factors may be taken into account in those areas. Indeed, it has been doubted whether the guidelines are followed in practice in all food-safety cases.[60] It should be noted that the Government will be

---

[56] See the Codes of Practice for food authorities, made under s.40(1) of the Food Safety Act 1990, and the empirical studies referred to elsewhere in this chapter.
[57] Enforcement Concordat (1998).
[58] See C. Andrews, *The Enforcement of Regulatory Offences* (London, Sweet and Maxwell, 1998), pp. 22–3.
[59] Ibid. p. 27.   [60] Ibid.

taking action under the Regulatory Reform Bill 2000 to issue enforcement codes. It seems that these will provide more formal rules than the Enforcement Concordat, although details are not yet available.[61] The factors examined below are those that are likely, in appropriate cases, to be considered when deciding whether or not to prosecute. They may also be considered when taking other enforcement action, such as the revocation of a licence, where that power exists.

The first factor which is likely to influence the decision to prosecute is the existence of *mens rea*, in particular intention, on the part of the trader. Some commentators have found the intent of the violator as being the single most important factor in the decision to prosecute.[62] Although the majority of consumer protection offences impose strict criminal liability, trading standards officers will be influenced by whether the offence is committed intentionally.[63] However, although the existence of intention is important to the decision whether or not to prosecute, it is irrelevant to the guilt of the defendant in the context of strict liability offences, and therefore generally will be inadmissible in evidence.[64] Where an offence is committed carelessly there is also more likely to be a decision to prosecute than where there is no culpability. Where the offence is committed without any carelessness a prosecution is unlikely for two main reasons. First, it may be seen as inappropriate by the enforcement authority because it will be unlikely to have a deterrent effect.[65] Secondly, it is unlikely to be successful as a trader who is not negligent is likely to be able to establish a due diligence defence, and so be acquitted. If the trader escapes liability by passing the blame onto an employee the authority may still be able to secure a conviction by targeting the employee under a bypass procedure, but evidence suggests a deep reluctance to do this.[66] If prosecution

---

[61] Cabinet Office, *Publication of Draft Regulatory Reform Bill* (Cm 4713 (2000)). See C. Scott and J. Black, *Cranston's Consumers and the Law* (London, Butterworths, 2000), p. 524.

[62] See W. G. Carson, 'Some Sociological Aspects of Strict Liability and the Enforcement of Factory Legislation' (1970) 30 MLR 396 and Richardson, Ogus, and Burroughs, *Policing Pollution*.

[63] Cranston noted an internal memo of one London Borough which stated '[t]his department will only prosecute if there is evidence of either dishonesty, fraud, sharp practice, gross negligence or flagrant breaches of the law'. Cranston, *Regulating Business*, p. 107. However, the author also noted that one chief officer stated that 'if the consumer is injured we prosecute. The consumer is not interested if it is a matter of fraud or accident' (p. 131).

[64] *Sandhu* [1997] Crim LR 288.

[65] This argument is less convincing where there is a due diligence defence because there is an incentive upon the trader to take care, as well as an incentive to avoid the harm which constitutes the offence.

[66] See Cranston, *Regulating Business*, p. 115 and P. Cartwright, 'Defendants in Consumer Protection Statutes: A Search for Consistency' (1996) 59 MLR 225.

is normally reserved for offenders who commit offences deliberately or, at the very least, carelessly, it could be argued that this 'reveals a de facto conversion of [the typical consumer protection offence] into one requiring *mens rea*'.[67] This, coupled with the ubiquitous due diligence defence, means that only blameworthy defendants should be convicted in practice.

A second factor that may influence a trading standards officer to prosecute is the existence of previous offences. Where repeat offences have taken place, particularly when they have been brought to the attention of the trader, prosecutions are more likely than when it is a first offence. Judges have criticised prosecutions of apparently innocent defendants on occasions.[68] However, it should be remembered that judges generally do not know the background to the prosecution, and in some cases there will be evidence of prior fault, both in terms of *mens rea* and in terms of previous contraventions. The Court of Appeal has quashed convictions where evidence of *mens rea* has been introduced on a strict liability charge, on the basis that such evidence is irrelevant and therefore inadmissible.[69] Evidence of previous contraventions may, however, be admissible where there is a due diligence defence, as they will be relevant to the question of whether the defendant has taken all reasonable precautions and exercised all due diligence.

A third factor that may have some influence on the decision to prosecute is the size of the firm, although the precise effect that this will have is unclear. Grabosky and Braithwaite suggest that prosecutions are less frequent for large firms than small firms.[70] By contrast, Cranston's research found an ambivalent approach on the part of trading standards officers to the prosecution of large firms. Some authorities were more reluctant to prosecute large firms because of the increased likelihood of the prosecution being vigorously contested; others expressed the importance of even-handedness between small and large firms, and some prosecuted large firms when small firms would be cautioned.[71] It should also be remembered that it is not only companies that can be prosecuted. Many consumer protection statutes allow for action to be taken against

---

[67] G. G. Howells and S. Weatherill, *Consumer Protection Law* (Aldershot, Dartmouth and Ashgale, 1995), p. 438. Carson found similar approaches being taken to enforcement of strict liability offences in factories legislation. See Carson, 'Some Sociological Aspects of Strict Liability'.

[68] See for example *Smedleys* v. *Breed* [1974] AC 839 and *Wings* v. *Ellis* [1984] 3 All ER 577.

[69] *Sandhu* [1997] Crim LR 288.

[70] Grabosky and Braithwaite, *Of Manners Gentle*.

[71] A related point is that small traders may be more easily persuaded that an enforcement agency is willing and able to prosecute than a larger trader. See Baldwin, *Why Rules Don't Work*, p. 325.

individuals. In some cases, only those who are part of the directing mind and will of the business may be prosecuted; in others junior employees and even private individuals become potential targets.[72] Evidence suggests that trading standards officers are reluctant to prosecute employees, feeling that they are the victims of their employers' wrongdoing.[73]

A fourth factor is the nature of the offence committed, in particular its seriousness. A general rule would be that the more serious the offence, the more likely it is to be prosecuted. However, identifying seriousness is problematic.[74] Seriousness may involve weighing up a wide variety of matters, such as the degree of culpability on the part of the defendant (was there intention, recklessness, or no identifiable *mens rea*), the type of harm caused or risked (physical or economic), and the degree of harm caused or risked (significant or minor) to name but a few. Hawkins found that in the context of pollution control it tended to be culpability that was the main factor in assessing seriousness: '[i]n all but the most massive pollutions, it is the component of moral disreputability – of wilful or negligent rule breaking or persistent disregard for the enforcement authority's authority – which can make the deviance serious'.[75] Despite these difficulties, it seems likely that enforcement authorities will, in the majority of cases, have a reasonably clear picture of how serious an offence is. Although it has been criticised as unsophisticated,[76] research by the criminologists Sellin and Wolfgang found considerable agreement among the public in ranking criminal offences, and disagreement about whether or not an offence is serious is likely to occur in relatively few cases.[77] It seems likely that enforcement authorities are more likely to act where physical safety is at issue than where economic interests are affected.[78] This may be because they are perceived as more serious. However, it should be remembered that apparently small offences may belie a greater wrong. Cranston notes how small offences 'may be symptomatic of a deeper

---

[72] Contrast s.1(1) of the Trade Descriptions Act 1968 which allows the prosecution of any employee acting in the course of a trade or business with s.20(1) of the Consumer Protection Act 1987 which limits prosecutions to an employee acting in the course of a trade or business 'of his'.

[73] Cranston, *Regulating Business*, p. 115.

[74] See ch. 1 and A. Ashworth, *Principles of Criminal Law* (3rd edn, Oxford, Oxford University Press, 1999), pp. 37–42.

[75] Hawkins, *Environment and Enforcement*, p. 206.

[76] Ashworth, *Principles of Criminal Law*, p. 38.

[77] T. Sellin and M. Wolfgang, *The Measurement of Delinquency* (1978). By contrast see Levi, who argues that 'views on seriousness vary by social class and in particular, commercial mores may differ from those of the mass of the people'. M. Levi, 'Business Regulatory Offences and the Criminal Law' 1984 5(6) *Company Lawyer* at 254.

[78] See Bragg, *Trade Descriptions*, p. 201.

malaise – a breakdown in supervisory proceedings, gross carelessness, or sharp practice'.[79]

A fifth factor to bear upon the decision to prosecute is the attitude of the firm. This has some overlap with other factors such as prior convictions and the existence of *mens rea*. However, a negative attitude to enforcement may exist independently of any prior fault. Code 2 of the Codes of Practice for enforcement for food authorities set out the factors to consider when deciding whether to prosecute, and they included the ability and willingness of the party to co-operate and the willingness to prevent the contravention recurring.[80] Hawkins' research on the enforcement of pollution control found that the attitude of the polluter was the most important factor enforcement authorities took into account when deciding on the appropriate response to a contravention.[81] A trader who fails to co-operate with an enforcement authority's investigation and who shows no sign of taking steps to tackle contraventions in the future is likely to find himself brought before the court. This is, of course, similar to the tit-for-tat approach championed by Ayres and Braithwaite, and discussed above.

One factor that is so influential upon the decision to prosecute that it might even be seen as a prerequisite is the belief that the prosecution will be successful. It has been noted elsewhere that enforcement agencies have a strong incentive to prosecute only those who are likely to plead guilty, with loss of a case being seen as too severe to be contemplated.[82] Richardson also found 'ample evidence that enforcement agencies are reluctant to prosecute if they fear they will lose'.[83] Andrews has even gone so far as to argue that 'some authorities will prosecute purely on the basis of a perceived expectation of conviction'.[84] The type of provision may be relevant here. Where a provision is vague, for example depending upon a judgement of reasonableness, an enforcement agency may think twice before prosecuting, whereas if the provision is more specific, the increased chance of conviction may make it more likely to be invoked.[85]

Ultimately, an enforcement agency is influenced by matters such as self-preservation and limited resources. In relation to self-preservation we should note the words of Hawkins: '[i]t is . . . in the careful and

---

[79] Cranston, *Regulating Business*, p. 130.

[80] See C. Scott, 'Criminalising the Trader to Protect the Consumer: The Fragmentation and Consolidation of Trading Standards Regulation' in I. Loveland (ed.), *Frontiers of Criminalisation* (London, Sweet and Maxwell, 1995), p. 149 at p. 169.

[81] Hawkins, 'Compliance Strategy' in Hawkins, *Environment and Enforcement*.

[82] Ibid.

[83] Richardson, 'Strict Liability for Regulatory Crime', p. 303.

[84] Andrews, *The Enforcement of Regulatory Offences*, p. 27.

[85] Baldwin, 'Why Rules Don't Work', p. 323.

sparing selection of cases for prosecution that the agency is best able to protect its own interests by showing that "something is being done"'. However, when a breach leads to harm which is sufficiently serious, prosecution is likely to follow as a matter of course, even in the absence of culpability. As well as furthering the aim of general deterrence, this 'serves to display publicly the agency carrying through its legal mandate as a credible enforcement agency'.[86] The image of the agency is clearly important. Prosecution has been said to have a ceremonial quality and, as Hawkins has emphasised, 'agencies feel exposed to public attention in the exercise of their authority – to endorsement of their policy or to the risk of public criticism of bullying or extravagance'.[87] Where there is a feeling among the public that an agency has been weak this may lead to increased enforcement, whereas a perception of over-bearingness might lead to a reduction in the number of prosecutions. Third-party influence, in terms of public, press, or interest-group pressure, may thus be a factor, as agencies feel the need to 'appease external constituencies'.[88]

In relation to resource limitations it would be impossible, given current levels of funding, to expect any regulatory agencies to prosecute as a matter of course, and some commentators have seen resource limitations as the prime reason for the paucity of prosecutions.[89] If this is so, it is a matter of grave concern. First, if some authorities have healthy budgets while others have paltry sums at their disposal then this may lead to unequal enforcement, a problem mentioned above. Secondly, if traders realise that the threat of prosecution is unrealistic for economic reasons, then those amoral calculators among them will feel inclined to contravene the law without fear of censure. The 'benign big gun' becomes illusory. However, it has been argued that agencies in some areas could increase their number of prosecutions significantly without any difficulty.[90] It may be that even if it were feasible to increase the number of prosecutions, this would be regarded as counter-productive and so avoided.

What this shows us is that while the emphasis of enforcement agencies is on seeking compliance through informal means, prosecutions remain an important weapon in practice as well as in theory. Several factors are likely to be considered in deciding whether to prosecute, but the most influential factors will be those pertaining to the overall approach of the trader towards the law, as evidenced by factors such as attitude to enforcement officers, *mens rea*, and commission of previous infractions.

---

[86] Hawkins, *Environment and Enforcement*.
[87] Ibid.
[88] Richardson, 'Strict Liability for Regulatory Crime', p. 302.
[89] Baldwin, 'Why Rules Don't Work' at 323.
[90] Hawkins, *Environment and Enforcement*

One further point to note is that the emphasis of our discussion so far has been on ensuring compliance with legislation with the threat of prosecution in the background. The focus of this work is, of course, on the role of the criminal law in consumer protection. However, it should be noted that prosecution is by no means the only course of action available to an enforcement agency. In some areas of activity, the agency may have the power to revoke the licence it has granted.[91] In others, it may have the power to impose a civil penalty.[92] Ayres and Braithwaite suggest that compliance with legislation is most likely where an agency displays an explicit enforcement pyramid. At the base of the pyramid will be where most action occurs (for example, negotiation and persuasion). Further up will be warning letters, civil penalties, criminal penalties, and so on, with the apex of the pyramid containing the most stringent, and least frequently used, sanction, such as licence revocation. Different types of sanctions will be relevant in different areas, but the shape of the pyramid will remain the same, with the most frequently used and most minor sanctions at the bottom, and the least frequently used and most severe sanctions at the top. There are a number of advantages to this. First, if there is a variety of sanctions, some minor and others severe, the threat of action is likely to carry more weight. An agency which has only severe sanctions at its disposal, such as revocation, may be unlikely to act in all but the most exceptional cases. It has been argued that as a result of this, stringent regulatory laws may lead to under-regulation.[93] Secondly, if severe sanctions are used only sparingly, and the emphasis is on less severe action, traders are more likely to comply willingly. The trader who is treated as a cheat and threatened with prosecution is more likely to dig in his heels and fight than the trader who is treated as a responsible citizen who has made a mistake. However, Ayres and Braithwaite conclude that while punishment should not be in the foreground, it needs to be in the background, and it needs to be significant: 'It may be that trustworthiness is best secured when the obligations of trust are owed to principals with great power over the agent, where the power is threatening but never threatened.'[94] Some commentators have noted that compliance strategies can swiftly turn into deterrence or retributive approaches.[95] However, the absence of effective sanctions remains an impediment. One of the difficulties with much UK consumer protection law is that the possible and

---

[91] For example, the Director General of Fair Trading can revoke consumer credit licences.
[92] For example, in relation to the Inland Revenue.
[93] See C. Sunstein, *After the Rights Revolution: Reconceiving the Regulatory State* (Cambridge, Mass., Harvard University Press, 1990), pp. 91–2.
[94] Ayres and Braithwaite, *Responsive Regulation*, p. 48.
[95] Richardson, 'Strict Liability for Regulatory Crime', p. 301.

likely penalties are so low, that power can seldom be seen as sufficiently threatening. This is a major cause for concern, and one that is considered further below.

Local enforcement and the home authority principle

We have seen that one fear of local enforcement is that it can lead to unequal enforcement in different parts of the jurisdiction. One of the characteristics of what Scott calls the 'regulatory crime paradigm' (of which consumer law is part) is the possibility of a non-uniform pattern of enforcement policy and practice.[96] The risk of non-uniform enforcement has troubled scholars for some time.[97] In an attempt to counter some of the deleterious effects of non-uniform enforcement, and to ensure consistency and co-ordination in all aspects of their work, local authorities under LACOTS operates the 'home authority' principle when it comes to enforcement of consumer protection legislation.[98] The home authority is the authority within which the firm's decision-making base is located. Normally this will be the head office, the main factory, or similar. The principle is designed to ensure uniformity of approach in trading standards matters, to avoid duplication of effort and to assist businesses in complying with the law. The home authority performs a variety of functions. For example, it acts on behalf of originating and enforcing authorities as the primary regulatory link to businesses within its area, and liaises with originating authorities likely to have special knowledge of problems at the point of production or service delivery.

The emphasis placed on the home authority does not mean that other authorities will not take action. Every authority is classed as an enforcing authority, and retains its statutory responsibility for enforcing the law. However, LACOTS has stated that the enforcing authority should have contact with the home authority, for example, by liaising with the home authority before embarking upon legal action and ensuring that relevant documents, cautions, and results of legal proceedings are communicated to the authority. The enforcing authority should also take account of advice given to a business by the home or originating authority.

There are other ways in which the dangers of non-uniform enforcement have been limited. Codes of Practice on enforcement have been

---

[96] Scott, 'Criminalising the Trader to Protect the Consumer' in Loveland (ed.), *Frontiers of Criminality* (London, Sweet and Maxwell, 1995) at p. 150.

[97] See Ashworth, 'Is the Criminal Law a Lost Cause?'

[98] LACOTS, which was set up in 1978, has the role of encouraging 'sensible and consistent' enforcement of food and trading standards laws and promoting best practice by local regulatory authorities.

established by central government which aim to ensure consistency and uniformity. The increasing use of industry standards to determine whether a trader has fulfilled the requirements of a due diligence defence may also lead to 'a more cohesive, coherent and responsive body of standards than the legislature can achieve'.[99] This may play a part in helping enforcement agencies to predict the outcome of cases and so facilitate uniformity in prosecution.[100] EC law requires effective enforcement on the part of member states, and it has been pointed out that uneven enforcement may create barriers to trade, for example where one state follows a deterrence strategy and another a compliance strategy. As we will see below, product safety is one area where European law has been particularly prescriptive in setting out the enforcement procedures that member states need to have in place.

A case study on enforcement: product safety

The main provisions relating to the enforcement of product safety law are found in the Consumer Protection Act 1987.[101] Chapter 5 examines the Secretary of State's law-making powers under the Act. In addition, the Secretary of State has at his disposal the enforcement powers considered below. Trading standards officers also have enforcement powers under the Act, albeit fewer than the Secretary of State. Although prosecution will be one of the prime weapons of trading standards officers, the Secretary of State rarely prosecutes for breach of product safety law. In the period 1 April 1993 to 31 March 1998 there were 1,640 prosecutions for offences under the Consumer Protection Act 1987, 1,588 of these being successful. In all these cases, the prosecution was undertaken by local enforcement authorities rather than by the Secretary of State.

The enforcement powers in this section may sometimes be used where there is no breach of the criminal law, but this will be rare. A prohibition notice or notice to warn can be served where the Secretary of State considers that goods are unsafe, and it appears that a prohibition notice cannot be challenged on the grounds that the product is, in fact, safe. However, it is suggested that it is correct to view these measures as part of the enforcement of criminal law, because they will generally only be used where unsafe products are placed on the market and therefore a

---

[99] Scott, 'Criminalising the Trader', p. 164, although Scott raises questions about how such standard setting is to be monitored and made accountable.

[100] The difficulties in predicting whether due diligence defences will be satisfied is a major problem for enforcement.

[101] See P. Cartwright, 'The Regulation of Product Safety' in G. G. Howells (ed.), *Product Liability* (London, Butterworths, 2000).

criminal offence is committed under regulation 7 of the General Product Safety Regulations. It is also an offence to contravene a prohibition notice, notice to warn,[102] or suspension notice.[103] The relationship between the enforcement procedures and the criminal law is so close that discussion of them is essential to an examination of the enforcement of criminal law.

Powers of the Secretary of State

Prohibition notices. Section 13(1) of the 1987 Act provides that the Secretary of State may serve on any person a prohibition notice which prohibits that person, except with the consent of the Secretary of State, from supplying etc. any relevant goods which the Secretary of State considers to be unsafe and which are described in the notice. This is aimed at preventing a named trader from supplying etc. dangerous goods without the Secretary of State's consent. The procedure is most useful where only a small number of goods and traders is involved. If a person affected by the notice objects, he must be given an opportunity to make representations in writing for the purpose of establishing that the goods are safe. The Secretary of State must then either consider whether to revoke the notice or appoint a person to consider the representations and investigate the matter further. Contravention of a prohibition notice is a criminal offence.

Prohibition notices are consumer protection focused in a number of ways: the consultation period only occurs after the order has been made, the notice can only be challenged by judicial review, and there is no requirement to pay compensation if it turns out that the goods were safe. In practice, however, they are rarely used. From 1988 to 1993, eighteen prohibition notices were made (related to only three products), and in the period 1993 to 1998 none was issued. The DTI's report for the latter period merely states that the need did not arise for prohibition notices to be issued over that period.[104] Although the prohibition notice could be a useful enforcement tool in appropriate circumstances, the reluctance to use it must be a matter of concern.[105] Might the reluctance to use the provision be evidence of capture? This seems unlikely. The Secretary of State, while no doubt eager to retain the support of industry, would

---

[102] Consumer Protection Act 1987 s.13(4).
[103] Consumer Protection Act 1987 s.14(6).
[104] *Consumer Safety: Report by the Secretary of State for Trade and Industry for the period 1 April–31 March 1998* (HMSO) para. 7.
[105] For an illuminating explanation of how prohibition notices might be used, see B. Harvey and D. Parry, *The Law of Consumer Protection and Fair Trading* (5th edn, London, Butterworths, 1996), p. 243.

risk too much criticism if he failed to take appropriate action against dangerous products.

Notices to warn. Section 13(1) of the 1987 Act also states that the Secretary of State may serve on any person a notice to warn which requires that person at his own expense to publish, 'in a form and manner and on occasions specified in the notice, a warning about any relevant goods which the Secretary of State considers are unsafe, which that person supplies or has supplied and which are described in the notice'. The provision aims to ensure that warnings are given about products' risks, and that the trader bears the cost of this. Some commentators have doubted the effectiveness of notices to warn because they are subject to a burdensome consultation process. This requires a draft of the proposed notice to be served on the trader and prevents action being taken until fourteen days have passed without any representations being made. A trader who wishes to make representations must be given an additional twenty-eight days in which to do so. Howells describes the procedure as both cumbersome and 'quite inappropriate for situations in which consumer safety is at risk'.[106] Although notices to warn have never been used, the DTI has noted two convincing reasons for this: first, because the Department can generally secure co-operation without having to enforce the power, and secondly, because in some cases publishing a press notice might be more effective.[107] The first reason shows the DTI acting as a 'benign big gun', securing compliance through the threat of action, with a powerful sanction in the background. Notices to warn have been described as a 'particularly potent threat', which can 'result in a supplier having to mount a media campaign warning consumers not to use the products concerned, with all the embarrassment and expense that entails'.[108] Howells disputes this, arguing that there are sufficient incentives already on traders to co-operate with the DTI, such as the desire to restrict civil claims in product liability law.[109] However, the limitations of the civil law have already been noted, and reliance on individual enforcement may be particularly inadequate in the area of product safety. Although many commentators accept the power of adverse publicity as a regulatory tool, and the power given to the DTI to create adverse publicity is considerable, this

---

[106] G. Howells, *Consumer Product Safety* (Aldershot, Dartmouth and Ashgale, 1998), p. 269. Indeed, where emergency action needs to be taken, it seems likely that the Secretary of State would take out a press notice, or act under another procedure.
[107] *Consumer Safety*, para. 9.
[108] C. Hodges, M. Tyler, and H. Abbott, *Product Safety* (London, Sweet and Maxwell, 1996), p. 152.
[109] Howells, *Consumer Product Safety*, p. 270.

can be achieved through other means. The Department sometimes issues press notices which draw attention to dangerous products and, as mentioned above, the Department has stated that this may be more flexible and more effective than using a notice to warn. Again, it seems unlikely that the reluctance to use the power is evidence of capture. Action does appear to be taken against products by more effective means.

Information powers. Section 18(1) states that where the Secretary of State considers that he requires information for specific purposes, he can serve a notice on any person who is likely to be able to furnish that information.[110] Again, this power has never been used. The Secretary of State's report for the period 1993 to 1998 stated that it had not been necessary to exercise the power because the necessary information had always been made available voluntarily. Again, the fact that the power has never been used may belie its utility, as the very existence of the powers may have acted as an incentive to disclose the information requested.

Powers of trading standards officers

Suspension notices. Section 14(1) of the Consumer Protection Act 1987 states that where an enforcement authority has reasonable grounds for suspecting that a safety provision has been contravened the authority may serve a suspension notice which prohibits the person on whom it is served for up to six months after the date of the notice from supplying etc. the goods without the consent of the authority. This provision aims to control the supply of specific dangerous products by controlling the behaviour of the supplier. Where the authority gives its consent, it can impose such conditions 'on the doing of anything of which the consent is required as the authority considers appropriate'. This gives the authority considerable power to dictate, for example, the terms upon which the goods are supplied.

The use of the term 'has reasonable grounds for suspecting' rather than 'suspects' ensures that the test imposed upon the authority is objective rather than subjective. The appeal procedure makes it clear that the key to success under that procedure is whether a safety provision has been contravened, rather than any fault on the part of the authority. Section 15(1) states that any person having an interest in goods to which a suspension

---

[110] The specific purposes mentioned in the provision are for deciding whether to make, vary, or revoke any safety regulations; to serve, vary, or revoke a prohibition notice; or to serve or revoke a notice to warn.

notice applies is able to apply to the magistrates' court for an order setting the notice aside. The magistrates will only make an order if satisfied
that there has been no contravention in relation to the goods of a safety
provision.[111] There is a further right of appeal to the Crown Court from
the magistrates' court under s.15(5)(a). In *R* v. *Birmingham City Council
ex p Ferrero Ltd*[112] the Court of Appeal held that there was relatively little
scope for judicial review because of the appeals procedure. The Queen's
Bench Division had granted judicial review of a decision by Birmingham
City Council to issue a suspension notice in relation to 'Kinder surprise
eggs'. The eggs contained small parts upon which a child had choked.
Taylor LJ stated:

> The real issue was whether the goods contravened a safety provision and the sec-
> tion 15 appeal was geared exactly to deciding that issue. If the goods did contra-
> vene the safety provision and were dangerous to children then, surely, procedural
> impropriety or unfairness in the decision-making process should not persuade
> a court to quash the order. The determining factors are the paramount need to
> safeguard consumers and the emergency nature of the s.14 powers.[113]

Suspension notices are personal to the person on whom they are served,
and are therefore aimed at the trader rather than the goods. This reveals
the limitations of such measures. Hodges, Tyler, and Abbott argue that
because the goods are already in circulation, 'the use of a suspension
notice against the manufacturer or importer will have little practical effect
in protecting consumers, and serving hundreds of individual suspension
notices on distributors and retail outlets is impractical'.[114] Where a large
class of goods is involved, it will be necessary to look to other methods of
control. It may be necessary for the Secretary of State to take action under
the procedures considered above. From April 1988 to April 1993, 1,702
suspension notices were issued. The Secretary of State's most recent five-
yearly report does not contain details of the number of notices issued.

Forfeiture orders. Section 16 of the 1987 Act permits authorities
to apply to court for forfeiture of any goods on the grounds that they
contravene a safety provision. Section 16(1) provides that an enforcement
authority may apply for an order for the forfeiture of any goods on the
grounds that there has been a contravention in relation to the goods of a
safety provision.

---

[111] Section 15(3).   [112] [1993] 1 All ER 530.
[113] Ibid. at 538–9.   [114] Hodges, Tyler, and Abbott, *Product Safety*, p. 146.

At the time of the 1987 Act's enactment this was hailed as the most important reform contained in the new legislation.[115] It recognises that other powers, such as suspension notices, will sometimes be inadequate to protect the public from dangerous goods: 'the goods may be so dangerous, and the trader so unscrupulous, that the only way the public can be protected is to apply for forfeiture'.[116] A limitation of suspension notices is that, by contrast, they leave goods with the trader. Although there needs to be contravention of a safety provision for a successful application for forfeiture there is no requirement that anyone be convicted of an offence. Forfeiture involves taking an action against the goods themselves, and there may be occasions where the enforcement authority believes that although the trader has done his best, and so should not be prosecuted, the goods should still be forfeited. From 1988 to 1993, 299 forfeiture orders were issued, with many more goods being voluntarily withdrawn.[117] Section 16(4) states that: a court may infer that there has been a contravention of a safety provision if satisfied that any such provision has been contravened 'in relation to goods which are representative of those goods'. This enables enforcement authorities to detain goods on a large scale, but only to test a small proportion.[118]

Under s.29(6)(b) of the 1987 Act, trading standards officers also have the power to seize and detain goods which they have reasonable grounds for suspecting may be liable to be forfeited. If no contravention has been established, the officer would again be liable to pay compensation. Any person who has an interest in the goods may appeal against their detention to the magistrates' court and then again to the Crown Court.

Enforcement and compensation

Whether an enforcement officer should be required to pay compensation to a trader in the event of the officer seizing goods which did not contravene consumer law is a matter of some contention. The issue tends to arise in relation to product safety, as it is less common to seize goods that pose a risk only to consumers' economic interests. Section 34(1) of the Consumer Protection Act 1987 states:

---

[115] K. Cardwell, 'The Consumer Protection Act 1987: Enforcement of Provisions Governing the Safety of Consumer Goods' (1987) 50 MLR 622 at 632.

[116] Lord Cameron of Lochbroon HL Official Reports 483 col. 920.

[117] No figures are available for the period after 1993.

[118] There is an appeal procedure under s.16(5) which states that a person aggrieved by the making of, or refusal to make, a forfeiture order may appeal to the Crown Court.

Where an officer of an enforcement authority exercises any power . . . to seize and detain goods, the enforcement authority shall be liable to pay compensation to any person having an interest in the goods in respect of any loss or damage caused by reason of the exercise of the power if –

(a) there has been no contravention in relation to the goods of any safety provision; and
(b) the exercise of the power is not attributable to any neglect or default of that person.

Identical provision is made by s.14(7) where goods have been made the subject of a suspension notice. It is not necessary to show a conviction, merely that contravention has taken place. This is important where the defendant is acquitted because he has a due diligence defence, as in that case there will still have been a contravention and so compensation will not be payable.

Particular controversy attaches to the situation where the enforcement officer has made a reasonable and honest mistake and there has been no contravention. Compensation will be payable if 'the exercise of the power [to seize goods or issue a suspension notice] is not attributable to any neglect or default by that person [the person who has an interest in the goods]'.[119] When will the exercise of such a power be said to be attributable to that person's neglect or default? Michael Howard, when Under-Secretary for Trade and Industry, suggested that an example would be where: 'a trader has refused to produce any evidence that might reasonably be expected about the precise origin of goods, relevant test certificates and so on and enforcement authorities have reason to suspect that the goods are unsafe'.[120]

The second issue which has caused particular concern is that of to whom the compensation is payable. It is payable to 'any person having an interest in the goods'. This obviously covers the owner, but presumably also includes those with a lien, and perhaps even others such as buyers, storers, and transporters who have a contract in relation to specific goods. A final difficulty concerns the extent of compensation payable. If it includes expectation loss, as it presumably does, the extent of liability could be enormous. It certainly appears not to be limited to the value of the product.[121] There is a risk that Local Authorities might find insurance premiums prohibitive, and so would feel compelled to

---

[119] Section 14(1)(b).
[120] Report of the Debate of the House of Commons Standing Committee, 30 April 1986 at p. 34.
[121] See Cardwell, 'The Consumer Protection Act 1987', p. 635.

self-insure.[122] They are also likely to exercise considerable caution before taking enforcement action, which has implications for consumer safety. Although in most cases the goods can be returned to the owner in their original state with little or no loss of profit, this will not be the case where the goods are perishable or there are other complicating factors. Lord Lucas demonstrates the objective of the provision as follows:

> It is quite possible to envisage circumstances where an authority was not acting unreasonably in detaining the goods, even though it transpired ultimately that the trader too had acted perfectly reasonably and that his goods were indeed perfectly safe . . . I do not accept it is the trader who should bear the cost of any damage he has suffered as a result of the exercise of those powers.[123]

Howells criticises the compensation provisions, arguing that exposure to compensation is a 'real restraint on the freedom of officers to act as they see best', and noting that similar penalties are not placed on the Secretary of State should he make similar mistakes.[124] This is argued to be particularly unfair for two reasons. First, trading standards officers are so frequently responding to emergency situations, and secondly, they have fewer resources than the Secretary of State to draw upon. Miller also demonstrates a degree of concern, saying that 'it is hoped that this will not unduly constrain officers who are exercising highly important powers of suspending the supply of potentially dangerous goods'.[125] The main fear from the point of view of consumer protection is that these provisions may deter enforcement authorities from acting except in the most serious circumstances.

It seems unlikely that trading standards officers have been captured by the businesses they regulate for a number of reasons. First, trading standards officers deal with such a wide variety of sectors that it is doubtful that the regulated could organise themselves sufficiently effectively to mount the necessary offensive. Secondly, there is no great tradition of trading standards officers moving from local authorities to work for business, and therefore the revolving-door syndrome appears not to be a significant issue. Thirdly, the local nature of trading standards work, and the independent nature of many authorities, means that a major national player would have some difficulty in achieving capture on a national

---

[122] K. Cardwell and P. Kay, 'The Consumer Protection Act 1987: Liability of the Enforcement Authorities' (1988) 6(7) *Trading Law* 212 at p. 214.

[123] HL Official Reports 485 cols. 920–1.

[124] See Howells, *Consumer Product Safety*, pp. 274–6.

[125] C. J. Miller, *Product Liability and Safety Encyclopedia* (London, Butterworths, n.d.), p. 164.

level.[126] Indeed, it has been suggested that the frequency with which some national players are prosecuted is evidence of the over-zealous tendencies of some authorities. To the extent that trading standards officers are unwilling to take enforcement action where a breach occurs, it seems likely that this can be explained on other grounds, such as the effectiveness of compliance strategies, the limitations of resources, or the inadequacy of certain enforcement powers.

General enforcement powers and economic interests

Where legislation is concerned to protect the economic interests of consumers, special enforcement powers such as those given to the Secretary of State to deal with dangerous products are less common. Instead, reliance tends to be placed upon prosecution as the main form of action. However, there are examples of procedures which are closely related to the criminal law that enforcement officers can rely upon. For example, several offences are created by the Consumer Credit Act 1974, and breaches of these, as well as being offences in themselves, may be used by the Director General of Fair Trading as a reason for revoking a consumer credit licence. Also, under the Control of Misleading Advertisements Regulations 1988 the Director General of Fair Trading can apply to the court for an injunction to ban an advertisement which is misleading. Misleading advertisements will tend also to be criminal offences under s.1 or s.14 of the Trade Descriptions Act 1968. The Director General has similar powers in relation to unfair terms under the Unfair Terms in Consumer Contracts Regulations 1994. There is also power under Part III of the Fair Trading Act 1973 which enables the Director General of Fair Trading to seek assurances from traders who carry on a course of conduct which is detrimental to the economic, health, safety or other interests of consumers in the UK and is unfair to consumers according to specified legislative criteria. As well as concerning economic interests in addition to safety, the provision deals with breaches of civil as well as criminal law. Breach of an assurance is not automatically a criminal offence, but breach of a court undertaking will be. Part III was examined in chapter 6 in the context of protecting consumers' economic interests.

    Enforcement Authorities are given a number of other general enforcement powers under consumer protection statutes. These powers tend to be similar in statutes that protect safety and those that protect economic interests. The Consumer Protection Act 1987 provides a useful

---

[126] Although the home authority principle may make this possible.

illustration as its general enforcement provisions apply both to offences pertaining to product safety, and those relating to misleading pricing.

One typical provision is that contained in s.28(1) of the 1987 Act. This provides that an enforcement authority may make, or authorise its officer to make, any purchase of goods for the purpose of ascertaining whether any safety provision or provision under Part III of the Act has been contravened. Section 29 is another typical provision, containing powers in relation to the search of premises and seizure of goods. For example, s.29(1) provides that a duly authorised officer of an enforcement authority may, at any reasonable hour, and on production (if required) of his credentials, exercise any of a number of powers. Whether a power is exercised at a reasonable hour will be a question of fact. Normal office hours will, presumably, always be reasonable, but where dangerous goods are suspected, and there is a need to act quickly, it is submitted that any hour could potentially be reasonable. Where certain additional criteria are established, enforcement officers are given further powers. For example, under s.29(5) if the officer has reasonable grounds for suspecting that there has been a contravention of any safety provision, he may require the production of records relating to the business, and seize and detain the goods. There is little guidance about what is meant by having 'reasonable grounds for suspecting' that there has been a contravention, although it will presumably be a lower standard than having reasonable grounds to believe. It seems that 'there must be some objective evidence which gives rise to the suspicion but there need not be enough to give rise to any degree of certainty'.[127]

Consumer protection statutes also tend to include provisions to prevent officers from being impeded in carrying out their duties. Under s.32 it is an offence intentionally to obstruct an enforcement officer or intentionally to fail to comply with any requirement made by him. It is also an offence for any person, without reasonable cause, to fail to give the officer the information or assistance that he may reasonably require. Likewise, it is an offence for a person to make a statement that he knows to be false, or recklessly to make a statement which is false in a material particular, in giving information required of him.[128]

---

[127] Bragg, *Trade Descriptions*, p. 205.
[128] The meanings of recklessness and knowledge in this context are not clear. It is submitted that knowledge probably includes wilful blindness (see *Roper* v. *Taylor's Central Garages (Exeter) Ltd* [1951] 115 JP 445). In relation to recklessness, there has been a tendency for the courts to give this a subjective meaning in recent cases, but as the 1987 Act is a regulatory statute, there may be good reason to give it an objective meaning here. See for example *MFI Warehouses Ltd* v. *Nattrass* [1973] 1 All ER 762. For a discussion of the meanings of recklessness in consumer protection see P. Cartwright, 'Reckless Statements, Trade Descriptions and Law Reform' (1996) 47(2) NILQ 171.

Criminal law and injunctions

A final point to note is that enforcement authorities may be able to use injunctions as a means of ensuring compliance with the criminal law. Section 222 of the Local Government Act 1972 provides that local authorities may institute civil proceedings where they consider it expedient for the promotion and protection of the interests of the inhabitants in their own area. An injunction may therefore be a powerful weapon. Normally the authority will have exhausted other remedies, such as prosecution, before seeking the injunction, but this need not always be the case. For example, where it is apparent that nothing short of an injunction will restrain the defendant, it may be granted. It has been said that an authority can seek an injunction where the defendant is 'deliberately and flagrantly flouting the law', but it appears that this test is too narrow. Bingham LJ identified three principles before an injunction can be granted. First, that the power will only be exercised with great caution; secondly, that there must be more than merely a breach of the criminal law, and thirdly, that the defendant's unlawful activities will continue unless restrained by an injunction. The injunction will only rarely be granted, but it may be useful where the powers possessed by the courts under statute are inadequate to deter harmful activity. For example, injunctions were sought on a number of occasions to prevent flouting of Sunday trading laws under the Shops Act 1950.

Conclusion

When the enforcement of consumer protection legislation is examined a number of points emerge. First, it is clear that the majority of enforcement agencies, including trading standards officers, use compliance strategies, which are designed to ensure compliance with legislation rather than punish for non-compliance. There are several possible reasons for this. Reasons which might give us cause for concern include an undesirable closeness between regulator and regulated leading to capture, a fear of the power and influence of the regulated, and the inadequacy of resources for enforcement. However, empirical evidence casts some doubt upon the widespread existence of these matters. Although enforcement agencies and businesses are sometimes close, this appears to bring as many advantages as disadvantages. Research upon capture theory and the revolving-door syndrome suggests that capture is uncommon. Indeed, Makkai and Braithwaite found that in the context of nursing-home regulation, tougher inspectors are more likely to find employment with the businesses they have regulated than their meeker colleagues.[129]

---

[129] Makkai and Braithwaite, 'In and Out of the Revolving Door', p. 75.

Enforcement agencies undoubtedly suffer from inadequate resources, and this is a matter of concern. However, it appears likely that even if resources were increased, the reluctance to prosecute would remain because of the benefits that compliance strategies are perceived to bring.

There appear to be good reasons for adopting a compliance strategy. Chief among these is that those enforcing the law see it as effective. Studies using mathematical techniques have borne out this view, although it seems likely that most enforcement agencies will base their decisions on their own experiences rather than on the minutiae of game theory.[130] A relationship of trust between agency and industry is valued by both, and despite the arguments made by some commentators for a deterrent-based approach, the advantages of negotiation and co-operation are likely to remain paramount.

Despite these arguments in favour of compliance strategies, some concerns remain. Where the absence of enforcement action such as prosecutions is due to the benefits resulting from compliance strategy, forbearance is to be welcomed. However, there may be other reasons for the reluctance to take formal action. First, lack of resources has been recognised as one reason for the dearth of prosecutions. To the extent that enforcement agencies would regard it as desirable to prosecute but are hamstrung by inadequate resources, this is a matter of concern. Secondly, enforcement agencies such as trading standards officers may be discouraged from taking action because of the legal consequences of making a mistake. This is of particular concern in the area of product safety where there is a statutory requirement to pay compensation, for example, where goods are wrongly seized. It is to be regretted that trading standards officers may be reluctant to seize goods which they believe to be dangerous for fear of having the goods declared reasonably safe. Thirdly, the legal requirements of some provisions make enforcement action difficult. In some cases, prosecutions require proof of *mens rea*, which is particularly difficult to establish in the case of a corporate defendant. In other cases there may be onerous obligations, such as the requirement to consult before issuing a notice to warn. Perhaps the most significant obstacle to a successful prosecution is the existence of a due diligence defence. It is argued elsewhere in this work that due diligence defences provide necessary protection for defendants from the potential harshness of strict liability, and indeed help to justify the imposition of strict liability. However, the

---

[130] For an application of game theory to enforcement see J. Scholz, 'Deterrence, Co-operation and the Ecology of Regulatory Enforcement' (1984) 18 *Law and Society Review* 79 and 'Voluntary Compliance and Regulatory Policy' (1984) 6 *Law and Policy* 385.

ease with which they appear to be established is a matter for concern, and the obstacles they place to conviction should be remembered. For these reasons it is suggested that due diligence defences be reformulated to make it impossible for corporations to escape liability by passing blame on to an employee.

On balance, the tit for tat enforcement strategy championed by Ayres and Braithwaite, which bears a close similarity to that utilised in the field of trading standards, appears to be the most desirable way of ensuring compliance with consumer protection legislation. Prosecution should not be an automatic reaction to contravention, but must remain both a theoretical and practical option for the trading standards officer. However, in order for tit for tat to work, there must be an adequate sanction, and preferably an adequate range of sanctions, to back it up. In some areas of consumer protection the sanctions are substantial, in others not so. Ashworth has urged legislators to 'avoid the fallacy that crime will go down if penalties go up', but it is difficult to deny that it is harder for enforcement authorities to apply pressure to delinquent businesses if they have weak powers at their disposal.[131] If consumers are to have confidence in the ability of enforcement authorities to ensure that traders comply with the law, the inadequacy of sanctions under some consumer protection statutes needs to be addressed.

---

[131] Ashworth, 'Is the Criminal Law a Lost Cause?', p. 251.

8   Conclusions

Criminal sanctions are frequently used to protect consumers from business wrongdoing. Whether the objective of the provision is to protect the consumer's health and safety, or her economic interests, the criminal law is central. This is not to say that other legal techniques will have no useful role to play. The law of contract provides a mechanism by which consumers' expectations can be protected and their bargains held sacred. Increasingly, it also has a say in the fairness and content of consumer transactions. But contract law suffers from certain inherent limitations that make it an insufficient means of protection. Transaction costs, in particular enforcement costs, may be prohibitive, and so the consumer's redress on paper may look more effective than his redress in practice. The doctrine of privity frequently prohibits non-contracting parties from benefiting from a contract, and remains an obstacle to redress in many cases. The law of tort may overcome some of the limitations of contract, for example, the privity requirement, but has little effect where the consumer suffers pure economic loss, and is again limited by the existence of transaction costs. Other legal techniques have important roles to play too, such as administrative controls and self-regulation. But it is the criminal law to which successive governments have looked to provide a means for protecting consumers from business malpractice.

Despite, or perhaps because of, the ubiquitous nature of criminal sanctions, criticism of them has been vocal. Regulatory offences, such as those dealing with consumer protection, have received the wrath of commentators at different ends of the political spectrum. From the 'New Right', the criticism has focused on the part that regulatory offences play in imposing burdens on business and discouraging enterprise. From the left, regulatory offences are perceived as a barrier to the creation of a principled criminal law. There is certainly truth in these criticisms. The precise cost of complying with criminal regulations is difficult to quantify, but is likely to be significant. An attempt to create a principled criminal law along the lines championed by Ashworth finds an obstacle in offences of strict liability, which can be established without proof of *mens rea*. In particular, it is difficult to argue for using regulatory offences if one starts from the proposition that criminal law must be a last resort, utilised only when all other measures are inadequate. This view appears to be shared by the post-1997 Government, with Lord Williams of Mostyn stating that new criminal offences will only be created in the most extreme of circumstances. Even champions of the consumer interest, such as the former legal officer of the Consumers' Association, David Tench, have come down against strict liability.

Against this formidable opposition, can the widespread use of the criminal law in consumer protection be defended? It is submitted that it can. First, the cost of complying with regulatory law is significant, but so will be the cost of complying with whatever regime is put in its place. Of course, this does not justify the use of the criminal law. The key is to determine which examples of regulation are most beneficial in which circumstances. No doubt the Better Regulation Task Force, which is charged with advising the government on improving the quality of regulation, will continue to identify areas of the criminal law which could be decriminalised. But this is no argument for the removal of all regulatory criminal laws. It is rather an argument for better focus, something which it is difficult to oppose. Secondly, regulatory offences appear to run counter to some principles of criminal law, particularly those favoured by Ashworth. Sometimes they deal with matters that could not be described as 'serious wrongdoing'. Sometimes they are enforced in a non-uniform way, ostensibly offending principles of equal treatment. However, it is doubtful that many societies would truly limit the criminal law to 'serious' wrongdoing along the lines sometimes suggested. It might be possible to take minor thefts out of the criminal arena, but would be politically unthinkable. Property is such a fundamental foundation of the social order, and the market system, that any attempt to treat deliberate appropriations as other than criminal seems highly unlikely. Furthermore, we have already noted the difficulty in establishing an acceptable test of seriousness. Many contraventions of consumer law which appear to be minor are revealed to be more serious on closer inspection. In relation to non-uniform enforcement, Ashworth is right to expect like cases to be treated alike. However, empirical evidence in the area of regulatory enforcement shows us that this is generally fulfilled, although there is room for improvement. Enforcement agencies emphasise similar principles when deciding whether to prosecute, and steps have been taken to formalise these in some areas, for example, food law. Whenever a prosecutor has discretion there is always likely to be a public interest factor in her judgement. Compliance strategies could be viewed as a variation of this.

A further criticism of regulatory crime relates to its use of strict liability. It is morally objectionable, it is said, to convict the innocent. This is a powerful argument, and one that is difficult to refute. But is there evidence that the morally innocent are convicted under regulatory statutes? Safeguards are built in at several stages. First, it is clear that the *mens rea* of the defendant is a major factor in deciding whether to prosecute, even when no *mens rea* is required by the provision in question. Secondly, a defendant who lacks any fault will almost invariably have a defence of due diligence. Such defences are designed to distinguish the defendant who has done all he reasonably could from the defendant who has not. The defendant who has not done all he should have, even if lacking intent, can be said to be at fault. Thirdly, fault is taken into account when sentencing. A defendant with little culpability should fear little by way of punishment. Statistics from the Director General of Fair Trading's Annual Report reveal that the courts are willing to discharge defendants where they deem it appropriate. There is still stigma to a conviction, as there should be, but surely less stigma for breach of a consumer protection offence than for many others.

Although the use of criminal sanctions in consumer protection has been defended, this does not mean that the status quo is to be supported. There are many areas where the law could be improved, and this book has sought to examine some of these. First, there is a lack of coherence between the leading statutes. Although most statutes impose strict liability, s.14 of the Trade Descriptions Act 1968 requires proof that the defendant was reckless or knew his statement to be false. The reasons for imposing a *mens rea* requirement have been examined and can no longer be accepted. Secondly, the statutes take different approaches to who can be prosecuted. The Trade Descriptions Act 1968 allows employees to be prosecuted under sections 1 and 14 and even private individuals to be prosecuted under s.23 if they cause offences to be committed. The Consumer Protection Act 1987 only allows a defendant acting in the course of any business of his to be subjected to criminal sanctions. The Property Misdescriptions Act 1991 provides that where a false or misleading statement is made in the course of estate agency or property development business, the person by whom the business is carried on shall be guilty of an offence, thus providing a rare example of explicit vicarious liability. However, it then provides that where an employee causes the offence to be committed, he shall be guilty of the offence. These differences are impossible to justify in principle. It is suggested that employees should not be subjected to liability under the criminal law for consumer protection offences. Even less should private individuals be subjected to the control of consumer protection law. Where private individuals or junior employees act dishonestly there are general provisions under which they can be held to account. Their liability should be limited to breach of those provisions.

Reform of the law relating to the liability of individuals can only take place alongside reform of corporate and vicarious liability. Since the creation of the doctrine of identification, and in particular its interpretation in *Tesco* v. *Nattrass*, the criminal law has been a weak instrument with which to hold corporations to account. Recent judicial re-examination of the doctrine has provided useful food for thought, as have a number of important writings. It is hoped that these initiatives will lead to a reconstruction of corporate and vicarious liability under which the prosecution of corporations for strict liability and *mens rea* offences is facilitated.

Perhaps the most serious threat to consumers is to their health and safety, and laws to protect consumers' physical integrity have been on the statute book for some time. The General Product Safety Regulations 1994 reveal many of the difficult policy issues that arise for a jurisdiction that wants to remove dangerous goods from the market but allow safe goods to circulate within the jurisdiction. The law in the UK draws a reasonable balance between these sometimes competing aims, but is marred by inadequate sanctions, and by obligations on enforcement authorities which sometimes put the interests of the consumer and the enforcement authority behind those of the trader. This can only be addressed by removing the obligations on enforcement authorities to pay compensation when goods are wrongly seized, and significantly increasing the sanctions for breach of product safety law.

Law governing the protection of economic interests is also in need of reform. Chapter 6 endeavours to identify a conceptual framework for protecting consumers' economic interests, something upon which literature is scarce. The law appears to focus primarily upon prohibiting false and misleading information, with attempts to encourage the supply of accurate information being relatively uncommon. It is suggested that this is an area in which the criminal law should play a greater part. Information deficits are a barrier to an efficient marketplace, but also cause social injustice. A considered disclosure regime can have enormous benefit, particularly for those vulnerable consumers who may be most at risk from information failure. The law also needs to clarify how misleading statements are judged. Social justice demands that traders take account of how the most vulnerable might interpret the information they supply, and the law should ensure that the interests of vulnerable consumers are not overlooked. However, economic interests are about more than merely inaccurate or inadequate information. Consumers are also entitled to expect that their legitimate expectations be fulfilled. The criminal law plays some role here, but has tended to shy away from addressing the difficult issues involved. The creation of a new criminal offence which protects these expectations would be a bold step, but one which could be justified on the basis of the benefits it would bring, and the extent to which traders are already obliged by the civil law to supply goods that are of satisfactory quality and fit for their purpose. Any attempt to reform the law which protects consumers' economic interests should take account of the increasing recognition of the importance of fairness in the marketplace. The civil law has led the way with its increasing emphasis on good faith and it is now time for public law to follow this lead. The possibility of creating a new criminal offence prohibiting unfair conduct has been considered, although deemed problematic. Instead, it is submitted that we should look towards the administrative procedures, in particular Part III of the Fair Trading Act 1973, to deal with unfair conduct. As it currently stands, Part III does not protect consumers' interests to the extent that they deserve, but a reformulated Part III could play an important role in tackling the unfair conduct which dogs the marketplace.

Calls for an expansion of the criminal law and the role of enforcement authorities might lead to fears of over-regulation, and it is important that the law recognises these legitimate fears. Effective enforcement is central to effective consumer protection. Enforcement in the UK takes place both at national and local level. It is apparent that enforcement powers could be improved, particularly with a reformulated Part III. It is also apparent that the majority of enforcement authorities use their powers sensitively and fairly. The use of compliance strategies has come in for criticism, but there is ample evidence that such an approach facilitates the effective enforcement of much regulatory legislation. There may be areas where the scarcity of prosecutions is a matter for concern, but they are sometimes down to inadequate powers rather than inadequate enforcement policies. It was suggested in chapter 7 that the best enforcement approach is a tit for tat policy, along the lines of that championed by Ayres and Braithwaite, a strategy that bears many similarities to the approach followed by enforcement authorities in the UK. Such an approach respects the interests of the genuine trader, eager to comply with her obligations, but takes a dim view of the trader who abuses the authorities' flexibility.

A number of themes run throughout this book. Perhaps the most obvious is that the criminal law has a central role to play in the protection of the consumer, and that the legislature should not shy away from the creation of additional offences where appropriate. Strict liability, backed up with due diligence defences, and integrated within a new conception of vicarious and corporate liability, is the favoured structure. Another theme is that the rationale for new laws should be both economic and social. Market failure provides a useful model upon which to consider the creation of new initiatives. However, laws based solely on addressing market failure are likely to ignore the interests of some of the most vulnerable in society. Social rationales, in particular distributive justice, should be considered, and laws designed to achieve them. Indeed, many existing examples of consumer law can be justified on both economic and social grounds. A consumer who has trust in the market not to dupe him, and the law to protect him if it does, is more likely to be able to play the role assigned to him in free market economic theory. Provided it is drafted carefully, enforced sensitively, and interpreted wisely, it is submitted that the criminal law can provide an effective and fair means of consumer protection.

Index